Dr Dent is Fellow, Dean of Divinity, and Chaplain of New College, Oxford.

Oxford Theological Monographs

PROTESTANT REFORMERS IN ELIZABETHAN OXFORD

C. M. DENT

OXFORD UNIVERSITY PRESS

Oxford University Press, Walton Street, Oxford OX2 6DP

London New York Toronto
Delhi Bombay Calcutta Madras Karachi
Kuala Lumpur Singapore Hong Kong Tokyo
Nairobi Dar es Salaam Cape Town
Melbourne Auckland

and associated companies in
Beirut Berlin Ibadan Mexico City Nicosia

Oxford is a trade mark of Oxford University Press

Published in the United States
by Oxford University Press, New York

First published 1983
Reprinted 1985

British Library Cataloguing in Publication Data

Dent, C.M.
Protestant reformers in Elizabethan Oxford. —
(Oxford theological monographs)
1. University of Oxford—History
2. Reformation—England
I. Title
274.2   BR377
ISBN 0-19-826723-1

Library of Congress Cataloging in Publication Data

Dent, C. M. (Christopher Mattinson)
Protestant reformers in Elizabethan Oxford.
(Oxford theological monographs)
Bibliography: p.
Includes index.
1. Protestant churches—England—History—16th
century.   2. England—Church history—16th century.
3. University of Oxford—Religion   I. Title.
II. Series.
BR375.D46 1983   280'.4'0942574   82-24588
ISBN 0-19-826723-1

Printed by Antony Rowe Ltd,
Chippenham

*For my
mother and father
in thanksgiving*

PREFACE

This study, in company with many other explorations of Elizabethan protestant history written in the last decade, was prompted initially by Professor Patrick Collinson's *The Elizabethan Puritan Movement*, which appeared in 1967, and, in particular, by Professor Collinson's argument there that 'the puritanism of Elizabethan Oxford has been persistently underestimated, and only rarely has due recognition been accorded to the influence of what was perhaps the most remarkable puritan society in either university, Magdalen under Humphrey's presidency' (page 129). Professor Collinson first aroused my interest in the history of the Elizabethan church whilst I was an undergraduate at King's College, London and has subsequently offered much helpful advice in the preparation of this study.

Following Professor Collinson's fertile suggestion, the research for this examination of Elizabethan Oxford was begun in the archives of Magdalen College. I gratefully acknowledge here the kind permission of the President and Fellows of Magdalen College, Oxford to use records relating to the life of their society. I owe a particular debt to Dr G. L. Harriss, Librarian and Archivist of the college, who brought to my attention the letter-book of George Wilton, a late sixteenth-century undergraduate, which the college purchased at Sotheby's in 1971. I am indebted to the governing bodies, librarians, and archivists of the following colleges in Oxford: All Souls, Balliol, Christ Church, Corpus Christi, Exeter, Merton, New College, Queen's, and University College for permission to refer to their manuscript and archive collections. Acknowledgement is also due to the Keeper of the Oxford University Archives, the Master and Fellows of Corpus Christi College, Cambridge, and the librarians of the British Library, Dr Williams's Library, the Inner Temple, the Lambeth Palace Library, and the Keeper of the Public Records for permission to consult materials in their possession. The staff of the Bodleian Library, especially those in Duke Humfrey's Library, willingly provided the hundreds of late sixteenth-century books and pamphlets which I read there.

This book could not have been written without the generosity of the Warden and Fellows of New College, Oxford, who
elected me to the Hastings Rashdall Studentship, which I held
from 1976 to 1979, during which time the greater part of the
research for this study in its original form as an Oxford doctoral
dissertation was completed. Dr B. R. White supervised that
dissertation and his constant encouragement and detailed
attention, both to the general argument and to its clearer
expression, saved me from many theological, historical, and
linguistic failings. Dr Penry Williams, fellow of New College,
read the entire work in typescript and not only helped me to set
the discussion within the broader world of Elizabethan government and society, but offered a large number of clarifications
and correctives. I also owe several suggestions to conversations
with Dr Jennifer Loach and with the examiners of my dissertation, Dr J. K. McConica and Dr Claire Cross. Mr J. H.
Eggleshaw assisted me with the complexities of sixteenth-
century Latin. As copy editor, Mrs Marny Leach brought good
order to a difficult typescript. At the Oxford University Press,
Miss Audrey Bayley has steered me through the trials surrounding a first-published work. Although I have received much help
from these and other friends, I alone am responsible for the
faults which remain.

In quotations, original spelling and punctuation have in
general been retained. Dates throughout are in New Style.

New College   C. M. D.
Oxford
Epiphany 1983

CONTENTS

PRINCIPAL ABBREVIATIONS

Airay, *Philippians*	Henry Airay, *Lectures upon the Whole Epistle of Saint Paul to the Philippians* (London, 1618)
BL	British Library, London
Bloxam, *Register*	J. R. Bloxam, *Register of the Presidents, Fellows, Demies of St. Mary Magdalen College, Oxford.* Vol. II (Oxford, 1867); Vol. III (1873); Vol. IV (1873)
Clark, *Register*	Andrew Clark (ed.) *Register of the University of Oxford.* Vol. II (1571-1622), part i, Introductions (Oxford Historical Society, x, 1887); Vol. II, part ii, Matriculations and Subscriptions (Oxford Historical Society, xi, 1888)
Collinson, *E.P.M.*	Patrick Collinson, *The Elizabethan Puritan Movement* (London, 1967)
DNB	*Dictionary of National Biography*, ed. Leslie Stephen and Sidney Lee, 21 vols. (London, 1908-9)
Macray, *Register*	W. D. Macray, *A Register of the Members of St. Mary Magdalen College, Oxford, new series.* Vol. II (London, 1897); Vol. III (1901)
O.L.	*Original Letters Relative to the English Reformation*, ed. Hastings Robinson, 2 vols (Cambridge, Parker Society, 1846-7)
OUA	Oxford University Archives
Porter	H. C. Porter, *Reformation and Reaction in Tudor Cambridge* (Cambridge, 1958)
PRO	Public Record Office
Reynolds, *Haggai*	John Reynolds, *The Prophesie of Haggai Interpreted and Applied in Sundry Sermons* (London, 1649)
Strype, *Annals*	John Strype, *Annals of the Reformation and Establishment of Religion during Queen Elizabeth's Happy Reign*, 2 vols., each in 2 parts (Oxford, 1824)
Wood, *Annals*	Anthony à Wood, *The History and Antiquities of the University of Oxford ... The Annals*, ed. John Gutch, Vol. II (Oxford, 1796)
Z.L., I	*The Zurich Letters, 1558-1579*, ed. Hastings Robinson (Cambridge, Parker Society, 1842)
Z.L., II	*The Zurich Letters, Second Series, 1558-1602*, ed. Hastings Robinson (Cambridge, Parker Society, 1845)

INTRODUCTION

A visitor to the Upper Reading Room in the Bodleian Library may find his eye drawn upward to the frieze of painted heads which surrounds the walls. A detailed inspection will reveal a procession of worthies, Christian saints and fathers, Greek and Roman writers, medieval schoolmen, heroes of the Renaissance, lawyers and scientists, reformers and divines, selected and arranged at the beginning of the seventeenth century by Thomas James, Bodley's first Librarian, to form two elaborate sequences illustrating secular and divine learning.[1] Conspicuously placed over the Tower Arch, a succession of theologians marks a break in the carefully-contrived pattern of faces. In the most prominent position of all, above the keystone, is John Reynolds, fellow and later President of Corpus Christi College, a friend of Thomas Bodley, literary opponent of Cardinal Bellarmine, and a translator of the Authorized Version. On his right is Lawrence Humphrey, President of Magdalen 1561-89, and once Bodley's tutor. For Thomas James, these two divines may have epitomized the Oxford contribution to the united protestant front against Rome. In this study, they also emerge as the most significant figures in the university's claim to be part of what Reynolds himself called 'the Reformed Church of England'. Elizabethan Oxford, though still a closed society and conservatively religious in character, developed in the course of the reign a cherished place within the European reformed tradition, not narrowly Calvinist and Genevan, but inspired by a variety of continental protestant centres. In the Bodleian frieze, Reynolds and Humphrey are framed by Erasmus and Luther on their right, and on their left by du Jon (Junius), the Antwerp pastor, Zanchius, the reformer of Heidelberg, and Marnix de Sainte-Aldegonde (Marnaeus), the moderate Dutch Calvinist. James was again no doubt principally concerned with their solidarity as opponents of papist corruption. They

---

[1] J. N. L. Myres, 'The Painted Frieze in the Picture Gallery', in *Bodleian Library Record*, 3 (1950), 82-91; 'Thomas James and the Painted Frieze', in *Bodleian Library Record*, 4 (1952), 30-51.

also represent, in large measure, that hybrid and broadly-based theological tradition described in the pages which follow. Theological controversy frequently leads to the production of written assertion and counter-assertion, polemic and apologetic. The structure of this study has therefore been determined, in some degree, by the focus provided by a series of controversies in the university and in individual colleges. The protestant history of Magdalen College is traced through the vicissitudes of 1575, 1578, 1585, and 1589. The reformed tradition in theology, broadly based as it was, is seen in conflict with free-thinking intellectuals, Francesco Pucci and Antonio del Corro, in the 1570s. Later controversies were based more on differences of ecclesiology, the failure of the university as a nursery for godly preachers and ministers as well as laymen, and the deficiencies of discipline and practice when measured against the pattern of the continental reformed churches, than on those variations in the interpretation of the doctrines of grace and assurance which so preoccupied the university of Cambridge in the closing decade of the reign. In 1586, a group of radical Oxford preachers, including John Reynolds, launched a violent sermon campaign in favour of lay eldership, a resident ministry, and more preaching, and against excommunication by laymen; in 1602-3, Vice-Chancellor Howson provoked from the 'precise' a spirited defence of 'the excellencie and necessity of devout and holy preaching' by some unguarded words in a university sermon. These issues, which are at the centre of the surviving documents, may further be illuminated by the increasing number of printed sermons, some of them from the Oxford press of Joseph Barnes, situated in the High Street at the west end of St. Mary's Church.

In one respect, this study has itself taken an unexpected turn. Undertaken with the intention of tracing the puritan history of Elizabethan Oxford, it has, in its final form, attempted to avoid the use of the term 'puritan'. This description was rarely employed by or of Oxford men in Elizabeth's reign, and when it was used, it was almost invariably a term of abuse, grudgingly accepted, if accepted at all, by those against whom it was directed.[2] The term 'protestant' has been here preferred,

---

[2] See, for example, the use in Magdalen College in 1580, below, 61; in 1589, below, 69, in Airay, below 205, and in Robert Bolton, below, 195.

as allowing greater latitude and gradation. Dr Rosemary O'Day has recently proposed a short definition of a puritan which sees him as a 'revivalist protestant' resisting 'the institutionalization of Protestantism within the English state', differing 'not in doctrine from the men who support the settlement, but in attitude. His spirit is essentially critical, revivalist and outspoken.'[3] This acute definition captures many of the characteristics of the university men who form the subject of this account, but does not, in the view of the present writer, sufficiently justify the use of the term 'puritan', even given 'the loosest possible definition'. 'Puritan' retains limiting connotations and suffers from having become the description of a historical stereotype. The protective atmosphere of the university rarely forced men to resist 'the institutionalization of Protestantism'. 'Critical' and 'revivalist' they were, 'evangelical' they were, if these terms denote a concern with preaching the gospel and interpreting the scriptures, especially in the backward corners of the land, and bringing the church, in the university and in the country, more into line with the churches of the gospel on the Continent. Yet these attempts at definition have historical overtones which originate outside the sixteenth century. The term 'protestant' is not without its own difficulties and ambiguities, as contemporaries realized, but it possesses an adaptability and flexibility which is central to this account, where men, in the confines of the university, not only changed course within their careers, but were rapidly supplanted by more radical young men in succeeding academic generations. For protestants, as for their contemporaries who chose the path of recusancy, the university and its colleges remained in Elizabeth's reign places apart, places exempt. The following chapters attempt to offer an illumination of some of the dark corners of this enclosed world. *Dominus illuminatio mea.*

---

[3] Rosemary O'Day, *The English Clergy: the Emergence and Consolidation of a Profession, 1558-1642* (Leicester, 1979), xii.

I
PROLOGUE: THE INFUSION OF PROTESTANTISM IN THE REIGN OF EDWARD VI

The reign of Edward VI marked a period of rapid transition in the protestant history of the university of Oxford, distinguished by the attempted reforms of the royal visitors, the assertion of militant action in one college, Magdalen, and the establishment of strong and enduring associations with the continental churches of the reform, especially Zurich. The King's accession, on 28 January 1547, was the signal in some parts of the country, as in Magdalen College, for supporters of a more insistent protestant outlook to reassert the outward face of reformed religion in a way which had been impossible in the repressive closing years of Henry VIII's reign. On Whitsunday, 29 May 1547, Thomas Bickley, fellow of Magdalen, rushed up to the altar during mass, snatched the tabernacle from the priest, and smashed it in pieces.[1] Other acts of iconoclasm followed.[2] Protector Somerset seems at length to have heard of the militancy in the college and wrote on 6 June 1548 urging that no 'undecent innovation' should take place, but that they should follow the example of Christ Church under Richard Cox. Despite this inhibition, the Order of Communion replaced the mass, ceremonies were discontinued, and the tabernacle was not set up again.[3] 'Sume fewe' conservative members of the college complained to the Council that these changes had taken place precipitately, through the rashness of young men; while President Oglethorpe and eighteen moderates protested that they had only acted in accordance with the Protector's instructions. At least seven radical members of the society

---

[1] Bloxam, *Register*, II, 301.
[2] Ibid.; Bloxam, *Register*, IV, 77.
[3] OUA/WP/B/24, letter from some fellows of Magdalen to the Council, after 6 June 1548; see also M. L. Bush, *The Government Policy of Protector Somerset* (London, 1975), 123-4; D. E. Hoak, *The King's Council in the Reign of Edward VI* (Cambridge, 1976), 175-6, 214-15.

did not put their names to the letter of complaint and were supported by other 'young men and boys'.[4]

The royal commission to visit the two universities was first issued on 12 November 1548, but a second commission, dated 8 May 1549, seems to have superseded it before any action was taken.[5] Before the visitors arrived, attempts, resisted in some colleges, were made to restrain elections to offices and fellowships, but a letter from Somerset, dated 1 January 1548, had already made it clear that the Council did not intend to inhibit the normal divinity disputations, despite the provisions of the Act against revilers (1 Edw. VI c. 1) and the mockery of the mass in ballads, plays, and sermons in London.[6]

The brief given to the Edwardine visitors was very comprehensive, including the examination of all colleges and halls in heads and members, bringing the rebellious to order by civil and ecclesiastical censure, reform of the curriculum, and examination of finances and statutes.[7] On 4 June, less than two weeks after they had begun their work, the visitors provided the university with a revised set of statutes, probably envisaged as a holding operation until the detailed visitation had been completed.[8] To each college they delivered a set of forty or more injunctions to regulate college lectures, biblical lections in hall, grace at meals, and chapel services. In general these were, like the university orders, moderate in tone but they swept away altars, images, statues, organs, and all other associations of Roman worship and abolished the mass and popish offices.[9] In some colleges, at least, the visual changes desired by the visitors had preceded their arrival. In Magdalen, all the wall paintings had been obliterated in 1547, but the high altar was not demolished until 1551, when the college purchased a new

---

[4] SP 10/5/12, Magdalen College to Somerset, 8 November 1548.

[5] SP 10/5/13, 12 November 1548; SP 10/7/6, 8 May 1549.

[6] Act against revilers in *Documents Illustrative of English Church History*, ed. H. Gee and W. J. Hardy (London, 1896), 322-8; OUA/WPβ/A/37; Wood, *Annals*, II, 94; Magdalen College Oxford Archives, Register of Admissions, 1539-1614, fo. 14.

[7] Wood, *Annals*, II, 96-9.

[8] Strickland Gibson, *Statuta Antiqua Universitatis Oxoniensis* (Oxford, 1931), 341-62, based on an eighteenth-century MS copy.

[9] Magdalen College injunctions in Macray, *Register*, II, 23-6; All Souls in *The Statutes of the Colleges of Oxford* (London, 1853), 85-9; additional statutes for Exeter College, dated 1548, Exeter College Archives, A. I. 5., Register, Vol. I (1539-1619).

communion table.[10] Silver plate to the value of £163. 8s 6d. was sold in 1549 because it was no longer needed and benefactions for the celebration of masses were converted into exhibitions, 'ex mandato regiorum delegatorum'. In Merton, the changes were more moderate. The last mass for the founder, Walter de Merton, was not said until 15 July 1548 and the proceeds of a considerable sale of plate in 1549 were used to buy books for the library.[12] In Corpus Christi College, where the number of convinced protestants was extremely small, the visitors' orders were sufficiently obeyed to allow the purchase of a communion table.[13] In New College, however, the founder's glass was saved from destruction when the fellows protested that they were too poor to replace it with plain glass.[14] The outward face of protestant worship was clearly apparent in some chapels; others remained virtually unchanged. The work of the visitors continued into 1550. In particular, they were faced with strong opposition in Magdalen College to their plans to close the grammar school and they delivered a second set of injunctions to the college, perhaps because of disputes raised by the original set, on 28 February 1550.[15]

On very slender evidence, Anthony Wood accused the visitors of wholesale spoliation of college libraries, especially that of his own college, Merton, and of the university library. This cannot be substantiated. When the Marian visitors demanded an inventory of Merton library in 1556, fearing the presence there of protestant books, it revealed that the college possessed 300 medieval manuscripts, and 200 printed books

---

[10] Magdalen College Oxford Archives, Liber Computi, 1543-59, fos. 42, 70ᵛ, 86ʳ, 98ᵛ, 99ʳ; Bloxam, *Register*, II, 271-2.

[11] N. R. Ker, *Oxford Libraries in 1556* (Oxford 1956), 17; Magdalen College Oxford Archives, Liber Computi, 1543-59, fos. 69ᵛ, 77ʳ, 78ᵛ.

[12] *Registrum Annalium Collegii Mertonensis, 1521-67*, ed. J. M. Fletcher (Oxford Historical Society, new series, xxiii, 1974), 143-4, 138; Merton College Muniments, no. 2798.

[13] Corpus Christi College Archives, Libri Magni, III, fos. 126ʳ, 146ʳ.

[14] New College Oxford, 1379-1979, ed. E. J. M. Buxton and P. H. Williams (Oxford, 1979), 47.

[15] Corpus Christi College Cambridge (hereafter CCCC) MS 127/23 (pp. 415-16), printed in *Visitation Articles and Injunctions*, ed. W. H. Frere and W. P. Kennedy (Alcuin Club, xv, 1910), II, 228-9. See also CCCC MS 127/25-8 for defences of the school; Bloxam, *Register*, III, 109-13.

most of which were less than twenty years old.[16] During the
reign of Edward VI, Merton also made over £70 available for
the purchase of books.[17] Though other colleges purchased
books at this period, protestant theology does not seem to have
found its way on to the shelves.[18] The Edwardine visitors must,
however, bear the responsibility for the loss of the university
library, though, in the short term at least, this was mitigated by
the fact that the teaching of juniors was increasingly concen-
trated in colleges and halls rather than the public schools of the
university.[19]

Cranmer's campaign to raise the intellectual standards of the
English ministry and associate the church more closely with the
continental reformed churches found expression in a series of
invitations to continental protestant refugees to make their
homes in England, among them Peter Martyr Vermigli, Ber-
nardino Ochino, Immanuel Tremellius, and later, Martin
Bucer. In March 1548, after spending some time in company
with Ochino with Cranmer at Lambeth, Martyr was appointed
to succeed the arch-conservative, Richard Smith, as Regius
Professor of Divinity at Oxford. Here his life was overstrained
and frequently disturbed. On 1 June 1550, he told Bullinger of
his daily 9 a.m. lecture, his work as moderator in theological
disputations, and, finally, the continual battle against the
papists.[20] Financially and socially at least, Martyr gained
greater security through his long-promised appointment to a
canonry at Christ Church, though his life in college was frequently disrupted, his windows broken, and he and his wife
Catherine, the first woman to take up residence, subjected to
abuse. Around Martyr, and a significant factor in sustaining

[16] Wood, *Annals,* II, 106-9; Merton College Muniments, no. 4277; Ker, *Oxford
Libraries in 1556,* 15.

[17] Merton College Muniments, no. 2798. N. R. Ker, 'Oxford College Libraries in
the Sixteenth Century', in *Bodleian Library Record,* VI, 3 (1959), 464 ff.

[18] On Corpus, see J. R. Liddell, 'The Library of Corpus Christi College,
1517-1617', Oxford B.Litt. thesis (1936), 36; on Magdalen, Paul Morgan, *Oxford
Libraries Outside the Bodleian: A Guide* (Oxford Bibliographical Society, 1974), 64; on
New College, R. W. Hunt, 'The Medieval Library', in *New College Oxford, 1379-1979,*
335-6.

[19] There is no record of the dispersal of the books in 1549-50. On 25 January 1556,
the Vice-Chancellor and proctors were authorized to sell *'subsellia librorum in publica
Academiae bibiotheca'*, OUA/NEP *supra*/Register I, fo. 157ʳ.

[20] *O.L.*, 481.

him, grew up a group of Swiss students.[21] Martyr had stopped
in Zurich on his flight from Lucca and formed a considerable
friendship with the ministers there. The first student to arrive in
Edwardian Oxford was John ab Ulmis, who may have lodged
in Broadgates Hall before Richard Cox secured him a place
in Christ Church on 1 January 1549. As the senior member of
the group, he not only stayed long enough to pursue the Arts
course and proceed MA in 1552, but was the prime influence in
the growth of the group.[22] Johann Andreas Croariensis and
Augustine Bernher joined him in the autumn of 1548.
Croariensis stayed for three years, but Bernher left after a short
time to become Latimer's secretary.[23] John Stumphius, returning to England with John Hooper, joined the group as a member
of Christ Church in the spring of 1549.[24] Alexander Schmutz
arrived in England at the same time and after a stay at
Westminster School came to Oxford, not leaving until December
1553.[25] Christopher Froschover, son of the Zurich printer, joined
them in November 1550.[26] A few later arrivals, John Conrad and
Henry ab Ulmis, Albert and Walter Blaurer, Joshua Maler, and
one other completed the circle.[27]

The reaction of the Swiss students to the university was,
almost without exception, favourable, though their letters
home may in part have been coloured by gratitude to their
Oxford patrons. Froschover commented on the severity of the
Oxford winter and of Lent; Croariensis complained in
February 1549 of the low intellectual standards, but he seems
to have changed his mind by the summer.[28] This group of
Swiss students would have found life in Oxford almost in-
tolerable socially, financially, and academically without their
English friends, especially at Christ Church. The benefit was

[21] See the comprehensive survey by Dr Claire Cross, 'Continental Students and the
Protestant Reformation in England in the Sixteenth Century', in *Studies in Church
History, Subsidia*, 2, ed. D. Baker (Oxford, 1979), 35-46.

[22] *O.L.*, 384-5, 389, 450. Cross, art. cit., 38-9.

[23] *Briefwechsel der Brüder Ambrosius und Thomas Blaurer, 1509-67*, ed. T. Schiess, III,
1549-67, (Freiburg-i-Br., 1912), 16; Cross, art. cit., 39.

[24] *O.L.*, 461; Cross, art. cit., 40.

[25] Cross, art. cit., 40.

[26] *O.L.*, 719.

[27] Cross, art, cit., 40.

[28] *Briefwechsel der Brüder Ambrosius und Thomas Blaurer*, 16, 43-4, 126-8.

not entirely one-sided however, since Oxford scholars were to be rewarded by the association with Bullinger, Gualter, Blaurer, and the Swiss churches. These contacts, reinforced by the hospitality offered to Oxford refugees in Mary's reign, may partially account for the strong associations between Oxford and Switzerland in the first two decades under Elizabeth.[29]

Foremost among the English patrons of the Swiss students was Richard Cox, Dean of Christ Church and Chancellor of the university from 1547 to 1552. Both John ab Ulmis and Stumphius spoke of his liberality and friendship, ab Ulmis encouraging Bullinger to correspond with him.[30] Henry Siddall, Canon of Christ Church, named by ab Ulmis 'my especial patron', was praised for his 'great influence, considerable erudition, exceeding uprightness' and was himself an infrequent correspondent of the Zurich church. On 4 October 1552 he wrote to Bullinger, expressing high praise of ab Ulmis and reporting on the progress of the reform in Oxford, adding that 'many of us are exceedingly united with you in spirit, though separated by sea, of whom I wish to be counted the chief'.[31] Just over a year later, Siddall was supervising Martyr's house-arrest in Christ Church and though Julius Terentianus, Martyr's servant, described him as 'a truly excellent man' he was a weak one, reverting to the old religion under Mary, only to embrace the protestant cause again in 1558.[32] James Courthorpe (Curtopp), his fellow canon, is also mentioned as a friend of Martyr and Bucer; like Siddall, he reverted to catholicism, giving evidence at Cranmer's trial.[33] Another member of Christ Church who prized his Zurich correspondence was the doctor Richard Masters, Sub-Dean in 1550 and a valued protector of the Swiss students.[34]

It is surprising to discover that the Swiss students had at least two friends in the conservative society of New College. Ralph Skinner, Warden from 1551 to 1553 and first Elizabethan

[29] See below, ch. IV.

[30] *O.L.*, 460-2, 385, 389, 450.

[31] *O.L.*, 467-8, Stumphius to Bullinger, 12 November 1550; *O.L.*, 311-12, Siddall to Bullinger, 4 October 1552.

[32] *O.L.*, 369-70, Terentianus to John ab Ulmis, 20 November 1553.

[33] G. C. Gorham, *Gleanings of a Few Scattered Ears during the Period of the Reformation in England* (London, 1857), 199, Martyr to Bucer, 11 November 1550.

[34] *O.L.*, 358-60.

Dean of Durham, was encouraged to correspond by ab Ulmis and praised Bullinger for his fatherly affection towards England.[35] Thomas Harding, an unlikely friend since he became Chaplain to Stephen Gardiner in Mary's reign, had met Bullinger on his way to Italy in 1548 and found in John ab Ulmis, Stumphius, and Croariensis a renewal of his acquaintance with the city and its ministers.[36] Thomas Caius (Keys), Registrar of the university until he was deprived for incompetence in 1552 and from 1561 Master of University College, greatly admired Bullinger and translated some of his Latin discourses.[37] In Magdalen, Owen Oglethorpe, the President, maintained the correspondence with Bullinger which he had begun in 1538.[38] A fellow of the college, Michael Renniger, 'a man of great learning and much attached to you', as ab Ulmis informed Bullinger, set out for Zurich at the beginning of 1551 with the intention of co-operating there in the printing of an English Bible.[39] Hugh Kirke, fellow of Magdalen from 1548, attracted Martyr's attention as a regular attender at his lectures, and Martyr supported his application for a preaching licence in April 1553.[40] Herks Garbrand, the Dutch bookseller in Oxford, whose family was also associated with Magdalen, seems to have entertained and given lodging to Swiss students.[41]

Martyr, his students, and their English supporters were encouraged by two visits to Oxford from Martin Bucer. In August 1549, Bucer came briefly but missed Martyr; in July 1550, accompanied by the proto-martyr, John Bradford, he stayed for eleven days.[42] He lodged with Martyr and preached in Christ Church a sermon which Lawrence Humphrey was able to recall in 1573.[43] Bucer's visit may have fortified Martyr

---

[35] O.L., 313-14, 5 January 1550.

[36] O.L., 309-11, 19 October 1551.

[37] O.L., 415, ab Ulmis to Bullinger, 22 August 1550.

[38] O.L., 124, 425, 31 December 1550; 448, 5 February 1552.

[39] O.L., 425-6, 31 December 1550.

[40] John Strype, *Memorials of the Most Reverend Father in God, Thomas Cranmer* (Oxford, 1853), II, 1002.

[41] O.L., 483-4, Martyr to Bullinger, 1 June 1550; Gorham, op. cit., 176, Martyr to Bucer, 6 September 1550.

[42] Gorham, op. cit., 97.

[43] Humphrey, *J. Juelli Episcopi Sarisburiensis, Vita* (London, 1573), 42-3; C. Hopf, *Martin Bucer and the English Reformation* (Oxford, 1946), 21; O.L., 490-2, Martyr to Conrad Hubert, lamenting Bucer's death, 8 March 1551.

after the confrontation with the conservative theologians in the university, especially the disputation on the eucharist in May 1549; but in September 1550, shortly after Bucer's return to Cambridge, Martyr had new difficulties to report. In the theological disputations at which, as Regius Professor, he had to preside, the subjects were being kept from him so that he had to speak extempore and in the presentation of BDs at Convocation, they had appointed a popish respondent.[44]

The Swiss students and their master opened an important link which foreshadowed developments in the Elizabethan university. In Magdalen College also, the events of 1547-53 are a seed-bed for the history of the remainder of the century. A group of militant reformers overturned a moderately conservative President, Owen Oglethorpe, replaced him with a reformer, and after a year were themselves expelled on the accession of Mary, to find the former President back in office, while they formed the most significant group of exiles from Marian Oxford. Oglethorpe had been elected President in February 1535. By the time of Edward VI's accession, he had already survived a period of considerable religious change. The immediate cause of his downfall was the election in Magdalen of a group of militant protestant fellows in the period 1539-48, including Henry Bull (elected 1539), Thomas Bickley (1540), Robert Crowley and Walter Bower (1542), Robert Whitton (1543), John Mullins (1545), Michael Renniger, Arthur Sawle, Robert Taynter, Thomas Bentham, and possibly John Boldren (1546), Thomas Williams (1547), and Lawrence Humphrey and Hugh Kirke (1548). During the last years of Henry VIII's reign, with new sympathizers arriving at every election, able to exercise influence over the young demies,[45] the group steadily grew in strength and the change in climate with the accession of Edward VI gave the opportunity needed to undermine and eventually oust the President. In a petition to the Council, probably of 1550, the militant members complained that Oglethorpe had little concern for the reformation

---

[44] J. C. McClelland, *The Visible Words of God* (London, 1957), 20-2; Gorham, op. cit., 80-2, 176-83; *The Commonplaces of Peter Martyr*, ET by Anthony Marten (London, 1583), 175, 248-50.

[45] Demies, the equivalent of scholars in other foundations, were so named because they received half the stipend of a fellow.

of religion, that he had slandered the royal visitors, and that 'agaynst the godlie, and those that be students, he is not onely in all things infest, but also is not ashamed to protest that he hatethe them for religions sake. Contrarie, the unlearned and papists he maketh muche of, and have all the rule of the college under hym.'[46] The signatories of this letter are ten of the militant fellows elected in the preceding decade.[47] To their petition, they appended a schedule of twenty-five articles of complaint, protesting at Oglethorpe's papist practices, and his hatred for those he called 'anabaptists', 'libertines', and 'gospellers'. Towards these he had acted in such extreme ways that whereas once there were twenty-five in the college who supported reform, this had been reduced to ten.[48] Within the enclosed collegiate society the temperature had been raised and factions created.

Oglethorpe in his defence protested strongly that he had not maintained papist practices, that he did not believe in transubstantiation, and that he had encouraged communion in both kinds, together with the catechizing of 'younglyngs'.[49] As a result of appeals and counter-appeals from the college, the Council became involved in a complicated procedure of intrigue and negotiation. In the spring of 1550, it seems to have been advancing the election of the militant, William Turner, and Turner himself was not above canvassing for the appointment.[50] Oglethorpe was now frequently an absentee, but for a time he managed to re-establish his position in the college. Trouble however revived at the beginning of 1552. Fifteen fellows wrote to the absent President, asking him to remain in office because they feared that if he resigned a militant who would advance the fortunes of the extreme party, now eight in number, would be introduced.[51] The surviving correspondence points to complex negotiations between court, Council, and college as various candidates for the presidency were reviewed.

[46] CCCC MS 127/21, printed in full, Bloxam, *Register*, II, 309-11.
[47] The signatories were Bickley, Mullins, Bower, Whitton, Renniger, Sawle, Taynter, Williams, Humphrey, and Kirke.
[48] Two copies of the articles survive in CCCC MS 127/22 and 127/27.
[49] Oglethorpe's letter is appended to CCCC MS 127/27.
[50] *O.L.*, 187; SP 10/10/34; SP 10/13/2; SP 10/13/14. Walter Bower seems to have been Turner's agent in the college.
[51] SP 10/13/2.

The eventual choice of the Council was Walter Haddon, who had spent his entire academic career in Cambridge, was a friend of Bucer, and had been Master of Trinity Hall for less than a year. The college resented external interference, but eventually bowed to the King's request that they elect Haddon, having been released by royal mandate from their oaths and statutes.[52] The radical party in the college had won its way and now had a President who shared its views. During Haddon's brief tenure, it came to control almost all the college offices. Thomas Bickley, by this time a royal chaplain, was elected Vice-President, John Mullins, Dean of Divinity, and Thomas Bentham and Robert Taynter, Deans of Arts. Only in the bursarial office, where the militant Walter Bower found himself in uneasy partnership with the conservatives Thomas Coveney and Richard Slythurst, did the advanced protestant party fail to gain complete direction of the affairs of the college.

The Vice-President's register records the swift collapse of this hierarchy on the accession of Mary. On 6 July 1553, Thomas Bickley noted the death of Edward VI, on 13 July, the installation of Lady Jane Grey as Queen, and four days later, the eventual accession of Mary. Uncertainty, rather than a definite conviction that the Roman allegiance would be restored, probably activated the sense of panic which overtook the college in the weeks following Northumberland's execution. Walter Haddon obtained a month's leave of absence on 27 August to attend to his own business.[53] On the following day, the Vice-President recorded the arrival in college of letters from the Queen commanding that all injunctions and ordinances contrary to the college statutes and made since the death of Henry VIII should be abolished.[54] During October and November, Thomas Butler was paid for reinstating the altars, though not all members of the college were compliant. Shortly after the accession, a priest was pulled away from the altar and forced to recant until the mass was made legal.[55] The

[52] Magdalen College Oxford Archives, Register E (1550-56), fos. 43[r], 96[v]; Bodleian Library, MS Rawlinson D 1087, fo. 53; BL, Lansdowne MS 3, nos. 5-9; BL, Additional MS 14026, fo. 150[r].

[53] Magdalen College Oxford Archives, Vice-President's Register, fo. 6[r].

[54] Ibid.; see also SP 11/1/11, Mary to the Vice-Chancellor and heads, 20 August 1553.

[55] John Foxe, *Acts and Monuments*, ed. J. Pratt (London, 1877), VI, 712.

advanced protestant members of the society began to
withdraw. On 27 September, Mullins and Bower were granted
six months leave; in the same month Humphrey and Boldren
were given leave to travel abroad, together with Robert
Taynter, and Kirke and Sawle requested short absences.[56]

Stephen Gardiner was restored to the see of Winchester
shortly after Mary's accession, and on 2 October issued a mandate for the visitation of the college, which began on 26
October. Nine fellows were expelled on the first day, Bickley,
Mullins, Bower, Bentham, Sawle, Williams, Kirke, Paley, and
Morwent.[57] Humphrey was not expelled, but held on to his
fellowship until 1555, when he was deprived through absence.
On 30 October, Oglethorpe returned as President having
received the votes of ten of the thirteen seniors.[58] Though nine
fellows were excluded, there is otherwise a surprising continuity of membership in the college throughout the Marian
period. Twenty-seven of the demies elected during the period
1547-58 were still in residence when Elizabeth came to the
throne.

Magdalen provided the only significant group of Oxford ex-
iles. Leaving Oxford late in the autumn of 1553, Lawrence
Humphrey made his way to Strasburg at much the same time
as Peter Martyr, finally released from house-arrest in Christ
Church. By the spring of 1554, he was among the students in
Zurich under the leadership of Robert Horne, Edwardine
Dean of Durham, who also included John Mullins, Thomas
Bentham, Michael Renniger, Thomas Spencer, once a fellow
of Magdalen and from 1547 student of Christ Church, and
William Cole from Corpus.[59] John Jewel, virtually the only
other protestant in Corpus, severely compromised himself in
the first months of the new reign, signing the Marian articles of
recantation. He withdrew from his college into Broadgates
Hall, where the Principal, Thomas Randolph, was a sympathetic ally. After acting as notary for Cranmer and Ridley at
their trial, Jewel fled from Oxford, taking refuge in Frankfurt

---

[56] Magdalen College Oxford Archives, Vice-President's Register, fo. 6^r.
[57] The nine deprived fellows were given £12 between them. Magdalen College
Oxford Archives, Liber Computi, 1543-59, fo. 161^v.
[58] Magdalen College Oxford Archives, Ledger E, fo. 51^r.
[59] *O.L.*, 751-2.

and Zurich.[60] Randolph was eventually forced to leave Broadgates and arrived in Paris in 1555, where Bickley also lodged before his removal to Orléans. Richard Tremayne, a member of Broadgates Hall since the mid-1540s and who had just been elected fellow of Exeter, fled to Germany.[61] Augustine Bradbridge, fellow of New College, was in Strasburg in November 1554 and later in Frankfurt and Geneva. Christopher Goodman, fellow of Brasenose and Lady Margaret Professor 1548-54, had permission to be abroad, but was deprived of his fellowship for absence in 1555. He journeyed to Strasburg, where he was in the company of Bradbridge, Arthur Sawle from Magdalen, and Henry Alcockson, once Chaplain of Magdalen Hall.

Without the group of fellows from Magdalen, there would be scarcely a history of Oxford exiles to record. The exile was not an astute political manoeuvre as Miss Christina Garrett claimed; the nine Magdalen exiles fled in 1553-4 by different routes and for different reasons.[62] The total of those leaving the university who have left any record is no more than seventeen, but they were joined abroad by at least seventeen other former Oxford men. This compares with seventy-six exiles, forty-four of them fellows or sometime fellows, listed by Dr H. C. Porter for Cambridge.[63] One Oxford head of house was an exile and he the most distinguished. Richard Cox was no longer in residence in Oxford when Edward VI died. He was imprisoned for a short time, on suspicion of complicity with Northumberland, but at the end of August fled abroad to Duisburg, then to Strasburg, and eventually to Frankfurt, where he was at the centre of the 1555-6 'troubles'. His future career was to lie outside Oxford as the first Elizabethan Bishop of Ely.

Dr Porter has observed that it is a mistake to see the exiles from Cambridge as a formative influence in the Elizabethan church.[64] In Oxford, as in Cambridge, the exile marked the end of an era, rather than the foundation in the university of a

[60] Humphrey, op. cit., 75; Wood, *Annals*, II, 122.
[61] Exeter College Archives, A.I.5., Register, Vol. I (1539-1619), 59.
[62] Christina Garrett, *The Marian Exiles* (Cambridge, 1938), 1. Details of the other Oxford exiles are from Miss Garrett's biographies.
[63] Porter, 91-8.
[64] Porter, 91.

new one. As in St. John's in Cambridge, the future tradition of
radical dissent in Magdalen College, Oxford was perpetuated
in Elizabeth's reign not by returning exiles, but by the sur-
facing once more of a tradition well established by 1553, if
thereafter temporarily eclipsed, and by the election of like-
minded men both on the eve of the exile, many of whom remained
in residence, and in the early years of the new reign.

II

THE ELIZABETHAN SETTLEMENT
AND THE DEMAND FOR REFORM,
1558-1573

Two famous virtues, namely, ignorance and obstinacy, have wonderfully increased at Oxford since you left it: religion and all hope of good learning and talent is altogether abandoned.[1]

Throughout his first summer in England, John Jewel provided Peter Martyr with gloomy descriptions of his beloved Oxford. Political and religious insecurity in the country at large was matched by a failure in the university to resume the activity broken off by advanced reformers in 1553. Unlike Cambridge, where four exiles returned to college headships, only Lawrence Humphrey resumed his place in Oxford. William Cole and Thomas Bickley were not to join him for another decade. Some of the Oxford exiles were shortly to occupy the chief seats in the Elizabethan church, Jewel as Bishop of Salisbury, Bentham at Coventry and Lichfield. Others became middle-rank ecclesiastics, John Mullins as Archdeacon of London, Thomas Spencer as Archdeacon of Chichester, Arthur Sawle as canon in Jewel's cathedral at Salisbury, and Michael Renniger as royal chaplain. Some, like Luke Purefoy, disappeared from the records after their flight into exile. Hugh Kirke and Peter Morwent decided to settle into country livings, Kirke at Hawkesbury in Gloucestershire, Morwent at Langwith in Derbyshire. There was little incentive to return to Oxford. Parkhurst, as depressed as Jewel at the university's prospects, advised Bullinger in May 1559 against sending his son there, for 'it is as yet a den of thieves, and of those who hate the light. There are few gospellers there, and many papists.'[2]

Jewel and Parkhurst hoped that the university would soon match the learned and godly society of the continental cities where they had been exiles and fulfil the hope of reform

---

[1] *Z.L.*, I, 11; see also 40, 45, 55.
[2] *Z.L.*, I, 29, 21 May 1559.

glimpsed in the reign of Edward VI, when Peter Martyr lived
and taught in Christ Church; but the initial purge of the university, through the activity of the royal visitors, was gentle and
conservative. It left more advanced protestants dissatisfied and
some colleges scarcely changed during the first decade of the
reign. In some societies demands for change were more insist-
ently expressed by members whose aim was to bring the university into greater conformity—in preaching the word, in
externals, and in the expulsion of papists—with the outward
face of the continental reformed churches. For men of this
calibre the pace of official reform was slow and cautious.

The royal injunctions, in part a reissue of those of Edward
VI, had already appeared by the time that the Queen wrote
to the Chancellor, the Earl of Arundel, on 27 May 1559, to
indicate that a visitation of the university was intended 'both
for the augmentation and maintaining of good learning, and
for the establishment of such uniformity in causes of religion
touching common prayer and divine service as by the laws of
the realm is ordained'. No elections to headships or fellowships
were to be made, no officers appointed, and no grants of land
agreed, until the visitation had taken place.[3] Arundel resigned
on 12 June 1559, despite entreaties from some members of the
university to stay and protect them, and eight days later Sir
John Mason resumed the office which he had held until 1556.[4]
The writ for the visitation is not extant, but was probably
issued at the same time as that for Cambridge, dated 20 June
1559. In Cambridge, the supremacy oath was to be applied and
subscription enforced on pain of deprivation, but it is unlikely
that such a thorough-going examination or reform was attempted at Oxford, since, in the summer of 1559, this would have
involved a wholesale ejection of heads and members which does
not seem to have taken place.[5] Nicholas Sander, one of the
fellows now excluded from New College, claimed that, though
the university had suffered much for the Catholic faith, the
visitors had not obtained the oath or subscription from more

[3] Magdalen College Oxford Archives, Admissions Register, 1538-1615, fo. 34^r.
[4] Anthony à Wood, *Appendix to the History and Antiquities ... Fasti Oxonienses*, ed. John
Gutch (Oxford, 1790), 97; OUA/NEP *supra*/Register I, fo. 184^r.
[5] Henry Gee, *The Elizabethan Clergy and the Settlement of Religion, 1558-64* (Oxford,
1898), 133-6; Porter, 104-5.

than one in twenty of the members.[6] The Queen may have been advised to deal gently with Oxford and a letter from the Vice-Chancellor at the end of September thanked her for so moderate a visitation, which had not only restored her authority, but gathered together what had been dissipated, restored what had collapsed, and brought almost all the scholars into obedience to the royal decrees.[7] It was a useful display of self-righteous loyalty, which can scarcely have deceived the Queen. The visitors, Sir John Mason, Sir Thomas Parrye, Treasurer of the Household, Sir Thomas Smith, Sir Thomas Benger, Richard Goodrich, Dr Richard Master, Alexander Nowell, and David Whitehead, seem to have been active from July to September.[8] In individual colleges, they did expel the outwardly non-conforming heads and members. In Trinity, Richard Slythurst, the first President (1555-9), refused the oath of supremacy and was deprived.[9] In Balliol, where the Bishop of Lincoln's commissaries were already active, Walter Wright, the Master, was unsettled and finally resigned in the face of the royal visitation, to be replaced by Francis Babington.[10] In Merton, Thomas Reynolds was deprived, and in the presence of Walter Wright, Archdeacon of Oxford, Thomas Whyte, Warden of New College, and Lord Williams of Thame, Thomas Gervys was elected Warden.[11] In Christ Church, the visitors removed the Dean, Richard Martiall, expelling some of the canons for refusing the supremacy oath.[12] Some prominent men had already fled, including Richard Smith, who was captured in Scotland and ordered to be brought back to conform in Oxford as an example to others.[13] The visitors also attempted

[6] 'Dr. Nicholas Sanders, Report to Cardinal Moroni on the Change of Religion in 1558-9' (1561), ed. J. H. Pollen, in Catholic Record Society, *Miscellanea*, I (London, 1905), 43.

[7] Vice-Chancellor and university to the Queen, 24 September [1559], in *Epistolae Academicae 1508-1596*, ed. W. T. Mitchell (Oxford Historical Society, new series, xxvi, 1980), 348; Wood, *Annals*, II. 141.

[8] SP 13/4/34.

[9] H. E. D. Blakiston, *Trinity College* (London, 1898), 75-6.

[10] Balliol College Archives, Register, 1514-1682, 82-3.

[11] *Registrum Annalium Collegii Mertonensis, 1521-67*, 189-91.

[12] Wood, *Annals*, II, 141.

[13] CCCC MS 114(A), 53, Council to Grindal and Parker, 23 August 1559; *Correspondence of Matthew Parker*, ed. J. Bruce and T. T. Perowne (Cambridge, Parker Society, 1853), 72-3.

to restrain the infiltration of former members and their ideas, and a list was drawn up of twenty-four Oxford men regarded as dangerous papists, over half of them members of New College. Some were confined, but others were permitted to remain at liberty, provided they did not visit the university.[14]

The limited royal visitation was immediately extended by a more thorough examination by ecclesiastical commissioners, in particular Parker and Grindal. In July 1560 they wrote to the Vice-Chancellor and proctors, complaining that many scholars were still resisting the religion established and its ministers. They were now less concerned to expel old recusants than to control the admission of new fellows, who were to take the supremacy oath, come to church 'orderly to abyde the hearing of devyne service', and receive holy communion; all those admitted to degrees were to take the oath, grace at meals was not to include prayers for founders or the departed, and commemoration of benefactors was to be limited to three occasions in the year. All those who continued in non-conformity were to be reported.[15] In Merton, Grindal, as an ecclesiastical commissioner, wrote to Warden Gervys on 3 December 1560 'prayenge yow to loke narowlye to suche as shalbe disobediente or shewe ani contempte of the godlye reformation in religion nowe established in the realme by publike authorite', but there is no evidence that real reform began in Merton until after Gervys's resignation in January 1562.[16]

The work of both royal and ecclesiastical commissioners was incomplete, so that more advanced protestant opinion continued to lament the impoverished state of the university. If the Queen and her bishops had intended a holding operation which would bring Oxford to some degree of outward conformity, those of more distinct reforming intention saw only decay and desolation. On 1 June 1560, writing from his cathedral city for the first time, Jewel told Martyr that 'every thing [in Oxford] is falling into ruin and decay; for the colleges are now filled with mere boys, and empty of learning'.[17] Young James Calfhill, who had delayed his ordination until the new reign and had

[14] Strype, *Annals*, I, part i, 411-17.
[15] Magdalen College Oxford Archives, Admissions Register, 1538-1615, fo. 84^r.
[16] *Registrum Annalium Collegii Mertonensis, 1521-67*, 197.
[17] *Z.L.*, 81; see also 77.

recently taken up a Christ Church prebend, preached at Paul's Cross in January 1561. An observer reported to John Foxe that Calfhill had revealed that Oxford was 'yet under the papistical yoke'.[18] 'Mere boys' predominated and this was shortly to become, as in Cambridge, the decade of the young don. The higher faculties suffered particularly, since they lacked men of the middle age-group, who had remained long enough in Oxford to proceed in their faculties. In 1560 there was no candidate for the DD, one in civil law, and three in physic, and in 1561 none at all in these three faculties.[19] The dearth of seniors is illustrated in the case of Humphrey, who did not proceed BD and DD until 1562, but was senior doctor in 1564. It was in divinity especially that the lack of suitable men was keenly felt, and as early as October 1560 representations had been made to the Queen. She wrote to the Lord Keeper, Nicholas Bacon, indicating that she understood the study of divinity was much decayed through lack of maintenance, and because of 'the alterance of the times' a large number had broken off their studies. Now the Queen proposed to confer exhibitions on suitable candidates nominated to her by the Vice-Chancellors, to encourage the study of divinity.[20] What the Queen fostered with one hand, she moved to take away with the other. Her declaration of 9 August 1561 forbidding heads of houses to marry was partly in response to a report that married heads had taken up residence in the country to the detriment of their students and of learning, and partly an indication of the Queen's desire to ban all clerical marriage. In Oxford, such a ban, had it been enforceable, would have inhibited Humphrey, Sampson, and many of their generation, who had adopted the position of the reformed churches on clerical marriage, and may have regarded it as a part of their witness against Rome.[21] In Merton, William Martiall, a staunch Catholic and Sub-Warden, denounced the new Warden, Thomas Gervys,

---

[18] Strype, *Annals*, I, part i, 354.

[19] OUA/NEP *supra*/Register I, fos. 192ᵛ-200ʳ; Wood, *Annals*, II, 147.

[20] SP 15/9/77, ? October 1560.

[21] SP 15/11/24, ? July 1561, request to the Queen; Inner Temple, Petyt MS 538, vol. 47, fo. 373, Queen's order from Ipswich, 9 August 1561; Cecil to Parker 12 August 1561, *Correspondence of Matthew Parker*, 148; John Strype, *The Life and Acts of Matthew Parker*, I (Oxford, 1821), 212-13.

because he was married but ended in prison for his pains.[22] Sir John Mason feebly informed Cecil on 11 August 1561 that the attempt to prevent the marriage of heads was too great a strain, though the Queen's new instruction would strengthen his hand.[23] The cause, however, was already lost. Nevertheless, the university depended on the goodwill of Queen and court. The Vice-Chancellor and others wrote to Cecil on 25 November 1561, praising his support for their cause. Although he allowed another to be their Chancellor, he was, in actuality and in deed, their 'chancellor', that is, their best patron who had freed them from their slavery.[24] Cecil's affection for Oxford was never on the same scale as that which he nourished for Cambridge, and Oxford was to wait until 1564 before it gained a Chancellor of similar stature and influence in Leicester.

One specific instance in which Oxford failed to attain the pattern of the continental reformed churches was in its provision of preaching. Wood reports that there were only two preachers at the beginning of the reign, Humphrey and Sampson, and records the testimony of Sir Henry Savile, 'that when he came first to the University about 1561, there was but one constant preacher in Oxon, and he only a Bachelaur of All Souls College'.[25] Savile may have been too pessimistic, yet as late as 1566, John Oxenbridge, then a student at Christ Church, assessed the total of Oxford preachers at only five or six.[26] Sampson was excluded from the pulpit after 1565, though Humphrey continued to preach regularly before the university. The bachelor of All Souls was, no doubt, Andrew Kingsmill, who matriculated as a member of Corpus about the time of Mary's acession, remained in the university throughout her reign, though his brothers were among the exiles, and migrated to All Souls to pursue his legal studies. None of his sermons has survived, but his *A Viewe of mans estate,* published posthumously in 1574, was clearly influenced by the Genevan theology.[27]

---

[22] SP 12/15/24, unsigned and undated petition on behalf of Martiall in prison.

[23] SP 12/19/9, Mason to Cecil, 11 August 1561.

[24] SP 12/20/29, Oxford to Cecil, 25 November 1561.

[25] Wood, *Annals,* II, 152.

[26] Bodleian Library, MS Tanner 50. fo. 35ᵛ.

[27] Andrew Kingsmill, *A Viewe of mans estate, wherein the great mercy of God in mans free iustification by Christ is very comfortably declared* (London, 1574), see especially sigs. B viii^v, C iii^v.

Another dedicated disciple of Geneva was Edmund Bunny. Wood records that when Merton College was unable to find a preacher among its members, it elected Bunny.[28] This took place on 11 December 1565. Bunny is noted as already having diligently studied theology and preached, and was senior in age and experience to the other probationary fellows of his election.[29] The influence of Calvin is demonstrated in his first published work, *The Whole Summe of Christian Religion*, dedicated to his patron, Grindal.[30] In 1580, he published an abridged Latin edition of Calvin's *Institutes*.

The new age was represented above all by Lawrence Humphrey. The only Marian exile of significance in Elizabethan Oxford, like his Magdalen friend of old, John Foxe, with whom he shared a refuge in Basel, Humphrey does not seem to have been considered for high ecclesiastical office.[31] Indeed, when Foxe heard of Humphrey's appointment to the presidency of their college, he wrote a reproving, though not entirely serious letter, accusing his old ally of 'deserting our flock and order ... that of the mendicant brothers, or, if you will, the preaching brothers'. He was delighted for Magdalen, and relieved to find in later correspondence that Humphrey had not 'left our company and gone up higher, riding ... in a white chariot'. Foxe's suspicion that office would not leave Humphrey unscathed was later to be amply justified, though he entrusted the education of his son Samuel to him.[32] In 1559, however, Humphrey was no doubt considered too militant for appointment in the church, where Elizabeth chose convinced but moderate reformers.[33] His name is not in the list of spiritual men without promotion of the spring of 1559 but does appear in a very different catalogue, 'certen godlie lerned preachers which have utterly forsaken Antichriste and al his Romishe rags'. It is interesting

---

[28] Wood, *Annals*, II, 152. Noted under the wrong year, 1563.

[29] *Registrum Annalium Collegii Mertonensis, 1521-67*, 258, 260, 262.

[30] Edmund Bunny, *The Whole Summe of Christian Religion* (London, 1576), esp. sig. * vii^r, and fos. 16-17, 25-6, and 31 where Bunny enunciates the doctrine of election.

[31] *Z.L.*, II, 21.

[32] BL, Harleian MS 416, fo. 140; ET by J. F. Mozley, *John Foxe and his Book* (London, 1940), 66.

[33] A list of those considered for bishoprics, in *Calendar of State Papers, Foreign Series, 1559-60*, ed. J. Stevenson (London, 1865), 138 (no. 323), 25 November 1559. Cecil's list of possible bishops, SP 12/4/39.

to find Humphrey here in the company of Thomas Sampson, Miles Coverdale, *quondam episcopus,* Lever, Foxe, Arthur Sawle, and many others, a total of twenty-eight, some of whom were never beneficed.[34] Humphrey had published his advanced ideas of reform in church and state before his return to England, and this may have caused his moderation to be suspect. His *De religionis conservatione et reformatione vera,* addressed from Basle on 30 August 1559 to Francis Russell, Earl of Bedford, argued that outward reforms, purging the church, and preaching the word, would be inadequate without inward repentance and cleansing.[35] A section of the work entitled '*Disciplina ecclesiastica*' makes a direct plea for jurisdiction and censure to be reinforced in the church no less than in the state. The Queen would not have rejoiced at his observation that the secular arm was not to interfere in religious matters.[36] Humphrey's address to the English nobility, published at the same time, entitled *Optimates, sive de nobilitate,* dedicated to Elizabeth, whose reign it hails as the beginning of a golden age, nevertheless encourages the Queen to press forward with reform: 'What your mightyest father Henrye began, youre godlyest brother furthered, that you, even you, should finishe and accomplyshe ... Proceede therefore, proceed, O most noble Quene wyth this your noble trayne in settyng like rooffe and ende to your beginninges.'[37] On his return from exile, Humphrey was to discover a very different Queen, in religious intention at least, from the one he had greeted from afar, and one who would not be moved by his rhetoric.

Humphrey seems to have been recognized again as a member of Magdalen, since with the permission of the President and fellows, he lived with his family in a house outside the college.[38] Although he was not considered for ecclesiastical office, Parker and the Queen's commissioners were advancing

[34] Historical Manuscripts Commission, *Report on the Pepys Manuscripts, preserved at Magdalene College, Cambridge* (London, 1911), 2-3 (= 'Papers of State', II, 701).
[35] Lawrence Humphrey, *De religionis conservatione et reformatione vera* (Basle, 1559), 17-18.
[36] Humphrey, op. cit., 27.
[37] Humphrey, *The Nobles or of Nobilitye,* ET of the *Optimates* (London, 1563), sig. A viii[r-v].
[38] CCCC MS 114(B), 939-40, Humphrey to Parker and Grindal, 17 September 1561.

his fortunes in Oxford. At first they attempted to instal him in the Lady Margaret chair. Francis Babington, Master of Balliol and Vice-Chancellor, a man known for his conservative religious sympathies, nevertheless greeted the prospect of Humphrey's appointment with enthusiasm, admitting that divinity was at a low ebb, and hoping that he would revive it.[39] The unsettled state of religious opinion in the university is illustrated by the fact that for some months it was hoped that Peter Martyr would return to his former chair. The Queen was reported to favour this and the ecclesiastical commissioners, meeting at Lambeth on 12 April 1561, had agreed that the archbishops and bishops should make a contribution to learned strangers to cover their stipends and expenses of travelling to take up residence in the universities.[40] Martyr's return would have provided a focus for reformed teaching in Oxford, but he felt constrained to continue to serve the city of Zurich. When, late in 1561, Zurich was willing for him to depart, old age and ill health prevented it.[41] Humphrey profited by Martyr's inability to return and was offered the Regius chair.

The arrival of Robert Horne, Bishop of Winchester, in the autumn of 1561 was a sign of new hope for the reforming interest. His visitatorial rights extended to five colleges: New College, Magdalen, Corpus, and more tentatively to Trinity and St. John's. His definite though moderate zeal for reform pointed to the prospect of a watershed in the imposition of a distinctively protestant settlement in at least part of the university. He had been associated with Humphrey, Cole, and Sampson in the English community, many of whom were young dons, in Zurich in the spring of 1554.[42] From 1555-7, he had maintained a moderate polity at Frankfurt, which, however, had collapsed in the face of the challenge of John Hales and his associates.

Horne began his visitation in September 1561.[43] After ten

[39] CCCC MS 114(B), 799, Babington to Parker, 12 June 1560.

[40] *Z.L.*, I, 20, 45, 55, 71, 77, 81; *Z.L.*, II, 13; Strype, *The Life and Acts of Matthew Parker*, I, 195.

[41] *Z.L.*, I, 46, 53-4, 71, 74, 77, 81; *The Commonplaces of Peter Martyr*, letters 43, 44, 63, section 5 (five sections separately paginated), 127-9, 164-5.

[42] *O.L.*, 752; see also 125-34.

[43] Mandate for the visitation, Magdalen College, dated 15 July 1561, Magdalen College Oxford Archives, Ledger F, 1556-80, fo. 66ᵛ.

days in Oxford he wrote to Cecil, on 26 September 1561, indicating his preliminary findings. He had attempted, he claimed, to bring the colleges not only into line with their founders' statutes, but also into conformity with the religion now established. The youthfulness of the university, and the lack of grounding of its members in divinity, had immediately impressed him. At any rate, this was the reason he gave for not pressing the students and fellows with controversial religious issues, though any thorough-going examination would have emptied New College and Corpus. Horne therefore limited his reforming intention, and sought only obedience to the Queen's supremacy, conformity to the Prayer Book, and assent to the royal injunctions. Given even this limited enquiry, Horne admitted that if he had acted peremptorily, he would not have left two people in one of the houses. In Magdalen, however, he detected the advanced protestant society in embryo: 'the College of Mawdlen I founde thoroly in those matters conformable, like as I did also many handsome and towarde in lerning and therewith in Religion forwarde'.[44] Horne had proceeded to the immediate deprivation of the President, Thomas Coveney, because many of the promising young men had threatened to leave if he continued in office.

Although it was clear to Horne that the future of the college demanded the installation of a president of distinctively protestant persuasion, this was difficult to achieve. Humphrey had friends within the college and outside it, but some members of the society resisted him. Richard Chambers, patron of Jewel in the reign of Edward VI, who had aided protestants from the universities to exile in 1553, and was himself an exile in Zurich and Frankfurt, accompanied Horne on his visitation.[45] Francis Russell, Earl of Bedford, an exile in Geneva, was also in Oxford at this time, to assist the citizens in the election of the Mayor, and 'to see what good shuld be done in this Visitation'. Both Bedford and Chambers, who seems to have acted as Horne's emissary to Cecil, were convinced that the protestant cause could be more effectively advanced in Magdalen than in

[44] SP 12/19/56, Horne to Cecil, 26 September 1561.
[45] Humphrey, *J. Juelli, Vita*, 32. John Strype, *Ecclesiastical Memorials*, III, part 1 (Oxford, 1822), 225. *O.L.*, 751-2.

any other college. Humphrey was the ideal candidate, but he needed to be 'ayded and advaunced', and Bedford suggested that letters from the Queen should be obtained, directing the fellows to give him their votes.[46] Though Bedford reported that the fellows were as well affected towards Humphrey as he could wish, Humphrey himself found resistance. A few days before the visitation, he had written to Parker and Grindal, indicating that the fellows were claiming, without justice, that his election would be contrary to the statutes and their consciences; he was not a gremial, and he was a married man. The candidate they favoured, Thomas Caius, was not only an outsider, but immoral.[47]

Humphrey's position was further complicated by the fact that Coveney had appealed against his deprivation, and it was not until 25 November 1561 that Horne wrote to say that his sentence had been upheld.[48] In the meantime, the forces working for Humphrey seem to have won over the fellows, and almost the entire fellowship gave him one of their two votes in the first ballot, the other candidates being equally convinced protestants, John Mullins (17 votes), Thomas Bickley (8), Michael Renniger (1), and James Bond, Archdeacon of Bath, (1). Humphrey received twenty-five votes in the first ballot, and was unanimously elected in the second ballot by the thirteen senior fellows.[49] The influence of the court however may have been a more powerful influence on Humphrey's behalf than any decisive change of religious temper among the seniors.

Even in 1561, Magdalen College was a place apart. Its distinctively protestant outlook, at least among the younger fellows, contrasted startlingly with the reports which Horne was making of Corpus and New College. In Corpus the ejection

[46] SP 12/19/55, Bedford to Cecil, 25 September 1561; enclosed SP 12/19/55i, Chambers to Bedford, 25 September 1561.

[47] CCCC MS 114(B), 939-40, Humphrey to Parker and Grindal, 17 September 1561.

[48] Magdalen College Oxford Archives, Vice-President's Register, unnumbered leaf, 7 from the end, recto, Horne to the Vice-President and fellows, 25 November 1561. See also ibid., 6 leaves from the end, Nicholas Bacon to the Vice-President and fellows. Bloxam, *Register*, IV, 111.

[49] Magdalen College Oxford Archives, Ledger F, 1556-80, fos. 68-70, Bloxam, *Register*, IV, 113-14.

of the President, William Butcher (Bocher), possibly a nominee of the royal visitors in 1559, was delayed because of a technicality in the statutes, and Chambers persuaded the bishop to delay the appointment of a successor until the Queen had commended 'an honest godlye manne ... otherwise the fellowes are so corrupted wyth false religion that theye will choose a papiste'.[50] In New College, many of the members refused the subscription, protesting that Horne did not possess sufficient authority. Only nine fellows and the Warden, Thomas Whyte, took the oath of supremacy and swore that the Prayer Book was in agreement with the true word of God. Chambers regretted that nothing could be done to remove the Warden, who had already taken part in the royal visitation, and hoped that authority could subsequently be obtained to deal with him. The younger members of the college were, unlike those in Magdalen, also staunch adherents of the old religion. Two of the young fellows, having refused to come to service in chapel, protested to the Visitor that their statutes allowed them nothing but the mass, and Horne handed them over to be punished by the Vice-Chancellor.[51] The college was not reduced to outward conformity until the Visitor or his commissary had returned three times between 1561 and 1566. In these years thirty-three fellows left or were expelled. Dr Penry Williams has argued that the loss, with the departure of men like Nicholas Sander, Thomas Stapleton, John Fowler, the Roman Catholic printer, and John Rastell, was in quality rather than quantity, and that thirty-three fellows out of seventy was a smaller proportion than the nine expelled from Merton's fellowship of fourteen. In any case, the college had a continuous supply of new junior fellows direct from Winchester, and fourteen probationers were elected in 1560 and ten in each year during 1561-4.[52]

One college out of sixteen, Magdalen, now had been provided with distinctively protestant leadership by a combination of internal design and external prompting. In another, Christ

---

[50] SP 12/19/55i, Chambers to Bedford, 25 September 1561.

[51] Bodleian Library, MS Top. Oxon. C 354, a transcript of part of Horne's Register, fos. 12^v, 14^v, SP 12/19/56, Horne to Cecil, 26 September 1561.

[52] New College Archives, MS Register of Members of New College, compiled by J. E. Sewell; *New College Oxford, 1379-1979*, 49; *Wood, Annals*, II, 144-5.

Church, there seems to have been a general desire among the canons and students to advance beyond the outward changes demanded by the visitors. Early in 1561, George Carew, Dean for two years since Martiall's deprivation, resigned to become Dean of Windsor. He had evidently been contemplating resignation for some time, since in August 1560 Lawrence Humphrey had heard a rumour that John Foxe was to be the new Dean.[53] In January 1561, the suggested successor was a man of very different religious complexion, Francis Babington, by this time Rector of Lincoln College. He was Leicester's protégé and chaplain, though by this time he seems to have been declining in favour. It is evident that in these years Leicester's patronage was by no means exclusively directed towards advanced protestants.[54] Christ Church had no intention of tolerating Babington's appointment, if it could be prevented. In January, twenty-two members of the house wrote to Leicester. They also wrote to Cecil, encouraging him to use his influence with the Queen on their behalf. The signatories included James Calfhill, now Sub-Dean, and Lawrence Humphrey as Regius Professor of Divinity. They argued that since their house stood as a light to the rest of the body of the university, to give it the light of salvation, they needed a dean of the highest calibre. They had considered the great multitude of learned men in the country and, they concluded, there was not one to be compared with Thomas Sampson, skilled in many languages, excellent in learning, of conspicuous merit in theology, and greater in pure religion, not only than Babington, but than any other man.[55]

In its eagerness to exclude Babington, Christ Church exaggerated the qualities of Sampson, who would have been practically unknown in Oxford at this date. His Cambridge career is obscure, though he may well have belonged to the small circle, all of them fellows of Pembroke or Corpus, which had surrounded the Strasburg reformer, Martin Bucer. By 1552

---

[53] BL. Harleian MS 417, fo. 114; Mozley, op. cit., 64.

[54] On Dudley's patronage, see Collinson, *E.P.M.*, 52-3, 62-3; and *The Letters of Thomas Wood, Puritan, 1566-1577*, ed. Patrick Collinson (*Bulletin of the Institute of Historical Research*, Special Supplement, 5, November 1960) xvi-xl; and V. H. H. Green, *The Commonwealth of Lincoln College, 1427-1977* (Oxford, 1979), 128-9.

[55] Bodleian Library, MS Rawlinson D 264, fos. 28-9, 30-1, Christ Church to Leicester; BL, Lansdowne MS 5, fo. 4[r-v].

Sampson had been appointed Dean of Chichester and before his flight to Strasburg on 6 May 1554 had been in hiding in London with Richard Chambers, who may later have been instrumental in commending him to Christ Church. He spent the years 1554-8 first in Strasburg, then in Zurich, Geneva, Frankfurt, and again in Strasburg.[56] Throughout the period, he maintained a relentless and questioning correspondence with Bullinger in Zurich and later with Peter Martyr. For the first year of his return to England, he was without employment, spending some time with Bentham at Lichfield and probably with Lever at Coventry.[57] Like other exiles, Sampson was frequently in demand as a preacher. He preached at Paul's Cross at Easter 1559 and Easter 1560, and on three occasions early in 1561 he preached at court.[58] Sampson appears to have been willing to consider the prospect of office in the church. Before he left Strasburg, he had questioned Peter Martyr on 17 December 1558 about the attitude he should adopt if offered high office. He seems in one sentence to expect such an offer, and in another to doubt if any such will come his way. Sampson's chief reservation at this time was not the question of the surplice, but the royal supremacy and the difference in character between episcopacy in the Church of England and the primitive institution, especially with regard to first-fruits, episcopal election, discipline, and dress.[59]

In the New Year 1560, Sampson clearly regarded episcopal appointment as possible. Cecil's list of possible bishops from spring 1559 had named him for Salisbury, though by June or July his name had been dropped.[60] In an anonymous letter of the same year, he is named as bishop-designate of Norwich.[61] On 6 January 1560, he wrote to Peter Martyr announcing the appointment of Cox, Grindal, Sandys, Barlow, Bentham, and

[56] For examples of his correspondence see *O.L.*, 170-83, *Z.L.*, I, 32-3; John Strype, *The History of the Life and Acts of Edmund Grindal* (Oxford, 1821), 31.
[57] 'The Letter Book of Thomas Bentham, Bishop of Coventry and Lichfield', ed. R. O'Day and J. Berlatsky, *Camden Miscellany*, XXVII (Camden Fourth Series, 22, 1979), 189-90, 231.
[58] *The Diary of Henry Machyn, citizen and merchant-taylor of London, AD 1550-1563*, ed. J. G. Nichols (Camden Society, 1st series, 42, 1848), 192, 231, 252, 254. Strype, *Annals*, I, part i, 408-10.
[59] *Z.L.*, I, 2, Sampson to Martyr, 17 December 1558.
[60] Strype, *Annals*, I, part i, 227-8, Cecil's list of possible bishops.
[61] *Calendar of State Papers, Foreign Series, 1559-60*, 138 (no. 323).

Jewel, but indicating that he was 'loitering on the threshold'. He had transferred his scrupulous concern to the cross and candlesticks on the altar in the royal chapel, and the lack of sermons at the Lord's Supper.[62] Whilst he protested, 'Let others be bishops; as to myself, I will either undertake the office of a preacher or not at all', it seems that, at length, he did not have to face the anguish of refusing episcopal office. Professor Haugaard has convincingly demonstrated that he was passed over for the see of Norwich, 'much to his feigned relief and deep chagrin'.[63]

Although the Queen passed him over for Norwich, within a year she had offered him the deanery of Christ Church, acceding to the wishes of the canons and students. The Queen granted him the deanery on 11 April 1561, though he delayed until 5 September before being installed.[64] After his installation, he sought the permission of Congregation to preach within the university in a doctoral habit, although not a doctor, and was given permission to do so until the following Comitia.[65] This request was prompted not by the feeling of lack of academic standing, but, presumably, because Sampson regarded the doctor's habit as less idolatrous than the surplice, though he need scarcely have worn this to preach. Only a week after Sampson's eventual installation in his deanery, James Calfhill, Sub-Dean, recorded in the Chapter Act Book that the Dean had convoked the chapter, and that with the unanimous consent of all the prebendaries it had been agreed that the altars, statues, images, tabernacles, missal books, and all other idolatrous and superstitious monuments remaining in the cathedral should be destroyed.[66] Henry Machyn may have been noting this, or a similar cleansing in another college, when he records in his diary, though dating it 5 September, 'This Friday ... was bornyd at Oxford, by the master of the colege of ... grett reches that myght have beene sene and gyffyne

---

[62] Z.L., I, 62-3.

[63] Z.L., I, 75-6; W. P. Haugaard, 'The Episcopal Pretensions of Thomas Sampson', in Historical Magazine of the Protestant Episcopal Church, xxxvi (1967), 383-6; and Elizabeth and the English Reformation (Cambridge, 1968), 48.

[64] Calendar of the Patent Rolls, 1560-63 (London 1948), 154.

[65] OUA/NEP supra/Register I, fo. 199ʳ, after 27 November 1561.

[66] Christ Church Archives, Chapter Act Book (also called The Sub-Dean's book and the Black Book), 100.

to ...'[67] Even before Sampson's arrival, the Christ Church chapter, probably under the influence of Calfhill, had staged a demonstration of filial piety to Peter Martyr and at the same time conducted an important propaganda exercise for the reformed tradition. On 11 January 1561, the remains of Catherine Martyr, who had died in Oxford in 1553, which had been disinterred from their burial place in the cathedral on the instructions of Cardinal Pole, were solemnly reburied. They were safeguarded from further disturbance, when a reversal of religious affection still seemed possible, by being buried together with those of St. Frideswide. Calfhill commemorated the event in writing, verses were hung upon the church doors in Catherine's honour, and a sermon was preached which condemned the papist cruelty which originally disturbed her bones. Oxford was not again to have Peter Martyr in its midst, but the act of homage to his wife symbolized, perhaps, the reinstatement of the university's link with the continental reformed churches.[68]

While there can be no doubt of the reforming impetus within Christ Church, even before the advent of Sampson as Dean, none of his capitular colleagues can have welcomed him more gladly than James Calfhill, Sub-Dean in 1560-1, and again in 1566-7. Calfhill had migrated from Eton and Kings to become a member of Christ Church in 1548. Though he became Dean of Bocking and Archdeacon of Colchester, he was frequently in Oxford, and succeeded Babington as Lady Margaret Professor, when the latter was deprived of all his preferments on suspicion of papist allegiance in 1564. Calfhill's opinions seem to have reflected those of Sampson. With his Dean, he was proctor in the lower house of the Convocation of 1563, and both were among the thirty-four members of that house, about one third of the total, who put their names to the Seven Articles, which, had they been adopted, would have abolished the cross in baptism, baptism by laymen, cope and surplice, as well as 'any other dress worn by the ministers of the word and sacraments used by the enemies of the gospel'. Kneeling at the communion would have

---

[67] *The Diary of Henry Machyn*, 266. The original manuscript is damaged.

[68] '*Historia de exhumatione Catharinae ... ac eiusdem ad honestam sepulturam restitutione*', at the end of Conrad Hubert, *Historia vera: de vita, obitu, sepultura ... Buceri et Fagii* (Strasburg, 1562), 196-203. Strype, *The Life and Acts of Matthew Parker*, I, 198-201.

been left to the discretion of the ordinary and superstitious singing abolished.[69]

Calfhill's radical opinions further annoyed the Queen in July 1564, when Walter Haddon complained that he had preached a very offensive sermon, but we do not know its subject.[70] Further evidence of his desire to abolish the remnants of popish superstition may be found, at length, in his *An Aunswere to the Treatise of the Crosse*, published in 1565. Here, he distinguishes three types of traditions in the church, first, those necessarily inferred from the scriptures, secondly, those directly contrary to the word, thirdly, indifferent traditions, not utterly repugnant to the word, nor necessarily implied in it, which may be kept for policy, for the good of the church or for order, though nevertheless, he argues, the church may have too many ceremonies.[71] A sermon preached at Paul's Cross, on 10 February 1566, on the same theme shows that he was well grounded in the teaching of Calvin. Before the age when controversy reigned, Calfhill encouraged his congregation to avoid both proud presumption of their own deserts and doubting of their salvation.[72] Both Calfhill and Humphrey seem to have taken the conservative Richard Cheyney, Bishop of Gloucester, to task on the subject of free will in 1568. Cheyney was also unjustly under suspicion of Romanist sympathies because of his stress on the patristic writings, and Calfhill devoted two sermons at Bristol to an attack on him.[73]

Whilst no evidence survives to determine the course of the further advancement of the protestant settlement in Christ Church, under the leadership of Sampson and Calfhill, in Humphrey's Magdalen reform proceeded apace. On 23 January 1563, the President and seven of the fellows were given authority to sell vestments and hangings from the chapel.[74] Already, in 1560 and 1561, provision had been made

[69] Strype, *Annals*, I, part i, 501-2; for amendments, see Haugaard, *Elizabeth and the English Reformation*, 353, and for a full discussion of the proceedings, ibid., 62-73.

[70] *Correspondence of Matthew Parker*, 218, Haddon to Parker, July 1564.

[71] James Calfhill, *An Answer to John Martiall's Treatise of the Crosse*, ed. R. Gibbings (Cambridge, Parker Society, 1846), 32, 267.

[72] Bodleian Library, MS Tanner 50, fos. 40-1.

[73] F. O. White, *The Lives of the Elizabethan Bishops* (London, 1898), 175-6; Strype, *Annals*, I, part ii, 277-83; SP 12/48/11, 7 October 1568; SP 12/48/16, 15 October 1568.

[74] Magdalen College Oxford Archives, Ledger F, 1556-80, fo. 87^{r-v}. Bloxam, *Register*, II, 335-6.

for an adequate supply of surplices. Troubles in the college never reached the level of those in St. John's College, Cambridge in 1564-5, but the President and some of the fellows began to express their unease about the significance of this garment as early as 1563.[75] The first sign of Humphrey's uneasiness with the surplice was indicated in a letter to Bullinger dated 16 August 1563. Sampson was probably in close touch with the President of Magdalen on this question, and had also written to Zurich in the gloomiest of terms the previous month.[76] Humphrey's letter, less agonized than Sampson's, enquired whether the cap and surplice could be considered indifferent, since they had for so long been associated with superstition, and secondly, whether, when lawfully commanded, the godly might wear these vestments. The letter is moderate in tone, and suggests that, given the latitude which collegiate enclosure allowed, and with the encouragement to conform emanating from Zurich, Humphrey, if not Sampson, might have been quietly contained in Oxford.

Lawful authority was not prepared to allow the matter to rest. At the end of 1564, Parker summoned Humphrey and Sampson to London and submitted to them a series of questions.[77] This was essentially a moderate initiative; several bishops and divines took part in the consultation, and though not all were able to give their whole-hearted support to the questions, among the signatories were Grindal, Bickley, and Horne. Humphrey and Sampson were only induced to sign with the vital Pauline proviso, '*Omnia mihi licent, sed non omnia expediunt. Omnia mihi licent, sed non omnia aedificant.*'[78] Further moderate discussions were rendered hopeless by the general attack on non-conformity which followed the Queen's letter of 25 January 1565. Recent argument has suggested that Parker himself may have asked for this letter to strengthen his hand, and that Cecil allowed him to see a draft of it before it was

---

[75] Bloxam, *Register*, II, 276; Porter, ch. vi, for the St. John's troubles.

[76] *Z.L.*, I, 130-1, Sampson to Bullinger, 26 July 1563. *Z.L.*, I, 133-4, Humphrey to Bullinger, 16 August 1563.

[77] Strype, *The Life and Acts of Matthew Parker*, I, 329-45.

[78] Strype, *The Life and Acts of Matthew Parker*, I, 345. Original with signatures of Humphrey and Sampson, BL, Additional MS 32091, fo. 201; another copy (? the bishops'), BL, Lansdowne MS 9, fo. 175.

delivered.[79] The letter makes especial mention of places normally exempt, including the universities, where 'varieties,
novelties and diversities ... either in doctrine or in ceremonies
and rites of the Church, or in the manners, usages, and
behaviour of the clergy' are to be investigated, and the Queen
furnished with a list of non-conformists.[80] Parker acted immediately, sending to his suffragans and to the universities a
demand that investigations be carried out and names of nonconformists certified to him, for report to the Queen, by the
end of February.[81] The Oxford Vice-Chancellor's report does
not survive and Richard Beaumont, Vice-Chancellor of
Cambridge, dispatched his on the last possible day, 27 February
1565, an indication of opposition to the enquiry.[82] Magdalen
College, Oxford, like Christ's and St. John's in Cambridge,
raised a complaint. On 26 February, Adrian Hawthorne, Vice-
President, and twenty-five of the fellows wrote to the
Archbishop, protesting that their founder, Waynflete, had laid
down in the statutes that no authority was to be admitted in the
college, except that of their Visitor, the Bishop of Winchester,
and that the Vice-Chancellor and proctors, now making
enquiries on Parker's behalf, had no rights. Further, they had
laid aside the vestments, not at the persuasion of their President, who was highly to be praised, but through the promp-
tings of their own consciences.[83] John Kennall, student of
Christ Church, who had been re-elected Vice-Chancellor on
the same day, 26 February, must have sent at least two names,
those of Humphrey and Sampson, to the Archbishop. Parker,
acting very swiftly, summoned them to London for interview
on 3 March, the same day as he sent the document later known
as 'The Advertisements' to Cecil. After examination on 3
March and 8 March, the Archbishop found the heads unwill-
ing to make any concessions, and requesting liberty to return to

---

[79] *Correspondence of Matthew Parker*, 223-7. Collinson, *E.P.M.*, 69-70.

[80] *Correspondence of Matthew Parker*, 226.

[81] Ibid., 227-30. Parker's letter to Grindal, 30 January 1565; presumably similar
letters were sent to the universities.

[82] MS 106, p. 627; *Correspondence of Matthew Parker*, 226.

[83] Inner Temple, Petyt MS 538, vol. 47, fo. 58 (misdated 1572 in the catalogue);
copy (correctly dated), Bodleian Library, MS Smith 79, fo. 97; printed in Bloxam,
Register, II, 337-8, without names.

Oxford.[84] Parker, frustrated with the obduracy of the two men, told Cecil that he intended to put the case in the hands of Leicester, elected Chancellor of Oxford in December 1564, or of the Council.[85] Meanwhile, during their enforced stay in London, Humphrey and Sampson were deeply involved in the cause of the London ministers, directed with equal militancy against the vestments. On 20 March together with Calfhill, alone among other Oxford figures, but with seventeen London ministers, including Mullins, Foxe, and Nowell, they sent a letter to the Archbishop and the ecclesiastical commissioners, expressing great grief that there should be dissent about such a small matter as the cap and surplice, and requesting that, because of their tender consciences, they might be allowed liberty to follow their own opinions.[86] Parker seems to have handed the matter of the Oxford heads over to Leicester, since at the end of the month they wrote to their Chancellor asking permission to return home, not only to consider the important matters laid before them at Lambeth, but also to prepare their Easter sermons.[87] By 29 April, Parker himself was determined that Humphrey and Sampson should either conform, or lose their places. He now demanded that they should wear the square cap appointed by the injunctions, wear no hats with their long gowns, wear a surplice with a non-regent hood in their collegiate choirs, according to the ancient custom, and communicate in wafer-bread, kneeling. When they refused, Parker informed them that he must report this to the Queen, though he admitted to Cecil 'as the deanery is at her Highness' disposition, and the presidentship of Magdalen at the election of the College, upon what ground and how to proceed I am in doubt. If it be the Queen's Majesty's pleasure that I write letters to both Colleges, that they be not reputed or accepted there in their rooms, or enjoy any commodity, I shall do her commandment. Resign I think they mean not; judicially to be deprived, against Mr Sampson my jurisdiction (after long pleading) might serve, yet so it cannot upon Dr Humphrey; but it is to be expended by the bishop of Winchester their

---

[84] *Correspondence of Matthew Parker*, 233-4.
[85] Ibid., 234-5.
[86] Lambeth Palace Library, MS 2019, fos. 1-2.
[87] BL, Lansdowne MS 8, fo. 136, 31 March 1565.

Visitor.[88] Parker had already been reminded that Magdalen was a place exempt.

Stalemate seems to have been reached in the case of Humphrey, who took refuge with Alice Warcupp, a widow sympathetic to his cause, at English in Oxfordshire, and from there asked Foxe to intercede on his behalf with his former pupil, the Duke of Norfolk.[89] Sampson was deprived of his deanery by the Queen's command, though the common lawyers raised doubts about the legality of the proceedings, and Thomas Godwyn was installed on 26 May.[90] Sampson in his poverty seems to have aroused the sympathy of the Christ Church chapter, which offered his son a studentship on 4 June.[91] Huntingdon and Pilkington also interceded on his behalf.[92]

Further action against Humphrey was taken through the agency of the Vice-Chancellor. In his reply to the commissioners, he complained bitterly that enforced conformity was robbing the church of some of its best pastors: 'the learned man without his cappe is afflicted, the capped man without learning is not touched'; and that while the protestants were divided over caps and surplices, 'as wee say a doubt or a question in Divinitie', the papists were mocking them.[93] He was to make a similar protest about the detrimental effect on the preaching ministry when 'The Advertisements' were eventually issued in March 1566. In a letter to Leicester, dated 18 April 1566, Humphrey revealed clearly why he had been able to keep his office in Oxford, while Sampson had been displaced, and why Magdalen then and later was to flourish as a haven of nonconformity. He began, 'I trust your L. wyl be our Chancelar and proctour in the universitie as Mr Secretaries withal in Cambridge: where Magdalen College is yet free, as I trust our

[88] BL, Lansdowne MS 8, fo. 143; *Correspondence of Matthew Parker,* 239-40.

[89] BL, Harleian MS 416, fo. 177, 20 May 1565.

[90] Strype, *The Life and Acts of Matthew Parker,* I, 368, 371. The grant to Godwyn is in *Calendar of Patent Rolls, 1563-66* (London, 1960), 324.

[91] Christ Church Archives, Chapter Act Book, 105.

[92] *Correspondence of Matthew Parker,* Sampson to Parker, 3 June 1565; Parker to Cecil, 4 June 1565; Parker to Sampson, 4 June 1565; Parker to Huntingdon, 4 June 1565, all from Inner Temple, Petyt MS 538, vol. 47, fos. 322-3.

[93] SP 12/36/64; undated, probably from this time, but possibly subsequent to the publication of 'The Advertisements'.

Magdalen College shalbe. If you both agree in yt, to helpe poer miserable Magdalena, by our gracious Elizabetha, your honours shall muche please god and do service to the Churche. Both Magdalians have long enioyed this gratious libertie: bothe are, as your L. knoweth, out of the universitie: bothe separate and exempte places, no common churches, nor open collegiate houses within the precincts of the walls.'[94] Humphrey's claim for an exemption was tenuously based, but the position of a college like Magdalen and the liberty of religious practice enjoyed there contrasted favourably, both with colleges under the royal eye, like Christ Church, and with the fortunes of parochial ministers under the more direct control of their ordinaries. Despite this degree of protection, Humphrey seems to have believed, as late as 2 June, that he might be deprived of his office and wrote to Leicester asking leave, at least, to stay at liberty and to have the right to preach, although he would be without a living.[95]

By July 1566, Humphrey and Sampson, believing that the church in Zurich had been unduly influenced by the case put forward by the bishops, particularly Grindal and Horne, joined with Coverdale to send a delegation in an attempt to win the sympathy of the Genevan church for their cause. The delegation, led by Percival Wyburn, shows that a younger generation of Oxford fellows also supported the cause Humphrey had laboured to advance. The two other members were Andrew Kingsmill, fellow of All Souls, Dean of Laws there, and brother-in-law of Bishop Pilkington, and Ralph Warcupp, student of Christ Church since 1563, and son of Alice Warcupp who had earlier offered Humphrey refuge.[96] As early as 20 January 1564, Kingsmill had written to Parker about the vestments. In lawyer-like fashion, he had outlined the conditions for things indifferent and urged that the habits, as a free

[94] BL, Additional MS 19400, fo. 89[r-v]. The letter is dated 18 April 1565, presumably Humphrey's error for 1566.

[95] Historical Manuscripts Commission, *Report on the Pepys Manuscripts*, 87-8 (= 'Papers of State', I, 605, 613).

[96] All Souls College Archives, Letters of Kings, Archbishops, etc., fo. 10 (no. 25), 27 November 1564. Pilkington to Kingsmill, *The Works of James Pilkington*, ed. J. Scholefield (Cambridge, Parker Society, 1842), 679-82. Warcupp translated Marloratus' *Prayers on the Psalms* in 1571; see Wood, *Athenae Oxonienses*, ed. Philip Bliss (London, 1813), I, col. 754.

matter, should not be forced on those whose consciences prevented them from wearing them.[97] Humphrey sent a letter commending the delegation to the continental churches, and Coverdale, Humphrey, and Sampson sent a joint letter to Farel, Viret, and Beza, making clear their view that the dispute was not merely about dress, but about unleavened bread and kneeling at the communion.[98] Beza received the delegation warmly, and Wyburn was dispatched to Zurich with a recommendation to Gualter that he should go to England to see the situation for himself. Kingsmill seems to have fallen under the spell of the school of Christ in Geneva, and, forsaking the imperfect school of Oxford, remained there, moving later to Lausanne, where he died in 1569.[99]

By the end of August 1566, when the Queen visited the university for the first time, Humphrey must have realized that his position was secure. Horne, the only authority who could have deprived him, had made no move to do so, though a visitation of his college took place the following month. During the royal progress through the university, Humphrey was much in evidence, his disputation in the Schools earning the commendation of the Spanish ambassador and the nobles who heard it. Meeting the Queen in his scarlet, Humphrey was not allowed to present himself without challenge: 'that loose gown becomes you mighty well,' said the Queen, 'I wonder your notions should be so narrow'.[100] She also demonstrated annoyance when, in his speech of welcome to Christ Church, Thomas Kingsmill, the Public Orator, praised her for having conferred as great benefits on the university as her brother, who had appointed Bucer and Martyr to the Regius chairs. She had recalled the followers of Martyr from exile, and had conferred the divinity chair, which he had previously held, on Humphrey, 'the constant hearer of Martyr, the heir of his merits and in age only inferior to his predecessor'.[101] Such high

[97] Inner Temple, Petyt MS 538, vol. 47, fos. 482-90.
[98] Z.L., II, 121-4. Macray, Register, II, 100.
[99] On Kingsmill's bequest to All Souls, see below, 94.
[100] This version of the Queen's remark is reported by F. Peck, Desiderata Curiosa, I (London, 1779), 276. Wood, Annals, II, 156, has a variant.
[101] Bodleian Library, MS Rawlinson D 837, fo. 22; William Roper, Vita D. Thomae Morie (London, 1716), (pages 69-179 = Epistolae et Orationes Aliquammultae Academiae Oxoniensis), 108.

praise of one who had so recently caused the Queen great trouble somewhat dampened her appreciation and she told the Orator, 'You would have done well had you had good matter.'[102]

In Magdalen, which had so long resisted outside incursions, new order was achieved through the visitation by Horne's commissary, Dr George Ackworth, in September 1566. After Ackworth had examined the fellows, he summoned the whole body on 20 September and censured them for their failure to wear the surplice, square cap, and other clerical dress. They were ordered to obtain these garments before 1 November and to wear the surplice on Sundays and festivals. Thomas Turner, examined with other contumacious fellows on 27 September, was accused of not wearing a surplice and square cap, and admitted that he had not done so for three years. He had called the Vice-President a papist, and had tried to expel one of his fellows, Thomas Doylie, from the college because he wore a surplice. Judging by the letter from twenty-five fellows to Parker in February 1565, a large proportion of the society had left off the surplice, but Turner, because of his outspokenness, paid the penalty of suspension from all votes until Passion Sunday, while his brethren seem to have escaped without punishment.[103]

In two other societies, a protestant settlement, far from being welcomed by the fellows, was definitively imposed from above. These colleges, through the agency of their Visitors, were to join Christ Church and Magdalen as seminaries for godly divines and preaching ministers. In Merton College, Thomas Gervys resigned in January 1562. The college supplied Parker with five names, three of them originally suggested by him. On the grounds that this was two more than the statutory provision, Parker overturned the process of nomination and appointed as Warden John Man, a former fellow of New College.[104] When Babington and Whyte arrived as commissaries

---

[102] Wood, *Annals*, II, 157.

[103] Magdalen College Oxford Archives, C 129; nineteenth-century transcript of part of Horne's Register relating to Magdalen visitations.

[104] *Registrum Annalium Collegii Mertonensis, 1521-67*, 209-10; *Registrum Matthei Parker*, transcribed by E. M. Thompson, ed. W. H. Frere (Oxford, Canterbury and York Society, 1928), 798-800. SP 12/21/57, fellows of Merton to Cecil, 28 February 1562.

to install Man on 30 March, they found such strong opposition
that, having delivered a reprimand, they were forced to retreat
for three days. When they returned on 2 April, they found the
gates locked against them, there was a scuffle, and Man was
eventually installed on 27 May, but only after a visitation had
rooted out the conspirators.[105] All of them were papists or
crypto-papists, who had attempted to restore some of the older
practices of the house, such as the singing of psalms in hall and
vigils in chapel. There was widespread failure to attend
services and some of the fellows appear to have secreted popish
service books, vestments, and ornaments, under the chapel
floor.[106] During the following year, at least four members
withdrew or were expelled and an exceptionally large number
of junior fellows, seven in 1562 and another seven in 1563,
entered the college. Those elected in 1563 included Thomas
Bodley.[107] Man failed in the task of establishing a stable protestant settlement in Merton, largely because he was frequently
absent as royal emissary to the court of Spain. After he had
severely reprimanded the college on 18 March 1569, shortly
after Man's death, Parker appointed as Warden one of his own
chaplains, Thomas Bickley.[108] The Archbishop was determined to have a strong head in office and writing to Leicester
on 29 March, he disclosed his hope that Bickley would work for
the good of the university and put an end to the intolerable
trouble which he had suffered from the college for ten years.[109]

In Corpus also the initial attempt to impose a distinctively
protestant settlement was unsuccessful. Horne secured the
election of Thomas Greenaway in 1562, but despite his interest
in the continental reformed tradition, the life of the society
remained at a low ebb.[110] In June 1566, Humphrey and John
Pierce, fellow of Magdalen and later Dean of Christ Church,

---

[105] *Registrum Annalium Collegii Mertonensis, 1521-67*, 211-16; *Registrum Matthei Parker*, 691. Wood, *Annals*, II, 148-51.

[106] *Registrum Annalium Collegii Mertonensis, 1521-67*, 198.

[107] Ibid., 216, 219, 226, 256. See also H. W. Garrod, 'Bodley of Merton', in 'Friends of the Bodleian', *Annual Report*, no. 13 (1938), 10.

[108] *Registrum Annalium Collegii Mertonensis, 1567-1603*, ed. J. M. Fletcher (Oxford Historical Society, new series, xxiv, 1976), 17-18.

[109] *Registrum Annalium Collegii Mertonenis, 1567-1603*, 20-1; *Registrum Matthei Parker*, 845-6; Historical Manuscripts Commission, *Report on the Pepys Manuscripts*, 152-3 (= 'Papers of State', II, 253).

[110] For Greenaway's bequest of reformed writings to the college, see below, 94.

wrote to Leicester reporting the decay of the college, and Ackworth's visitation in September revealed great hatred of Greenaway, some of it, though not declared as such, religious in motivation. Hieronymous Reynolds and George Atkinson, the Chaplain, seem to have conspired to conceal the chapel plate, hoping, no doubt, for a swift return of the old religion.[111] In 1568, when Greenaway resigned, an open split was revealed between the senior fellows, conservative in religion, who proposed the election of Robert Harrison, recently removed from the college, and fourteen fellows, the majority of them elected since the beginning of the new reign, who petitioned Ackworth to prevent the election of a man of Roman Catholic sympathies, clearly a reference to Harrison.[112]

The college did not, however, expect the introduction by the Visitor of his former friend from exile, William Cole. When Horne, or his commissary, came with the new President to admit him, they found the gate closed against them, and it was not until a commission from the Queen had been sent, dated 21 July 1568, that Cole was finally settled in his place. Cole had spent the exile in Zurich, Strasburg, and Geneva. He was known as an opponent of the vestments and had remained abroad as preacher to the Merchant Adventurers in Antwerp after 1559, possibly because of his intense dislike of the ceremonies of the Church of England.[113] In Antwerp he had followed the advice of Grindal and adopted the manner of the local reformed churches in ceremonies, not wearing the surplice because the 'high Almayne churches use none'. In ecclesiastical discipline he had been assisted by six 'seniours'.

---

[111] Humphrey and Pierce to Leicester, Historical Manuscripts Commission, *Report on the Pepys Manuscripts,* 88 (= 'Papers of State', I, 609). Ackworth's visitation is described at length in Thomas Fowler, *The History of Corpus Christi College Oxford* (Oxford Historical Society, xxv, 1893), 110-23, from Horne's Register at Winchester. Accusations against Greenaway are in BL, Additional MS 6251, fos. 6, 16, and Corpus Christi College Oxford MS 280 (c), fos. 239-40, the '*Fatalis Oratio*' of Simon Trippe.

[112] Fellows of Corpus to Ackworth, Corpus Christi College Oxford MS 280(c), fo. 238 ʳ, not dated.

[113] Evidence of Cole in exile is suplied in *O.L.,* 751-2, and Corpus Christi College Oxford MS 318, fos. 88-111, 129, 134, 152-6. The letter from Coverdale, 22 February [1560] MS 318, fo. 134 reveals Cole's dislike of the ceremonies. See also Corpus Christi College Oxford MS 297, fo. 18. Collinson, *E.P.M.,* 50, identifies the preacher to the Merchant Adventurers with the later President of Corpus.

The visitation of Corpus in 1568 which installed him, expelled three more papists, Edmund Reynolds, Miles Windsor, and George Napier; and among the junior fellows, for example John Reynolds (admitted 1563) and John Barefoot (admitted 1562), there were signs that Corpus, like Magdalen, might become a nursery for the godly. Cole's own reputation, like that of Humphrey, began to decline within a few years of his admission. Administration of the college estates during his presidency seems to have been chaotic and the only significant gap in the *computi*, the bursar's annual accounts, is during this period.[114]

The events of 1568 mark the end of the first phase of the establishment of a protestant settlement in the university. In two colleges, Christ Church and Magdalen, reform had been introduced with the full co-operation of the majority of the fellows and the active encouragement of a smaller number. Two heads, known in the university and in the country at large as favourers of a more advanced protestant settlement, had been installed, though Sampson had been deprived after only four years in office. From 1565 until 1568 Humphrey alone in Oxford represented the former exiles and 'godlie learned preachers'. By this time even he was settling into a conforming mediocrity of outlook and though he continued to appeal for ministers who were under pressure to subscribe to be granted toleration, the more radical brethren in his own college and those who produced *An Admonition to the Parliament* in 1572 no longer counted him an ally.[115] Among the colleges of Oxford, however, Magdalen stood for further reform at a time when other societies were resisting the imposition of protestant heads and the intrusion of protestant fellows. In Merton and Corpus, the Visitors with their supporters, mostly among the younger fellows, were successful; but in Queen's, Exeter, and New College, for example, there were few signs of any distinctively

[114] See J. G. Milne, *The Early History of Corpus Christi College Oxford* (Oxford, 1946), 24; Fowler, op. cit., 124-56. See also '*Dialogus...qui inscribitur Nuttus*', Bodleian Library, MS Rawlinson D 463, fos. 3ᵛ, 11ᵛ, 12ʳ, which reveals that the younger members of the college favoured Cole.

[115] Historical Manuscripts Commission, *Report on the Pepys Manuscripts*, 88 (= 'Papers of State', I, 613); BL, Harleian MS 417, fo. 124ᵛ; BL, Harleian MS 449, fos. 1-16; BL, Lansdowne MS 24, fo. 52, February 1574; Humphrey promises Cecil his conformity over vestments.

protestant outlook among the members, or interest in the continental reformed churches, until after 1575. In Oxford as a whole, after the turmoil of the first decade, there followed four years of tranquillity until the first shocks of the activity of a new and younger generation of reformers began to be felt in 1572.

However in London, as early as 1567, it was evident that the more extreme reformers were gathering in congregations separate from the parish churches. They would not allow their followers to attend the preaching of Humphrey, Sampson, or Lever for although they admitted that these men had suffered much to obtain liberty in the matter of *adiaphora,* they now refused to join with them.[116] In Oxford this split between moderates and extremists was not to be revealed until the publication of the *Admonition to the Parliament* in 1572. John Field and Thomas Wilcox were at work on their *Admonition* almost as soon as the new parliament was announced in March 1572. Field was a BA of Christ Church, and seems to have withdrawn to Oxford again in 1566-7 after thirty-seven London ministers had been suspended in March 1566 for their refusal to wear the vestments. In January 1567, Field was in Broadgates Hall, just opposite his old college. He was in contact with Humphrey and was much influenced by him at this time.[117] The *Admonition,* however, was to present a much more extreme course than that favoured by the President of Magdalen. The *Admonition* proper, the work of Wilcox, lamented the failure of the English church to measure up even to the outward face of a reformed church. The second part of the work, by Field, 'A view of popishe abuses yet remaining in the Englishe church, for the which the godly ministers have refused to subscribe', was much more vituperative in its attack on the bishops, church courts, private patrons, and the services and ornaments of the Book of Common Prayer.[118]

The *Admonition* seems to have been available in Oxford soon after its publication, perhaps as a result of Field's attempt to

---

[116] *Z.L.,* I, 201-5, Grindal to Bullinger, 11 June 1568.

[117] BL, Harleian MS 416, fo. 185, Field to Foxe, 26 January 1567; Collinson, 'John Field and Elizabethan Puritanism', in *Elizabethan Government and Society,* ed. S. T. Bindoff, J. Hurstfield, and C. H. Williams (London, 1961), 129-30.

[118] Collinson, *E.P.M.,* 85-6 and 109-21. W. H. Frere and C. E. Douglas, *Puritan Manifestoes* (London, 1907, repr. 1954), 5-19. 'A view of popishe abuses' follows, pp. 20-37.

see that it was placed in the hands of influential persons. Some men in Field's old college, Christ Church, were apparently persuaded to champion the cause, while the Carnsew brothers, across the road in Broadgates Hall, noted in their diary that on 24 December (probably 1573) they had 'red the bookes sett forthe by the puritaynes to the parlament'.[119] In November 1572, Whitgift published his *Answere to the Admonition* and the controversy with Thomas Cartwright began, marking a revival of the movement in the spring of 1573. At least one member of the university was cautious about Cartwright's attitudes. An Oxford commonplace book, assessing Cartwright's work, allows that which Cartwright was not prepared to grant, namely, that ecclesiastical government which differed from the apostolic model might be permitted. The author admitted that the Church of England stood in need of amendment, but concluded that the failure of reform was not due to government orders, but to lack of their execution and the large number of dispensations.[120] This seems typical of the moderate position being adopted in Oxford at this time. Humphrey, despite his friendship with Field, made it quite clear that he did not sympathize with the *Admonition*. He recalled, in a letter to Gilby, that when he had presented the Queen with a New Testament in 1566, he had prayed that God would open her heart to further reform.[121] There is no suggestion here of reformation without tarrying for the magistrate. He also visited Field and Wilcox in jail, but showed their cause no affection.[122] Grindal, writing to Bullinger in July 1573, rejoiced that neither Humphrey nor Sampson were supporting the young men who were canvassing the proposals of the *Admonition*.[123].

When the second phase of the controversy was initiated by the Cartwright-Whitgift writings, only a few Oxford men were aroused. Arthur Wake, Canon of Christ Church, who must have been a contemporary of Field, despite a warning from the

[119] SP 46/15, fo. 219^r. This is an early use of the term 'puritan'.
[120] Bodleian Library, MS Selden *supra* 44, esp. fos. 21^r, 22^r-28^r.
[121] Cambridge University Library, MS Mm. I. 43 (Baker 32), 431, Humphrey to Gilby, 17 January 1573.
[122] Inner Temple, Petyt MS 538, vol. 47, fo. 481^r. Report by the Newgate jailer on visitors to Field and Wilcox.
[123] *Z.L.*, I, 292. Grindal to Bullinger, 31 July 1573.

Bishop of London's officials to have a consideration of the troubled times, used a Paul's Cross sermon at the beginning of August 1573 'to railing against this present state and confirming good what Cartwright set down in writing'. Sandys, exasperated by the proceedings, tried to apprehend the preacher but found that he had returned to Oxford, where he was protected by the liberties of the university. Wake, however, seems to have given up his permanent place in Oxford. He retreated to Northamptonshire, but was deprived of his living at Great Billing in the same year. In another incident, reported by Sandys to Leicester and Burghley, some of the London young men came to Balliol and attempted to get Adam Squire, the Master, to put his hand to their petition in favour of the Admonitionists.[124] Even before Wake's sermon, the Council had written to the Vice-Chancellor, warning him of reports that members of the university were devising 'to find fawltes with the boke of the uniforme Order of Common Prayer'. They had been attempting to alter the forms of service, and cause dissent in the minds of the people, and schism in the church. The Vice-Chancellor was asked to apprehend any who so disturbed the peace and to use the power vested in him and the Bishop of Oxford to control book publication. The *Admonition* was specifically mentioned.[125] In general, the Council need hardly have been troubled with the possible existence of radical cells in the university. To this, there was one exception, Magdalen College, where Lawrence Humphrey, now in no risk of expulsion for his own opinions, presided uneasily over the rising generation of radicals.

---

[124] BL, Lansdowne MS 17, fo. 96.

[125] OUA/NEP *supra*/Register KK, fo. 148ʳ, 9 July 1573; Wood, *Annals*, II, 173. Wood wrongly attributes the encouragement of this movement to Humphrey and Cole.

III

A HOUSE DIVIDED: DISTURBANCES IN MAGDALEN COLLEGE, c.1575-c.1589

This house, which should be a house of prophets, and of the sonnes of the prophets, will becom a receptacle of Papists, athists, ruffians, idle bellies, unlearned and ungodly parsons.[1]

In the autumn of 1585, as the Bishop of Winchester, Thomas Cooper, rode into Oxford from the south-west, he could not have failed to observe that his college of Magdalen, which he had first entered as a chorister fifty-two years earlier, splendid amidst its water-meadows, stood apart from the other towers and spires of the Oxford sky. Waynflete's foundation, exactly one hundred years old when Elizabeth came to the throne, was *'opere magnificum, et ad vitae studiorumque commoditatem aptissimum'*.[2] Magdalen under Lawrence Humphrey was in so many ways a place apart; in numbers, in income, in activity, rivalled only by the King's new foundation, 'so famous, so excellent in art, and still so rising', *Aedes Christi*.[3] When rents were assessed for the Queen's second visit to the university in 1592, Magdalen was exceeded in wealth only by Christ Church, and with rents of £1,200 Waynflete's college outstripped all other foundations, apart from New College at £1,000, more than twice over.[4] In numbers, with its 40 fellows, 30 demies, commoners, battlers, and poor scholars, its total of 246 members in 1612 could be rivalled only by Queen's College, which, under two reforming provosts, had buttressed its relatively meagre foundation with no less than

---

[1] Simon Pett to the Bishop of Winchester, 1585. Macray, *Register*, II, 117.

[2] Nicholas Fitzherbert, *Oxoniensis in Anglia Academiae Descriptio* (Rome, 1602), reprinted in *Elizabethan Oxford*, ed. C. Plummer (Oxford Historical Society, viii, 1887), 14.

[3] Shakespeare, *Henry VIII*, Act IV, scene 2.

[4] John Gutch, *Collectanea Curiosa*, I (Oxford, 1781), 190-1. Christ Church rents totalled £2,000, Magdalen £1,200, New College £1,000, while Merton claimed only £400, Queen's £260, and Balliol £100.

192 commoners.[5] In religious activity, Magdalen surpassed
them all, 'perhaps the most remarkable puritan society in either
university', as Professor Patrick Collinson has described it,
and certainly a college, torn as it was by violent disturbances,
throughout Humphrey's presidency, which brought the issues
of religious reform closer to the daily lives of several generations of students, many of them future ministers, more drama-
tically than any other society in Oxford or Cambridge.[6]

The two faces of Lawrence Humphrey, this ambiguous per-
sonality, dominate the history of the university in the middle
years of the reign. In 1561, his position was precarious; poor
and unsettled like many of his fellow exiles, his attempts to
secure lucrative office were not without excuse.[7] Later, he
might have been justly accused of lining his pockets at the
expense of the society, building for himself and his family a
position of security and of some prosperity. William Inkforbye
and Roger Inkforbye, his brothers-in-law, held many college
offices, one as college steward, in which office he had no skill
and daily damaged the college lands, according to the complaints of one fellow to the Visitor in 1585.[8] His son, John, was
elected a fellow in 1579, and other members of the family
followed him into the fellowship. As his standards of conduct
and management declined, so Humphrey's desire to reform the
discipline and ceremonies of the church abated and he settled
into a studied mediocrity. Already *cancellarius natus* in 1565,[9] by
the 1570s he had become the elder statesman of the university,
serving as Vice-Chancellor for a period of unprecedented
length, 1571-6, and close in the confidence of the Earl of
Leicester. In March 1571 he was installed as Dean of
Gloucester, and in 1574 it was rumoured that the Queen

---

[5] Ibid., 196-207. In 1612, Christ Church had 240 members, including all the clerks,
commoners, battlers, etc., Magdalen had 246, New College 130, Merton 93, and
Queen's 267.

[6] Collinson, *E.P.M.,* 129.

[7] In January 1562 he petitioned for a Christ Church prebend claiming 'I come bare
from exile', but was unsuccessful; SP 12/21/28, 25 January 1561, Humphrey to Cecil.
The prebend went to Westphaling, SP 12/22/1, 3 March 1562, the canons and
students having failed to nominate Humphrey.

[8] Macray, *Register,* II, 113.

[9] The *cancellarius natus* is the member of the university, normally the senior DD, who
takes the Chancellor's place on a vacancy, until a new Chancellor is elected.

intended to advance him to the episcopate.[10] His former pupil, Francis Hastings, wrote to urge him to accept a bishopric if offered and Humphrey in reply admitted that it was no sin to desire the work of a bishop.[11] Writing to Cecil on 6 February 1576, he confessed that his submission in the question of vestments might have offended some and he yet hoped that in any proclamation of this subject 'one clause maie be added for Ministers and students in the universitie, and a plain signification given, that it is enioyned, not so muche for an ecclesiasticall ceremonie, as for a civile policie and ordinance'.[12] This he believed would 'satisfie many in conscience', though in Humphrey at least by 1576 the ecclesiastical politician appears to have triumphed over the scrupulous and learned preacher.

Within Magdalen, the serious disturbances in 1565-6 over the wearing of the surplice and the Visitor's Injunctions of 1566 reveal that the society was far from tranquil, but Humphrey himself seems to have been highly regarded.[13] In June 1570, Horne wrote to the President, commenting: 'I ioye not a littell that your state is suche as I heare noe complainte of anye disorder amonge yowe which is toe me an argumente that yowe be *integrum corpus, eadem sententia.*' However, he referred to certain doubts about the statutes which needed resolution if they were not to break out into 'petite quarells'.[14] It was doubts of this kind, simmering below the surface, which eventually rocked the college. William Judson, a Dean of Arts, died aged 24, on 25 April 1575. On 9 June the thirteen senior fellows were summoned to the hall by the President to elect his successor.[15] Thomas Cole, William Powell, and Nicholas Lombard refused to take the oath or proceed to the election and Humphrey summarily expelled them from their fellowships. Henry West, Ralph Smith, and Walter Enderbie were also expelled, but later Humphrey withdrew his sentence against them. Theodore Tansey, William Garbrand, and John Travers, brother of the more celebrated Walter, who were not

---

[10] Strype, *Annals,* I, part ii, 144.

[11] Huntington Library, San Marino California, Hastings MSS, HA 13766.

[12] BL, Lansdowne MS 24, fo. 52; Strype, *Annals,* I, part ii, 518-19.

[13] Inner Temple, Petyt MS 538, vol. 47, fo. 58; see above, 35.

[14] Magdalen College Oxford Archives, Vice-President's Register, fos. 37ᵛ-38ᵛ.

[15] Bloxam, *Register,* IV, 119. The delay was probably caused by a divergence of opinion over whether a new election was necessary until after the audit.

among the thirteen seniors, attempted to meddle in the election
and caused a disturbance in hall. Tansey and Garbrand were
deprived of commons, and Travers, who behaved irreverently
when summoned by the college officers, was referred for correction to the Visitor.[16]

The controversy, which led the six fellows to refuse to take
the oath, concerned the interpretation of the statute *De numero
scholarium* in respect of five fellows, claimed by the complainants to be *non socii* because they were in breach of
statute.[17] Humphrey seems to have given the six fellows a
second chance to take the oath and proceed to the election of a
new Dean of Arts, but according to his account they had gone
to play bowls, though they protested that they 'stayed at home
until two of the clock at afternoon, not being called, and then
went with other ancients and godly preachers to exercise
ourselves'.[18] When they continued obstinate, the President
maintained that according to statute he had no alternative to
expulsion. The five fellows they challenged had already been
confirmed in their places by the Visitor, so their complaint was
invalid. Horne upheld this judgement, refuted the doubts
raised by Cole, Powell, and Lombard, and gave definitive
sentence against them.[19] Strength of opinion within the college
caused the three fellows to seek redress at the hands of the Privy
Council and twenty-four senior and junior colleagues persuaded them to stay in their places, threatening to leave the
college with them if they demurred. The President faced outright rebellion from a substantial proportion of the junior
fellows, but he and the Visitor were determined to stand firmly
by their interpretation of the statutes.

The first hint that this was more than a simple matter of
college discipline is indicated in a letter of Nicholas Lombard to

---

[16] Magdalen College Oxford Archives, Vice-President's Register, fo. 36[r]. Bloxam,
Register, IV, 119.

[17] The five fellows whose rights in the college were disputed were Christopher
Gregory, who had not taken orders in the appointed time, Thomas Brickenton, who
had been presented to a living but had not resigned his fellowship, Roger Inkforbye
and Christopher Wade, who claimed lawyer's places but without the consent of the
Dean, and Edmund Lillie, who had failed to take orders. SP 12/105/20 contains the
complaints against the five.

[18] SP 12/105/15.

[19] SP 12/105/7; SP 12/105/15; Bloxam, *Register*, IV, 124-7.

Francis Mills, dated 26 June 1575. Mills, a contemporary of Andrew Kingsmill in All Souls, later his literary executor and now one of Walsingham's secretaries, may have had personal connections with the deprived fellows. Lombard explained that the President 'whether upon to muche precisnes in religion on our part, or malice towardes Mr. Powell ... and Mr Cole in a trifle and matter of no weight has expelled us to the utter discredit, overthrow of our noble house, and the discouragement of all other towardly divines in our College'. The junior fellows, the 'precise', had viewed Humphrey's mismanagement and capricious judgement as incompatible with the society of a godly college. Their grievances included his inordinate covetousness, taking leases into his own possession, the maintenance of non-resident ministers in the college, and the lack of respect for ancient servants and tenants of the house. They viewed these abuses not only as shameful to the honour of the house, but as 'the slander of the gospel', 'the quenching of Gods spirit in his children', and 'the battering of our consciences', making it evident that they opposed the President on grounds of conscience and religion as well as statute.[20]

In the face of this crisis, two parties emerged with supporters inside the college and without. Humphrey had the support of the Visitor, who upheld his sole right to interpret the statutes. According to Lombard, writing to Laurence Tomson, another of Walsingham's secretaries who had been a fellow of Magdalen from 1559 to 1568, the President's party numbered twelve, including the five fellows 'tolerated against the statutes'.[21] At the end of June Humphrey sent Wade and Gregory, together with a young bachelor, William Cotton, 'his sattelites hanging on his sleeve to clawe me', as Lombard dubbed them, to present his own case to the Visitor. The party opposing the President was larger, but, as Lombard told Mills and Tomson, they were powerless against 'the fat bulls of Bashan, unless the Lord rayse up your spirits and stir up the good gifts of godly men to assist us'.[22] Fourteen junior fellows sided with the three expelled seniors, and included several who

[20] SP 12/103/67, 26 June 1575.
[21] SP 12/105/2, 2 July 1575.
[22] SP 12/103/70, 29 June 1575.

would later come to prominence in movements for further reform in religion, among them John Barebon and Edward Gellibrand.[23] The Magdalen fellows were supported by a large number of members of the university who wrote to Leicester protesting that Cole, Powell, and Lombard had been unjustly treated in view of the 'good opinion conceived of them generally for their discrete zeale in profession of true religion and for their honestie and good behaviour'.[24] The letter was signed by a diverse body, including both the proctors, John Underhill and Henry Savile, the Master of University College, William James, together with eleven students of Christ Church, nine fellows of Exeter, eight fellows of Magdalen, five fellows of Queen's, three fellows of All Souls, three fellows of Corpus, and fifteen others, most of them fellows of colleges and senior men elected in the 1560s, except in Magdalen where the division between those who supported the President and those who opposed him was based on seniority. Among the signatories are Henry Robinson and John Reynolds, but in general the group cannot be singled out for its religious radicalism. The effect which the expulsions would have on the ministry of the church in general concerned them all and in particular the fellows of Magdalen, who sent an accompanying letter referring again to the sharp and unjust sentence on the three fellows, 'to theyr hinderaunce and slaunder, the great discouragement of many towarde in divinite' and the damage of the college.[25] In general, the university may have been moved by the evidently unjust dealing of Humphrey, for in so small a society as sixteenth-century Oxford, the corrupt state and maladministration of Magdalen cannot have passed without notice.

The strongest hope of the expelled fellows was the agency of Laurence Tomson. Tomson not only shared the religious aspirations of the younger fellows, but knew Thomas Cole well. They had both been granted leave of absence from Magdalen in 1565 to go abroad, though their place of residence is unknown. Later, Tomson spent some months in Geneva where he probably met Beza, and in 1568-9 was in Heidelberg

---

[23] SP 12/105/7, 4 July 1575.
[24] SP 12/105/12, 10 July 1575.
[25] SP 12/105/13, ? 10 July 1575.

with the 'puritan ambassador', George Withers.[26] He published a version of the New Testament based on the Latin text with Beza's commentary.[27] In 1574, he became one of Walsingham's secretaries and at once began to advance the fortunes of godly preachers and zealous ministers who were suffering for their non-conformity.[28] In July 1575 he took up the cause of the young fellows of Magdalen, regretting that it had become a lively source of conversation at court, when it should have been kept 'within the well-fenced cloisters and walls'. Writing to Humphrey, Tomson professes his good opinion of his former President, but regrets that his government of the college has not been as good as it might have been. As for the young ministers, loss of their places would be death and a blemish on their ministry for ever. [29] Effect on their future ministry was Walsingham's concern also. The Secretary, prompted no doubt by Tomson, heard the arguments on both sides and confessed that the troubles had caused him great personal grief because of the 'love which I have borne a great while to the head'. Nevertheless, he had found the expelled fellows 'godly and honest, and ministers ... not to be touched in any respect for their conversation and behaviour. How they travailed also in preaching the word, both in the town and elsewhere abroad, it is so well known that thanks are given to God for the profit the church hath received by them.' Walsingham was, however, not only concerned with the welfare of the ministers. The troubles in Magdalen posed for him a potentially divided front against the Church of Rome. He had no doubt where the fault lay: the President had been severe and unjust and, commented the Secretary, if he had been as good a governor as he was thought to be a man, he would not have been so hasty to proceed to the unnecessary election. He hoped that, if the six fellows in question had

---

[26] Collinson, *E.P.M.*, 81, 111.

[27] Basil Hall, 'The Genevan Version of the English Bible', Presbyterian Historical Society of England, *29th Annual Lecture*, 1956.

[28] Irena Backus, 'Laurence Tomson (1539-1608) and Elizabethan Puritanism', in *Journal of Ecclesiastical History*, 28, no. 1 (January 1977), 17 ff.

[29] SP 12/105/1, 1 July 1575.

indeed held their places in breach of statute, this could now be overlooked.[30]

On 11 July, writing to Humphrey, the Visitor upheld his sentence of expulsion of Cole, Powell, and Lombard and instructed the President, whom he criticized for failing to maintain a steady position, that 'if there remain any which by words or otherwise maintain this faction, put an end to it'.[31] Five days later, however, in a reply to a letter from Walsingham, Horne claimed that he had done his best to quench the fiery coals in Magdalen and that he was loath to see Cole, Powell, and Lombard expelled from their places. Sending a copy of his letter to the college, he expressed the hope that the quarrel might be resolved by further examination, 'that living together in brotherly society, you may grow to be fruitful workmen and profitable members in the Church of God'.[32] The eventual resolution of the dispute is not recorded. Lombard died later that year; Cole and Powell disappear from the records, Smith and West remained in the college, the former to take a prominent part in later disputes, the latter to suffer expulsion for immoral behaviour in 1578. Enderbie resigned in August 1575, and was instituted to the vicarage of Bulkington, Warwickshire.[33] The Bishop of Winchester's visitation in 1576 may have been an attempt to impose a complete settlement, but no records of it have survived. Attempts to control the unruly young were continuing on the day that the bishop's mandate arrived for the visitation. On 26 July 1576, Garbrand, Gellibrand, and Staple were deprived of commons, for criticizing and beating Wade and for outrageous speeches against the President, officers, and state of the whole college.[34] It is clear that in the eyes of the younger members, Humphrey's government never regained respect. Laurence Tomson's inter-

---

[30] SP 12/105/16, 11 July 1575. Extensive correspondence throughout the early summer in SP 12/103/70-73, SP 12/105/2, and SP 12/105/20 discussed the precise interpretation of the statute *De numero scholarium*. SP 12/105/15 is a declaration stating Humphrey's case to which the expelled fellows have penned nineteen answers.

[31] Magdalen College Oxford Archives, Vice-President's Register, fo. 36ᵛ; Bloxam, *Register*, IV, 128-9.

[32] SP 12/105/19, 16 July 1575.

[33] Macray, *Register*, II, 184. Magdalen College Oxford Archives, Vice-President's Register, fo. 37ᵛ.

[34] Magdalen College Oxford Archives, Vice-President's Register, fo. 38ʳ; Magdalen College Oxford Archives, Ledger F, 1556-80, fos. 265ᵛ, 272ʳ.

vention in the 1575 dispute may have won him the admiration
of more advanced reformers, but aroused the deep suspicion
of the officers and seniors. Richard Stanclyffe, fellow of Magdalen from 1564-1580, told Tomson that at a recent meeting
with the officers, he had heard him accused of planning the
ruin of the church and attempting the subversion of the colleges, including Magdalen, through the alienation of their
lands, preferments, and possessions.[35]

For a time, peace was restored after the visitation, but the
disturbances which again shook the college in the late summer
of 1578 revived dissent, again initially focused on the interpretation of the statutes. The dispute concerned the confirmation as fellow of John Everie, son of the Queen's serjeant-at-
arms. The Queen had written to the college, recommending his
election as a probationary fellow, on 19 May 1577.[36] There was
some resistance to royal interference, Everie's year of probation was stormy, and in the end he was expelled. An appeal to
the Visitor secured his reinstatement and brought on the
fellows a condemnation for unseemly canvassing. The faction
in the college which had resisted the Queen's wishes was led by
John Barebon, Vice-President that year, and he, together with
Ralph Smith, who had narrowly escaped expulsion in 1575,
John Daye, a senior fellow, Timothy Fisher, and two
bachelors, John Batner and Thomas Durdant, were summoned
to attend on the Visitor.[37] The house was in uproar, according
to Daye, and Gellibrand, writing to John Foxe on 26 August,
related that the Visitor, in summoning the six fellows, had
called them 'rebels against their President, hypocrites and factious men'.[38] Daye excused himself from attendance on the
grounds of ill health; Barebon, Batner, Durdant, and Fisher
were expelled from their fellowships, though Smith retained his
until 1585. At the same time Henry West was excluded for

[35] SP 12/125/38, 24 July 1578.
[36] Magdalen College Oxford Archives, Vice-President's Register, fo. 43[r]. Macray,
Register, III, 64-5.
[37] Magdalen College Oxford Archives, Vice-President's Register, fo. 42[v]. Macray,
Register, III, 65.
[38] John Daye to Julius Caesar, 26 August 1578, BL, Additional MS 12507, fo. 44.
Daye remained a fellow until 1586. Edward Gellibrand to John Foxe, 26 August 1578,
BL, Harleian MS 416, fo. 194.

bringing great slander to the college and speaking against the officers. He was such a notorious offender that the Visitor did not need to examine him.[39]

The events of August 1578, like those of the summer of 1575, have at first sight the appearance of a dispute between the President and a group of rebellious fellows about the management of the society, in this case the intrusion of a fellow, contrary to the statutes, but at the Queen's request. The presence of John Barebon as leader of the opposition suggests that preciseness about the interpretation of the statutes went hand in hand with religious radicalism. Barebon had been a fellow since 1571; his opinions, which Anthony Wood calls 'Ramist', had already caused him trouble in May 1574, when he was allowed to incept only on condition that he confessed he had offended the other regent masters by his contentious behaviour.[40] In Magdalen he seems to have established some early contacts with Northamptonshire, though he himself came from Gloucestershire. By 1578, the year of his expulsion, he had begun to attract a circle of pupils. The young Robert Ashley was commended to him by his brother, but, Ashley noted, 'My tutor Barebon with Travers, Durdant and other learned and wise men was, for reasons I do not know, expelled from the college before my arrival.'[41] The reference to John Travers in Ashley's account is evidently an error, since he is not mentioned in the other accounts and he was a member of the college until at least 1585. It would nevertheless be in keeping with his known opinions to have him numbered among the precise associates of Barebon. The notebook of another young member of Magdalen, George Wilton, confirms the suspicion that Barebon's expulsion was in part due to his religious opinions. Wilton, whose home was probably in Daventry, came up to Magdalen in the autumn of 1578. Like Ashley, he appears to have been previously commended to Barebon, who had agreed to be his tutor. Wilton seems to have arrived in the college immediately after Barebon's departure and records his impression in a series of letters to his contem-

---

[39] Magdalen College Oxford Archives, Vice-President's Register, fo. 42^r. Macray, *Register*, II, 183.

[40] OUA/NEP *supra*/Register KK, fo. 170^r; Wood, *Annals*, II, 176.

[41] BL, Sloane MS 2131, fo. 17^v.

poraries and friends, including three to Barebon himself. The first letter, dated 2 November 1578, to his contemporary in Magdalen Hall, William Dawe, is a highly-coloured picture of the state of the college. Writing from Barebon's chamber, Wilton lamented that their most beloved tutor had been falsely and maliciously accused by those set to destroy his reputation. To Wilton, this was a double blow, for he had not only lost a friend, but no longer had a tutor. The expulsion of the other fellows is noted and Wilton includes Fisher, Durdant, Batner, and West, but not Travers. He observes that for right or wrong Everie had been made a fellow.[42] Dawe's reply offers pious comfort, recommending to Wilton the consolation which the Christian may find in the Scriptures.[43] It is remarkable that in the series of letters, which cover the years 1578-85, Wilton never mentions the President, either as a controlling force in college affairs or as an influence for good. In the vacuum caused by Humphrey's mismanagement, there was ample scope for factious dealing and the manipulation of office-holding. After the annual elections at the end of 1578, Wilton, writing to Robert Albany, another contemporary in Magdalen Hall, noted that Roger Inkforbye had been elected Vice-President in succession to Barebon, Wade, William Inkforbye, and Droope as bursars, Bisse as Dean of Divinity, and Cullen and Boughton as Deans of Arts. This has the appearance of an attempt to control radical movements in the college by the appointment of an establishment agreeable to the President. None of these men was of outstanding ability. The two Inkforbyes represented the President's family interest, Droope was censured by Gellibrand in 1585 for his failure to read his divinity lecture, and James Bisse was severely criticized at the same time for his continual neglect of duties as Reader in natural philosophy.[44] Albany's reply reflects the miserable state of the college, viewed through the eyes of an undergraduate. He lamented that the most pious and studious members of the college were jeered at, that wickedness went unpunished and all manner of evil flourished, while the best men were

---

[42] Magdalen College Oxford MS 617, 1-2.

[43] Ibid., 4; see also the correspondence 7 November 1578 with Edmund Abdye, Magdalen Hall, which records the same events, ibid., 5-8.

[44] Ibid., 14. Macray, *Register*, II, 101.

turned out. Nothing else could be expected but that the whole society would be ruined.[45]

Wilton's early letters disclose the existence of a close circle of his friends in Magdalen and Magdalen Hall. Three of the young men came from Northamptonshire: David Dryden, probably son of John Dryden of Ashby Canons, George Greene, and Wilton himself, which suggests a connection with Barebon before they came to Oxford. Barebon himself appears to have remained in Oxford for at least a year after his expulsion from Magdalen. He was admitted chaplain at Merton on 15 April 1579 and is listed with the chaplains in July of that year, but disappears before the next list in April 1580.[46] He preached at All Saints', Oxford in July 1579, and probably again in the New Year 1580.[47] In 1580, he seems to have retired to Northamptonshire, where, according to Ashley, '*mediocre beneficium eum expectabat*'.[48] This was Charwelton, where he received his Oxford friends and pupils and from where he directed the activities of the Daventry *classis* in the 1580s. Wilton's affection for his tutor is unbounded. A letter, dated 27 December 1578, delights that Barebon has retained his equanimity amidst such tempestuous events. Wilton confesses that nothing is more important to him than his patron's welfare, and a relationship of trust was established which survived not only during Wilton's Oxford career, but into the 1590s, when he was a schoolmaster in Crediton.

One of Wilton's contemporaries, Samuel Foxe, son of the martyrologist, was at the centre of a disturbance which brought about his expulsion in 1581. If Wilton and his tutor Barebon represented a group in the college pressing for change, Foxe was a moderate and a supporter of the President. The troubles in which he was involved reveal the society from a different perspective, with the radical members now seen as the persecutors rather than the persecuted. The first fifteen years of Humphrey's presidency seem to have reinforced rather than weakened John Foxe's affection for his old friend. In 1574, he

---

[45] Magdalen College Oxford MS 617, 15.

[46] *Registrum Annalium Collegii Mertonensis, 1567-1603*, 114, 117, 124.

[47] Bodleian Library, MS Rawlinson D 273, 262-4, 282. Three of Barebon's sermons are noted by John Rogers but without year and out of chronological order.

[48] BL, Sloane MS 2131, fo. 18^r. After Barebon's departure, Ashley, with others of his pupils, was commended to John Harding, fellow from 1579.

sent his elder son Samuel, then 14, to seek election as a demy of Magdalen. His expectations were considerable: 'I send you my foxlet that he may become an academic ... not to grow wealthy, but to feed his mind on the humanities and cultivate his talents. Take him under your protection, and do for him what you have done for so many others, not for our merits, which are none, but from your inborn piety and generous nature.'[49] The troubles of 1575 had not yet broken, but Foxe cherished a different view of Humphrey from that of Laurence Tomson. He requested that his son be given a room and a tutor. The choice of tutor could hardly have been less appropriate, though Edward Gellibrand's radical opinions had not yet revealed themselves. At first Samuel Foxe established a good relationship with Gellibrand, then in his early thirties. The young MA also regarded John Foxe as a wise confidant and when trouble arose in the college in 1576 after the visitation over the wearing of the surplice and academic dress, he wrote to Foxe hoping for some advice which might soothe his anguished conscience. The exchange of letters illustrates the difference in temper between the now moderate Foxe, carefully weighing categories and circumstances, and Gellibrand, impetuous in his rejection of anything suspected of papist association.[50] Foxe's reply is cautious and measured; the question of vestments is not to be treated simply or unilaterally. The majority of such garments have been tainted by their association with popish idolatry and superstition. Into this category fall the chasuble, alb, amice, stole, and maniple. These are in no circumstances to be used in the Church of Christ. However, there is another distinct category of dress, that of cantors and scholars, in fact laymen not priests, and worn not only in church but in the town, in the street, and in scholars' chambers. Into this class fall the gown, academic cap, and surplice. Vestments of this kind are neither good nor bad in themselves; they are *adiaphora* and may be used in suitable circumstances. Foxe then lists the circumstances to be considered: time, place, persons, causes, legitimate authority,

---

[49] Mozley, *John Foxe and his Book,* 108; ET of BL, Harleian MS 417, fo. 112^v.

[50] Although the 1576 Injunctions do not survive, the 1585 Injunctions of Bishop Cooper, para. 28, advocate the adherence of the college to Horne's Injunctions of 1577 (*sic*, i.e. 1576), and particularly the third chapter, *De vestitu clericali sive habitu scholastico,* in particular wearing gowns in the street. Macray, *Register,* III, 23.

method, and intention. Vestments, on the other hand, must
never be worn when they challenge true piety, fundamental
doctrine, the glory of Christ, or the true marks of the church.
The letter is an impressive performance, and can have left
Gellibrand in no doubt of the fundamental distinction between
moderate courses, weighing evidence and circumstances and
dividing categories, and the path of extremism, seeking perfection and acting for conscience.[51]

This early friendship and confidence was placed under
severe strain in the following five years. The incompatible
outlook of Samuel Foxe and his tutor led, probably in the
spring of 1577, to a letter from John Foxe to Humphrey, asking
that a different tutor be provided. Humphrey talked with both
pupil and tutor. He reported that Gellibrand was exceedingly
angry and threatened litigation.[52] However, for the sake of the
father and the son, Humphrey proceeded to appoint a new
tutor, Ralph Smith, described to John Foxe as, in the President's view, faithful, diligent, and benevolent. The choice of
the new tutor is significant. The breach of 1575, when
Humphrey had temporarily excluded Smith, must have
healed, though Smith remained radical in outlook. This may
have been the reason why Samuel Foxe continued to find the
college uncongenial. In December 1577 he left suddenly for
France without leave of absence, and after frantic enquiries by
his father returned and was received into the college again
without disciplinary proceedings.[53] He must have settled down
by 1579 when the college elected him probationary fellow and
confirmed him in his fellowship the following year. His own
account of his career records that it was shortly after this that
he was 'repelled by a contrary faction [and] restored by the
Queens letters mandatory'.[54] The more radical members of the

[51] Bodleian Library, MS Rawlinson C 936, fos. 7-8; BL, Harleian MS 416, fo. 195
seems to be Gellibrand's reply to Foxe, written at the same time of the Bishop's third
visitation, 1576. The Bishop has not come in the spirit of love, but with a rod.
Gellibrand's letter to Foxe evidently arises from visitation enquiries into the wearing
of the surplice and academic dress.
[52] Bodleian Library, MS Rawlinson C 936, fos. 5-6. Humphrey to Foxe, with
Foxe's draft reply scribbled on the back. By 1578, relations between Gellibrand and
Foxe seem to have been restored. On 26 August 1578 Gellibrand wrote in very friendly
tone to 'The Reverend in Christ and his friend [*assured,* added above] Mr Foxe',
describing the expulsions of August 1578. BL, Harleian MS 416, fo. 194.
[53] BL, Harleian MS 417, fos. 116^r, 117^r, 103; BL, Lansdowne MS 679, fo. 46^v.
[54] BL, Lansdowne MS 679, fo. 46^v. Foxe, as frequently, gives the wrong date.

college appear to have developed a dislike for Samuel. The
hostility gradually mounted and John Foxe tried to intervene
by letter, protesting his love for his old college, while
Humphrey attempted to moderate the activities of the extremists. Eventually, Samuel was expelled and John Foxe realized
that it was not the result of any crime he had committed, but
because he had found himself caught up in the continuing
religious and social tensions of the college. In a letter to an
unnamed bishop, Foxe delineates the lines of factious activity
which had been built up within the college.[55] The 'thrice-pure
puritans', as he calls them, had been sharpening their arrows
against him because he had chosen the side of modesty and
public tranquillity.[56] Their chief aim was to oust the President
and because young Foxe was known to be on the President's
side and had studied under him, he had been expelled from his
fellowship. John Foxe's private grief, however, receded into
the background as he considered the dangers to the church in
general. He confessed to the Bishop his anxiety at the gathering
strength of a new race of hypocritical 'monks', who 'require
everything to be formed according to their own strict discipline
and conscience [and] who will not desist until they have
brought all things into Jewish servitude'. Foxe's attitude is
characteristic of that of the former exiles to the new generation
of extreme reformers, typified in Magdalen by Samuel Foxe's
erstwhile tutor, Edward Gellibrand. For Foxe, a temporary
respite was achieved through the intercession of Cecil, and he
was restored to his fellowship by royal mandate. He escaped
the troubles of 1584-6 through travels abroad and though he
retained his fellowship until 1590, he was frequently absent
from the uncongenial society of Magdalen.[57]

Thomas Cooper became Bishop of Winchester in April 1584,
and must rapidly have realized that a comprehensive visitation
of his old college could not be long delayed if it was not to
dissolve in uproar. The events of the preceding ten years can

---

[55] BL, Harleian MS 416, fos. 152-3. Foxe also wrote to his old friend Daniel Rogers
requesting him to seek Grindal's help on his son's behalf. BL, Harleian MS 417, fo.
104[r-v]; fo. 117[r] is a copy of this letter.

[56] The term 'puritan' is here used in its contemporary sense, and as frequently, as
a term of abuse.

[57] BL, Lansdowne MS 679, fos. 43[v]-45[v].

have left him in no doubt that the college had been filled with young hotheads, who had perpetuated their tradition of radical dissent from generation to generation, while the President, whether through idleness or corruption had persistently failed to control them. Accordingly, all members of the college, senior and junior, were given notice on 21 June 1585 of a complete visitation in the early autumn.[58]

Whereas the evidence for the 1576 visitation is totally deficient, that of 1585 is well documented. Five depositions from fellows survive together with the twenty-eight injunctions which Cooper delivered to the college on 28 October. The complainants examined by the Bishop represent the same strain of radical opinion which had come to the surface in 1575, 1578, and 1581. First in line stand the comprehensive *comperta* of Edward Gellibrand, now fifth in seniority among the fellows, a BD, licensed preacher and one of the bursars of this year.[59] His list of complaints is characteristically directed towards transgressions of the statutes. This is a less obvious feature of the other *comperta*. William Cooke takes his place among the radical members of the society for the first time at this visitation. He was still only a BA, but had already been discommoned in November 1583 for insulting the Vice-President.[60] Simon Pett, the third witness, was equally unable to control his tongue. In February 1584, he had been deprived of commons for a week '*propter verba invidiosa, nociva, scandalosa et susurra*' against the Vice-President, James Bisse, and the Dean of Divinity, Robert Tinley.[61] Richard Boughton, the Vice-President, delivered his deposition *ex officio*; his own record, despite his prodigious activity as a college officer, was not untainted in the eyes of the radicals, who charged him with immorality. Edward Lord's deposition, concentrating for half its length on the religious state of the college, throws into high relief the aspirations of the godly.[62] Lord, like Pett and Gellibrand, was already a fairly senior member of the fellowship; he had been elected in 1575.

[58] Magdalen College Oxford, Ledger G, 1580-92, fo. 130^v.
[59] Macray, *Register,* II, 101-5.
[60] Macray, *Register,* III, 82-3.
[61] Ibid., 68.
[62] Lord's deposition, a folder paper in a box marked 'Magd. Letters', Magdalen College Oxford, Library Office, was evidently not known to W. D. Macray.

His career as a puritan minister began in the same month as Cooper delivered the visitation injunctions. On 12 October 1585, Lord was presented to the Warwickshire living of Wolston, five miles from Coventry. The patron, Robert Wigston, was a great supporter of the Marprelate tracts, and Lord was soon to find himself once again associated with Gellibrand, with Gellibrand's father-in-law, John Oxenbridge, Rector of Southam, and with Cartwright, Fen, and others in the activities of the Warwickshire *classis*.

The *comperta* of the four radicals reveal wide agreement and while collusion cannot be ruled out, their complaints represent a general dissatisfaction which had come to the surface many times during the preceding decade. Gellibrand's deposition ends with the plea that 'spedely order may be taken for the reforming of all abuses and disorders: first for the worship of God, then for the societie of men; that every man may both yeld to others, and have himselfe that reverence, dutie, obedience that is meete: whereas now all thinges, places, persons ar ful of disorder and confusion'.[63]

'First for the worship of God...': for Gellibrand and his associates, worship comprised more than the service of the chapel. For Edward Lord, there was a lack of godliness: 'we have bene very dissolute and negligent in the worship and service of God', in neglecting public prayer in the chapel, or coming late, or leaving before the end of the prayer, or failing to observe the celebration of the 'holy banquet', the Lord's Supper. He also complained that very few commoners attended the Sunday catechism lectures.[64] Gellibrand added the further grievance that 'here is no reverence in the world given to the Word, but a continual murmur at dinner and supper, as the noise of a swarme of bees'.[65] Surprisingly, the depositions are full of accusations that papists had been allowed to remain in the college. This is a strange claim, since it comes at a time when Humphrey was openly confuting 'the adversary' from the pulpit. In 1582 and 1585, he published two extensive works and an Ash Wednesday sermon attacking the doctrines and

---

[63] Macray, *Register,* II, 105.
[64] Lord's deposition, fo. 1[r].
[65] Macray, *Register,* II, 102.

practices of the Jesuits in England. The presence of papists in his own college casts severe doubts on his degree of control there. 'Sir Browne', claimed Gellibrand, 'enveied against Calvin and Beza; highly commended Campian to be the excellentest man that hath been brought up in this University; saide that by the same reasons the authority of the bishop of Rome may be defended by which the authority of our bishops is maintained.'[66] Richard Easton had been reconciled to the Church of Rome, and had received the first tonsure at Reims.[67] William Sterill, described as deeply suspect by both Lord and Pett, seldom received communion, was a companion of those who had gone to Reims, and had tried to maintain that the authority of the church was above that of the Scriptures. No member of the college appears to have suspected that Sterill was acting as a government spy on the Jesuit campaign in England. The doubts expressed about his religious opinions demonstrate how effectively he played his double role.[68] Paul Browne, vilified above, cannot have gained favour from the fact that he had been advanced to his fellowship in 1582 as a result of the Queen's letters on his behalf.[69]

'Then, for the societie of men...': in exercises, elections, management, and office-holding, the whole society was out of joint. First, among the causes of mismanagement stand the President and his family and the other officers. The accumulated grievances of the past decade were reviewed before the Visitor. Cooke complained that Humphrey had taken the college copyholds into his own hands, cut down and spoiled the woods, and allowed a large number of commoners to enter the house. Some of these were fellow-commoners, sons of gentry and nobility, and according to Cooke, they had caused great disorder. Since they were not members of the foundation, they refused to submit themselves to the authority

[66] Macray, *Register,* II, 115. Cooke, ibid., 108, attributes the same statement to Thomas Walker. See also ibid., 117, where Humphrey is described as 'a great frend and favorer' of the papists.

[67] Macray, *Register,* II, 104, 109, 114; Lord's deposition, fo. 2ᵛ.

[68] Macray, *Register,* II, 114; Lord's deposition, fo. 2ᵛ; Macray, *Register,* III, 80-2. There are frequent references to Sterill in the State Papers Domestic, 1585, 1586, 1591, 1602, and 1603.

[69] Macray, *Register,* II, 114; III, 88-90; Bloxam, *Register,* IV, 204; Lord's deposition, fo. 2ᵛ.

of the deans and other officers.[70] Simon Pett accused Humphrey and his family of ruining the college finances, woods, and farms. The President, he said, had used partiality in elections of demies, probationers, and college officers and in appointing men who were negligent and unlearned.[71] Gellibrand and Cooke complained that in the election of fellows and demies the restricted counties were disregarded, that places were brought and sold, and that strangers entered the society, while demies were left without promotion.[72] Complaints about corrupt elections are a constant refrain of the precise throughout the reign.

The final category of complaints concerned the disuse of academic exercises, the laxity of readers, and the general corruption of collegiate life. Deans were frequently absent, disputations had lapsed, lectures were seldom read. Lord was grieved that the divinity lectures called collations happened so seldom that there was little or no profit from them.[73] Pett was concerned with the wider church when he desired the Visitor 'to sett downe an order for our impropriations, that they may be annexed to our vicarages, that soe the livings might be sufficient to maintaine able and learned ministers; whereas now we have very ignorant, unlearned and bad ministers allmost in all our vicarages'.[74] The year was 1585, the year of the puritan surveys of the ministry. The college must have been a boisterous place, particularly after dark. Gellibrand witnessed to breach of statute 'by having dogges, hounds, greyhounds, dice, cardes, usual in chambers, at the accustomed time of the yere Lords of misrule, stonebowes, playing at ball against the church windowes, coursing of dogges, singing of roundes, throwing of stones in the night, to the trouble of study and sleep'.[75] Lord believed that discipline and order were so far decayed with so much blasphemy and swearing among the members, even fellows and scholars but especially commoners, cooks, and butlers, that 'this house will not long continue'.[76]

[70] Macray, *Register*, II, 110 (Cooke), 103 (Gellibrand), 111 (Pett); Lord's deposition, fo. 1ᵛ.
[71] Macray, *Register*, II, 112-13.
[72] Macray, *Register*, II, 101 (Gellibrand), 109 (Cooke).
[73] Lord's deposition, fo. 1ᵛ. See also Macray, *Register*, II, 106, 111, 118.
[74] Macray, *Register*, II, 116-17.
[75] Macray, *Register*, II, 102, 110.
[76] Lord's deposition, fos. 1ᵛ-2ʳ.

Gellibrand, Pett, Cooke, and Lord emerge as the ringleaders of the precise party of opposition to Humphrey. Associated with them may have been Richard Cullen (recorded as saying that Humphrey's government was 'no better than the government of Nerva'), John Harding, Anthony Garnance, William Gilbert, William Hooper, and Henry Chitty, all of them named as supporting witnesses in the depositions to the Visitor.[77] Harding, Chitty, Hooper, and Cooke were also members of the party which opposed the election of Bond as President in 1589. Garnance, Gilbert, and Cooke appear among the correspondents of George Wilton. Though Wilton was summoned to the visitation, he left the college that summer after he had incepted. However, his notebook records the deterioration in the society, apparent even to one of the junior members, which he now sees as 'a den of brigands, a haven of epicures, and a refuge for humbugs, gluttons, and gourmands'.[78] Wilton and his friends seem to have found a refuge of godliness with Barebon, whom they visited from time to time at Charwelton. On 12 December 1582, Wilton told Thomas Sanderson that he had been at a 'fast', presumably one of the series held by the godly, with Barebon *'quem 'αθειοι Oxonienses extinctum dixerunt'*. It was very far from the end for Barebon.[79]

Bishop Cooper's Injunctions, issued on 17 October 1585, deal comprehensively with every aspect of college discipline and management. Chapel services are regulated, with holy communion on the first Sunday of each month and more frequently, if possible. Members of the college were to be present at least four times a year. All the abuses in lectures, exercises, and the failure of readers to perform their duties; in elections and appointments, the mismanagement of college documents, lands, and estates are extensively reviewed and corrected. Little is said of moral abuses and recusancy, which form so extensive a part of the *comperta*, except for a ban on fellows and scholars making such frequent visits to the town.[80]

---

[77] Macray, *Register*, II, 112-14; III, 72.

[78] Magdalen College Oxford MS 617, 54 (my translation).

[79] Ibid., 141-2.

[80] The copy of the injunctions delivered to the college is Magdalen College Oxford Archives, *Chartae Regiae*, 79. The injunctions concerning the chapel are printed out by Bloxam, *Register*, II, 339-40. Injunction 8 concerning the Grammar School is in Bloxam, *Register*, III, 131-3; the remainder of the injunctions, 6-7, 9-28 are in Macray, *Register*, III, 11-24.

The wearing of the surplice is given a prominent place in the injunctions, which would seem to suggest that it was as contentious in 1585 as it had been in 1565 and 1576. At the beginning of the visitation, Cooper prescribed that until the use of the surplice had been restored, gowns and hoods should be worn in chapel for services on Sundays and Holy Days. Those who failed to wear them were to be deprived of commons, for a day for the first offence, a week for the second, a month for the third, and until reform in the case of repeated offences.[81] The *comperta* give no clue that the wearing of the surplice was still contentious in the college, but with scrupulous fellows such as Gellibrand, it is inevitable that it should have been a focus of dispute. The injunctions seem to indicate that the surplice had fallen into complete disuse, and this is partially confirmed by an entry in the *computi* for 1586, which indicated that after a gap of some years £10.4s.8¾d. was paid for surplices.[82] Similar troubles about wearing the surplice erupted in University College the following spring.[83]

The decline of Lawrence Humphrey dates from the 1570s. Despite his lax government of the college, he continued to be active in university affairs in the 1580s. By 1588, there are signs that his health had begun to decline and he died on 1 February 1589 at the age of 57. He had been a member of Magdalen for forty-two years and President for twenty-eight of them. To contemporaries, Humphrey's death may not have appeared a watershed; leadership in the preparation of godly ministers and laymen had long since passed from Magdalen to Queen's, where Provost Robinson was reaching the high point of his tenure, and where John Reynolds had joined him in 1586. In some respects, however, Humphrey's death does mark a moment of change. The tide of opinion in the country was turning against reformers of all shades of opinion. Leicester had been succeeded as Chancellor of Oxford by Hatton. Whitgift had for a long time wished to increase his control over the university and was to be instrumental on Hatton's death in securing the nomination of Buckhurst rather than Essex as Chancellor. Humphrey was succeeded in the

[81] Bloxam, *Register*, II, lxxviii.
[82] Macray, *Register*, III, 24.
[83] BL, Additional MS 38492, fo. 80.

Regius chair not by John Reynolds, who had a great deal of support in the university, but by Thomas Holland, soon to be Rector of Exeter on the Queen's recommendation; a man, who despite his reputation as an energetic head shared many of Whitgift's desires to impose conformity and stability in the church.[84]

The Queen's letter nominating Nicholas Bond as Humphrey's successor was the culmination of a series of royal attempts to interfere in the internal affairs of the college. All these attempts, on behalf of Everie, Samuel Foxe, Paul Browne, Sterill, and Wade had been staunchly resisted by the radical party in the college. In February 1589, the Queen spoke of the need for 'good order' in the college, her special care for its government, and the choice of a new governor 'as is agreeable to the Statutes of that House, and the good meaning of the Founder, and likely to repair and reform the late decays and disorders'.[85] Such a man, she suggested, was one of her chaplains, Nicholas Bond, 'a man well approved of Us for his good parts, and well known to you as Fellow of that house for the space of many years'. Whitgift may have been the principal agent in this nomination; he had already suggested Bond for the Mastership of the Temple in 1584, when Hooker was the successful candidate, and for the Deanery of Worcester in 1586, when the Queen herself took some exception to him. In 1589, she had no such reservations: 'we ... will and command you, and every of you, immediately upon the receipt hereof ... to nominate and elect unto the place of your President the said Dr Bond, against whom, so sufficiently qualified, we assure ourselves you can make no objection'.[86] The Queen's letter was reinforced by a letter from the Privy Council, again perhaps the work of Whitgift.[87] The Visitor may also have been involved on Bond's behalf.[88]

---

[84] OUA/NEP supra/Register L, fo. 296r, 9 May 1589. The Chancellor is to be asked that Reynolds be appointed in succession to Humphrey.

[85] BL, Harleian MS 4240, fo. 95r-v; Harleian MS 6282, fos. 126v-127r; Macray, Register, II, 172-3.

[86] Macray, Register, II, 171-2.

[87] The Privy Council letter has not survived, but is referred to in the petition of the fellows opposed to Bond. Macray, Register, II, 175.

[88] This is argued in A Dialogue, wherin is plainly laide open, the tyrannicall dealing of L. Bishopps against Gods children (n.p., 1589), sig. D 3v.

Despite the Queen's rapid action on Humphrey's death, the
opponents of Bond had already mounted a campaign against
him. Among other charges, it was well known that he was a
non-resident pluralist.[89] His opponents spoke of his 'lightness
in behaviour' and 'small skill or care of matters in our House',
presumably a reference to his lack of ability as Dean of Arts,
1570, Bursar, 1571-2, and Vice-President, 1572.[90] During the
campaign, Bond's opponents picked up a story that in a sermon preached in about 1570, he had spoken controversially.
The sermon has not survived, but may have defended the
presence of non-residents in the university.[91] His ability at
dancing is lampooned in the *Dialogue* associated with the
Marprelate tracts.[92]

Bond's supporters describe their opponents as 'the puritans'
and make it clear that opposition to him was focused on the
campaign to improve the ministry and discipline of the church.
They record how 'all the precise sort in the University of
Oxford, as well Heads of Colleges as other principal men of
that note, do account themselves interested in the election, as
appeareth by their continual recourse to Magdalen College
since the decease of the late President, by their daily conference
and consulting with certain of the same House of the said faction, intending thereby to frame themselves a strong party, if
they could place in that famous College such a Head as they
might be assured would favour and maintain their disorderly
course against the Church Government now established'.[93]
The opponents of Bond represented, in large measure, the
same party which had opposed Humphrey and his mismanagement in 1585. Outside the college, it is difficult to envisage
heads of houses who might have given encouragement, unless
Robinson of Queen's was one. Within the college, the principal opponents of Bond set up Ralph Smith as their candidate.
Fourteen of them addressed Burghley on 21 February 1589.[94]

---

[89] SP 12/107/95, non-residents in Oxfordshire, ? March 1576. Bond, the Queen's
Chaplain, is recorded as having a benefice at Brightwell and another thirty miles distant. 'Above all charges there he hath an unpreaching minister.'

[90] Macray, *Register*, II, 175.

[91] Ibid., 176.

[92] *A Dialogue*, sig. D 3ᵛ. Immoral behaviour is also indicated.

[93] Macray, *Register*, II, 174.

[94] BL, Lansdowne MS 59, fo. 14ᵛ.

The list is headed by John Harding. The success of the radical party in the college may be judged from the fact that he was Vice-President in this year. Some suspected that his election had been corruptly obtained.[95] Henry Chitty had been an opponent of Humphrey in 1585; John Kirke, Paul Balguay, William Hooper, John Pusie, Thomas Phippes, and Stephen Batt were all junior fellows. The five remaining signatories were all accused by their enemies of a variety of radical, in some cases presbyterian, opinions. William Cooke, no newcomer to the battle with authority, was reported to have refused subscription to the Prayer Book and Articles, when due to be ordained. Robert Parker and Henry Frencham were similarly accused of refusing subscription. Parker emerges as an uncompromising radical. He maintained openly in the hall that the calling of bishops was unlawful, and had notoriously abused Thomas Godwin, Bishop of Bath and Wells, an old member of the college.[96] He had been sconced in 1587 for refusing to wear surplice and hood, a serious offence since they had been re-enforced by the Visitor in 1585.[97] Parker's later career confirms his radical, presbyterian opinions. His *Scholasticall Discourse against Symbolizing with Antichrist in Ceremonies*, published anonymously in 1607, brought forth a royal proclamation for his arrest and he fled to Leyden, later settling in Amsterdam, where he died in 1614. The *Scholasticall Discourse* is bitter in its attack not only on ceremonies, but on the two-faced bishops who play at being puritans when they talk with papists, and then are papists when they talk with puritans.[98] Another of the signatories, Richard Jefferay, had conformed by the time that he preached at Paul's Cross in April 1604.[99] Ambrose Webb, fellow from 1584, was accused of being 'a great patron of Martin Marprelate, and a publisher of his seditious libels'.[100] Edmund Gellibrand, possibly a younger

---

[95] BL, Harleian MS 4240, fo. 94ʳ, declaration by eighteen fellows that Harding did not canvass for votes. The names correspond largely with those in the letter to Burghley.

[96] Macray, *Register*, II, 177.

[97] Macray, *Register*, III, 90-1.

[98] Robert Parker, *A Scholasticall Discourse against Symbolizing with Antichrist in Ceremonies; Especially in the Signe of the Crosse* (? Amsterdam, 1607), 8, 67, 135.

[99] Richard Jefferay, *The Sonne of Gods Entertainment by the Sonnes of Men* (London, 1605), 36.

[100] Macray, *Register*, II, 177.

brother of Edward, had already been marked out as one who appeared in chapel *'sine habitu sholastico'*.[101]

By the end of February the parties had gathered and the battle lines were drawn. The radical party represented a wide cross-section of the college, not merely the younger element. Many more senior men may have been moved by a desire to resist royal interference; only a few were extreme radicals, or advocated presbyterian courses. The subsequent events are confused because of the complex procedure laid down by Waynflete to ensure fair and valid elections. Each of the fellows who had completed his year of probation was to nominate two candidates. This process was to continue until two of those nominated had the majority of votes among all, but if the nomination was prolonged beyond two days, then the senior candidates in the ballot were to go forward to the second stage. The election proper was confined to the thirteen senior fellows. Each had one vote for either of the candidates nominated by all. All thirteen fellows were bound by oath to take part in the election.[102] Smith's party made great play of their oath to maintain the statutes.[103]

The election was tumultuous. There was considerable lobbying on both sides, by those who maintained that the statutes must be preserved at all costs, and those who believed that the Queen's mandate overruled all local considerations, fearing that resistance to her demand might bring her indignation against the college.[104] There was also considerable activity outside the college. Young Richard Jefferay was so perplexed by the proceedings that he asked for his father's advice and was told to vote for the same candidate as Henry Chitty did.[105] Harding, as Vice-President, took the opportunity of a sermon an hour before the election, perhaps a part of the proceedings, to make his opinion clear. He stated that elections were solely at God's direction and that no other power should control

---

[101] Macray, *Register*, III, 102-3.

[102] BL, Harleian MS 6282, fos. 146-7 is a seventeenth-century account, explaining the election procedure for those who are not members of the college.

[103] Macray, *Register*, II, 175.

[104] 'Considerations' of the fellows declaring for Bond. Harleian MS 4240, fos. 95ᵛ-96ʳ; BL, Harleian MS 6282, fo. 127; Macray, *Register*, II, 174.

[105] Macray, *Register*, II, 177. This must have been at nomination, since Jefferay was not one of the thirteen seniors.

them. Though his sentiments were masked in a heavy
academic disguise, the couplet he quoted from Virgil clearly
impugned the Queen's right to interfere.[106] Gellibrand was
unable to curb his tongue. He refused to listen to the entreaties
of colleagues to respect the Queen's command and claimed
that letters to the college had been manipulated. His final out-
burst, 'that he might as well give a voice to Tom Diggons, whom
he knoweth to be a very fool, as to Mr Dr Bond, whom it pleased
her Majesty so highly to commend', must have raised the
temperature of the proceedings.[107] In some quarters, there was
suspicion of a solemn covenant among the fellows to elect
Smith, and Gellibrand is reported to have rallied his party with
the cry, 'my masters, follow your colours'.[108]

With feeling running so high, it was almost inevitable that
the election in chapel should have been disrupted. While the
preparation for the second stage was in progress, Swithin
Strowde, one of Bond's party, believing that Smith's supporters would have a majority, seized the nomination papers
from the scrutineer and tore them in pieces. Smith's party
responded by writing the name of their candidate on pieces of
paper and throwing them down on the communion table. The
scrutineer, evidently a Smith supporter, declared that Smith
had eight votes, a majority. Bond's party claimed that because
they had not cast their votes, when all thirteen were bound to
vote, the election was invalid. In this stalemate, for which the
statutes provided no clear guidance, Bond's party seems to
have sought renewed support from Queen and court. Smith's
supporters buttressed their case with a legal opinion. Their
adviser, Mr Chippendale, argued that although the scrutiny
had been omitted, everything of substance had been performed
for a valid election. He also indicated that some of Smith's
potential voters had been forcibly hindered.[109]

If the law was for Smith, the Queen was for Bond and it
seems that the Visitor also gave his voice on this side. On 4
April, the Queen signed letters patent, declaring the election

[106] Macray, *Register,* II, 177.
[107] Ibid. The unfortunate Diggons was a former fellow of the college, a Sussex rector, and prebendary of Chichester. Macray, *Register,* III, 188.
[108] Macray, *Register,* II, 177.
[109] BL, Harleian MS 4240, fos. 196-8; Harleian MS 6282, fos. 128-32.

invalid and appointing Bond on royal authority alone. Bond presented these letters to the college on the following day and was declared President.[110] Inside and outside the college, the affair was subjected to scorn from the precise: 'I pray you can you tel me', says the Puritan in the *Dialogue* 'I have heard that Dr Bond is made master of Magdalins in Oxford, contrarie to the statutes of the Universitie: whereas one Master Smith was first elected, according to the orders of the house before him, he being one that stands for the reformation in our corrupt Church government.' Jack replies: 'It is very true, Sir, I can assure you of that, and he may wel be called the *Bonde* of iniquite for any goodnes is in him: he looks I can tell you to be a Lorde Bishop of the Divell shortely.'[111]

Jack's prediction was not fulfilled. Bond died in office in Magdalen in February 1608. In the university, as Vice-Chancellor from June 1589, he became a powerful, if not always compliant, instrument in Hatton's campaign to reduce Oxford to religious and social conformity.[112] In his own college, the precise dwindled away and those who had supported Bond in the 1589 election became officers of the house. The tradition of radical dissent, maintained through many vicissitudes since 1547, had, however, ended only for a time and a season. John Harding, in a brief presidency, 1608-10, restored its fortunes, and early seventeenth-century Magdalen became again the bastion of that preciseness which it had first embraced in the reign of Edward VI.

[110] BL, Harleian MS 6282, fo. 145ʳ. The letters patent include the statement that the Visitor had found the election invalid. The right to appoint therefore devolved personally to the Queen. Magdalen College Oxford Archives, Ledger G, 1580-92, fo. 279ᵛ is a copy of the Queen's mandate, and fos. 280ʳ-281ᵛ, Bond's oath to the statutes.

[111] *A Dialogue,* sig. D 3ᵛ.

[112] For further details of Bond's office as Vice-Chancellor, see below, ch. VI.

IV

OXFORD AND THE REFORMED TRADITION: THE UNIVERSITY AND THE CONTINENTAL REFORMED CHURCHES

'Oh Zurich! Zurich! how much oftener do I now think of thee than ever I thought of England when I was at Zurich.'[1] John Jewel's heart-felt cry of affection in the perplexity of the first months in Elizabeth's England was still being echoed in Oxford fifteen years after the English exiles had returned from the banks of the Limmat and Lac Léman. The links between Oxford and the cities of the exile, and with other continental centres, are now represented by the slenderest of surviving evidence, but sufficient traces remain to indicate that the university was not as isolated from the European reformed churches as is assumed in the contrast of reactionary, inland Oxford with progressive Cambridge, facing Europe across the Fens and the North Sea.

For the first two decades of the reign, Oxford men viewed Zurich as a centre of reform at least as significant as Geneva. The writings of Calvin and his successor, Beza, had by no means achieved the total dominance in English minds claimed by those who equate the influence of the continental reformed tradition with the dissemination of Calvin's *Institutes,* catechisms, and commentaries.[2] Oxford and Zurich were drawn together by the attraction which the Swiss city exercised upon a very small circle of resident or former Oxford men. John Jewel remained in close correspondence with Zurich until his death in 1571; John Parkhurst continued to write from Norwich for another four years; Thomas Sampson, while Dean of Christ Church, exhausted the patience of his Zurich friends by his scrupulous questioning. Lawrence Humphrey and

---

[1] *Z.L.*, I, 23.
[2] This is the most significant fault in the pioneering study by C. D. Cremeans, *The Reception of Calvinist Thought in England* (Urbana, Illinois, 1949).

William Cole provided a base of operations for a group of young Zurichers gaining experience in Oxford from 1573 to 1579. In doing this, they were returning the acts of kindness shown by the Zurich reformers to the Marian exiles. Writing his life of Jewel in 1573, at the time that the first Swiss students were settling in Oxford, Humphrey recalled the sparkling intellectual circle of committed reformers into which he and the future Bishop of Salisbury had been privileged to be received as exiles. He praised the charity shown by all the citizens and in particular Froschover, the printer, in whose house he had lodged, Bullinger, Pellican, Bibliander, Simler, Wölphius, Lavater, Zwingli, and Gesner.[3] William Cole was a member of the same party and, when called upon to help Rudolph Gualter the younger in 1573, wrote to Gualter's father in warmest praise of the city: 'The kindness, most honoured sir, which I experienced from you beyond all others at Zurich, can never escape from my memory; wherefore I wish you to believe that, although I am very far removed from you in person, in mind and inclination I shall always be a Zuricher.'[4] Cole's reflections were sometimes less cordial however, since his exile was a period of impoverishment and misery. When Horne visited Corpus in 1576 and observed the dissonances between President and fellows, he alerted Cole to the possibility that he might have to leave the college. Cole replied, 'What, my good Lord, must I then eat mice at Zurich again?'[5]

Financial considerations and the possibility of patrons, rather than the fame of Oxford as a centre of the reformed tradition, drew Rudolph Gualter the younger away from Cambridge and London. His father, a member of a Zurich patrician family, was one of Bullinger's chief assistants and became principal minister in 1575. He had visited Oxford as a young man, had stayed in Magdalen and was entertained by John Parkhurst, then a junior fellow of Merton. During Mary's reign, Parkhurst became a refugee in Gualter's house. Now he and Edwin Sandys found Gualter the younger and his companion, Rudolph Zwingli, Bullinger's grandson, places in Cambridge. Zwingli died in June 1572 and Gualter soon

[3] Humphrey, *J. Juelli, Vita*, 89-90.
[4] *Z.L.*, II, 222.
[5] Wood, *Annals*, II, 166.

became restless.[6] He visited Oxford in July, called on Lawrence Humphrey, and decided to migrate.[7] The move caused Parkhurst not a little trouble and his protégé does not seem to have been entirely without blame. His father was continually concerned about his conduct and expressed the hope that in Oxford Humphrey, who knew him, would correct him. It took a year, until July 1573, to make the arrangements for him to reside in Magdalen.[8]

The presence of the son of one of the most influential leaders of the Zurich reform renewed the contacts of the exile and provided for the reopening of correspondence. A 'true Zwinglian' was resident in an Oxford college and Humphrey told Gualter senior that this was very agreeable to him and to the whole body.[9] At first, the religious conservatism of the university, the large number of papists, and the lack of interest in reformed writing impressed the young Gualter unfavourably, though to him, as to others, Magdalen was the exception.[10] He found the university more pleasant than Cambridge, but this was due to the climate, his accommodation, and the fact that Humphrey had made himself responsible for his expenses, rather than to the religious temperature.[11] Humphrey and Cole both promoted his interests vigorously and, with Humphrey as Vice-Chancellor, Gualter was allowed to incept a month after his arrival.[12] He stayed in Oxford for a year, gained the affection of the President of Corpus as 'a youth excellent in morals and pious in religion', and returned to Zurich at the request of his father and Simler, to become a minister in the church and to

---

[6] *Z.L.*, I, 189-91. For further discussion see Claire Cross, 'Continental Students and the Protestant Reformation', esp. 51-4.

[7] *Z.L.*, II, 210, Rudolph Gualter the younger to Simler, 29 July 1572.

[8] The correspondence of Parkhurst is printed in *The Letter Book of John Parkhurst, Bishop of Norwich, Compiled during the Years 1571-5*, ed. R. A. Houlbrooke (Norfolk Record Society, xliii, 1974-5), esp. 73-4, 189-90; *Z.L.*, II, 211-12; Lambeth Palace Library, MS 2010, fo. 88ᵛ.

[9] *Z.L.*, I, 289, Humphrey to Rudolph Gualter, 28 July 1575. 'True Zwinglian' may be less a reflection on his doctrine than on the fact that his mother was a daughter of Zwingli.

[10] *Z.L.*, II, 218-19, Rudolph Gualter the younger to Simler, 20 July 1573.

[11] *Z.L.*, II, 218-19.

[12] Clark, *Register*, II, part i, 368. Gualter was incorporated MA on 8 October 1573.

marry.[13] Gualter and his son do not seem to have considered Oxford unsuitable as a seminary for the ministry of the reformed church, and had higher hopes of the academic discipline of the university than of some corrupt German academies.[14] The young Gualter may have brought the influence of the church of Zurich to Magdalen College, and John Reynolds and other members of Corpus retained a respect for him, rejoicing that he was still interested in their affairs, though now separated from them by many miles and preoccupied with public and private duties.[15] They were saddened by his death at the age of 25 in 1577.[16]

Another small group of Swiss students resided in Oxford in 1577-9. They reopened the contact with Zurich and, through Humphrey, brought the university into touch with Berne and with Abraham Musculus, minister at Zofingen in the Aargau, whose father's works Humphrey had read in proof for his Basle host, the printer Froben, in 1555-6. Wolfgang Musculus the younger made a favourable impression in Oxford in 1577 while visiting that city, Cambridge, and London.[17] The following summer, Humphrey established him with two other Zurich students in Broadgates Hall and they were matriculated as members of the university.[18] Johann Rudolph ab Ulmis was the son of John ab Ulmis, one of the circle of Swiss students in Oxford in the reign of Edward VI; his companion was John Huldrik à Vachnan. Humphrey found them places, but was unable to offer them financial assistance; William Cole also supervised them closely; and the Earl of Bedford wrote on their behalf.[19] Financial hardship probably dictated their return to

---

[13] Parkhurst refused to allow him to go home in the spring of 1574; Parkhurst to Gualter sen., 6 February 1574, *Letter Book of John Parkhurst*, 82. Humphrey's testimonial on behalf of the university, 30 July 1574, *Z.L.*, II, 219-20; Cole's recommendation, *Z.L.*, II, 256.

[14] Gualter to Richard Cox, 26 August 1572, Lambeth Palace Library, MS 2010, fo. 16.

[15] *Z.L.*, II, 279. Reynolds to Gualter the younger, thanking him for some verses he had written on the death of Parkhurst, August 1576.

[16] *Z.L.*, I, 324; *Z.L.*, II, 307.

[17] Humphrey to Abraham Musculus, *Z.L.*, II, 298-9, 3 March 1578 and *Z.L.*, II, 301, 5 June 1578.

[18] Clark, *Register,* II, part ii, 82, 20 July 1578.

[19] *Z.L.*, II, 307-8, Cole to Gualter, 28 February 1579; *Z.L.*, II, 306-7, Bedford to Gualter, 28 February 1579.

Zurich in the spring of 1579. In Broadgates Hall they could scarcely have arrived at a more propitious moment. George Summaster, Principal from 1575 to 1619, was enlarging the hall and seems to have encouraged the admission of students of advanced protestant tendencies. Contemporaries of the Swiss students were George Case, one of those who refused subscription to Whitgift's Articles in 1584, Edward Philipps, a noted godly preacher in Southwark, and Roger Squire, later a resolute non-conformist in Devon; Isaac Colfe, son of Amandas Colfe, one of the Huguenot refugees in Canterbury, entered the hall in 1579.

There is no record of any student visitor from Geneva in Oxford until 1578, when John Castorllius was matriculated as a member of Magdalen Hall on 22 December.[20] Nothing more is known of him until 1587 when, under the name Castollus, he appears as one of the sponsors of a collection in the university for French refugees.[21] Jean Hotman arrived in Oxford at the beginning of 1581, as guardian to the sons of Lord Paulet, English ambassador in Paris. In a letter to Dr Wake, presumably William Wake, student of Christ Church, he commended himself as an alumnus of Calvin and the Genevan church.[22] Another of his wide circle of Oxford friends was Laurence Bodley, whose family he must have known while they were exiles in Geneva. Even a man as well connected as Hotman, one of an international Calvinist élite with influential friends at the English court, needed sympathetic allies in Oxford, and his life in Christ Church appears to have been frugal. He was the son of a distinguished Huguenot family; his father, Francis Hotman, *sieur* de Villiers Saint-Paul, a friend of Calvin, had been a professor at Valence, where his son was educated. Jean became professor at Caen in 1584, but was forced to withdraw when the Wars of Religion began anew and accompanied his English patron, Leicester, in his mission to the Low Countries in 1586-7.

[20] Clark, *Register*, II, part ii, 72.
[21] See below, 86-7.
[22] *Francisci et Iohannis Hotomanorum Patris ac Filii et Clarorum Virorum ad eos Epistolae* (Amsterdam, 1700), 262-3. Hotman incorporated on 6 March 1581, Clark, *Register*, II, part i, 379 where LLD Valentia must be an error for his father. F. Schickler, *Les Églises de Refuge en Angleterre* (Paris, 1892), I, 244.

Hotman mounted an extensive campaign to secure an Oxford place for another Genevan student, Samuel le Chevalier. Chevalier was the son of Antoine-Rudolph le Chevalier, exile for religion in England in Edward VI's reign, who had become Professor of Hebrew at Geneva in 1559.[23] Hotman's correspondents in Oxford, no less than fourteen in number, included John Reynolds, Lawrence Humphrey, Henry Savile at Merton, and Tobie Mathew at Christ Church. Chevalier is described as a citizen of Geneva and a young man of erudition. Oxford, Hotman asserted, would judge him as favourably as Geneva had done, but there is no evidence that he was matriculated. Another Genevan, Isaac de Cardencia (Cardenas), moved over to Oxford from Cambridge in the autumn of 1584. Like Hotman, he was well connected at court and had been used in diplomatic service by Walsingham. This was probably the cause of the Queen's letters to secure him a place in Merton College, where he was admitted fellow on 31 August 1584.[24] Cardencia and Hotman brought Oxford into the circle of Beza; they also widened the awareness of their contemporaries of the political and religious implications of the wars in France and the precarious state of Geneva, threatened by the armies of Savoy. Apart from the incorporation of Villiers in 1576, the only other Genevan mentioned in the university records is one Abraham Carter, matriculated, improbably from Hart Hall, in July 1586. By this time Genevan visitors were coming to have the status of political refugees.[25] Political uncertainty after the rejection of the alliance with Berne produced not only a continuous flood of exiles from the beleaguered city, but constant appeals for financial assistance. These did not go unheeded. Merton College, always ready to aid refugees, made a collection on Easter Day 1590 for the city and people of Geneva, under attack from

[23] Samuel incorporated BA at Cambridge from Heidelberg in 1570, and became fellow and Hebrew lecturer at Corpus Christi College, Cambridge. J. and J. A. Venn, *Alumni Cantabrigienses*, Part I, i (Cambridge, 1922), 331. Hotman to Humphrey from Windsor, Christmas 1582, *Epistolae*, 308.

[24] *Registrum Annalium Collegii Mertonensis, 1567-1603*, 172; Merton College muniments, no. 2419.

[25] For Villiers, see below, ch. V; for an account of Genevan political fortunes in this period see E. W. Monter *Calvin's Geneva* (New York, 1967), ch. 8.

Catholic troops. The religious motive was strong and subscription was encouraged throughout the university, urged on by letters from Whitgift and supported by the Vice-Chancellor and heads of houses.[26] Magdalen College granted the city a donation from the common fund at the same time.[27]

The direct influence of Heidelberg, university city and capital of the Calvinist Palatinate, does not compare with that of the Swiss cities, yet should not be overlooked. Two of its principal theologians, Ursinus and Zanchius, exercised a major attraction for Oxford divines in the latter part of the reign. Frederick III (1559-76) found competing groups of Lutherans, Calvinists, and Zwinglians on his accession, and chose Calvin's view because he believed it to be based on scripture and reason. He gathered in Heidelberg a group of Calvinist ministers, most of them refugees, as impressive as those in Geneva or Zurich.[28] They maintained close contacts with the Swiss cities, with the French churches, and in England with Walsingham, Leicester, and Sir Philip Sidney, all three of whom were connected with Oxford.[29] One of the earliest Heidelberg students to visit Oxford was John Philip, son of the baron of Alt-Sax, who was incorporated MA on 18 May 1574.[30] Rudolph Gualter senior, commending him to Bedford, had hoped to establish him at court, but when this failed he was found a place at Oxford, probably through Humphrey's agency. In the company of Gualter's son, he returned to Europe in July 1574.[31]

When Frederick III died, his successor Ludwig VI turned the Palatinate over to Lutheranism, but under John Casimir,

---

[26] *Registrum Annalium Collegii Mertonensis, 1567-1603,* 261. Merton collected £3.10s.0d. at the Easter Day communion and added a further £2 from the common fund. For Whitgift's correspondence with Geneva see Lambeth Palace Library, MS 2010, fos. 56, 58, 60 concerning the collection.

[27] Macray, *Register,* III, 27.

[28] The principal ministers and theologians were John Emmanuel Tremellius, Zacharias Bär (Ursinus), Kaspar von Olewig (Olevianus), Pierre Toussain, Pierre Boquin, Francois du Jon (Junius), Hierome Zanchi (Zanchius), and Datherius. Many had studied at Geneva and had lived in Switzerland, Italy, France, the Netherlands, and England.

[29] See C.-P. Clasen, *The Palatinate in European History, 1555-1618* (Oxford, 1966).

[30] Clark, *Register,* II, part i, 379.

[31] *Z.L.,* II, 214-15. Humphrey provided him with a testimonial on behalf of the university dated 30 July 1574. *Z.L.,* II, 216, 260.

protector for his nephew from 1583, Heidelberg university again became a refuge for persecuted foreigners, or those in search of a more zealous Calvinist haven. Casimir had first-hand knowledge of Oxford. In February 1579, at the time that he had set up his court at Neustadt-an-der-Hardt, in exile from the Lutheran hegemony in Heidelberg, he was entertained by Leicester, who brought him to the university. Though he was not very religious himself, despite the title 'Joshua', he was a firm Calvinist, had fought with the Huguenots in France, and was ambitious to play an international role in the defence of protestantism.[32] In 1577 he tried to unite all the European Calvinist churches in a confession of faith, and in 1591 he almost succeeded in uniting German protestants in the League of Torgau. His *Collegium Illustre* at Neustadt was a powerful instrument in the dissemination of Calvinist ideas. Nothing is known of his Oxford visit apart from his expenses recorded by the Vice-Chancellor, Martin Culpepper of New College.[33] His affinity with Leicester was no doubt a result of similar diplomatic concerns. The Heidelberg Catechism, drawn up at the request of Casimir's father, Frederick III, had been prescribed as a set work of the first order in the Oxford Catechetical Statute only a month before his visit.[34]

A direct result of the visit was the commendation by Casimir through Leicester of Johannes Bernardus.[35] Bernardus had studied for ten years at universities in Germany and like many of the foreign visitors to Oxford was poor. He asked Hotman for money in 1582 and evidently spent his time on the academic grand tour.[36] He supplicated for an Oxford BD in June 1583, when he refuted the doctrine of transubstantiation.[37] At the same time, he intended to go north to the universities in Scotland. He was back in Oxford by 1586, when Humphrey wrote to commend him to Jacobus Regius (de Konink),

---

[32] He attempted to overturn the *Reservatio Ecclesiastica* of the 1555 Peace of Augsburg and was active with military and financial help for French Huguenots and the Dutch.

[33] Wood, *Annals*, II, 194.

[34] Clark, *Register*, II, part i, 155-6.

[35] *Ecclesiae Londino-Batavae Archivum*, ed. J. H. Hessels, III, part ii (Cambridge, 1897), 827-8. Bernardus to the Dutch Church, London, 1586.

[36] Hotman, *Epistolae*, 312.

[37] Clark, *Register*, II, part i, 380.

minister of the Dutch Church at Austin Friars in London, explaining that he wished to return to his native Moravia, despite the desire of the university that he should remain in Oxford and proceed DD, but that he was too poor to travel.[38] Nothing further is known of him. Balthasar Voegger, another Heidelberg student, was matriculated as a member of New College in June 1582.[39]

Lawrencè Humphrey, discredited by many of the advanced protestant fellows in his own college, stands at the centre of the circle of continental reformed influence in Oxford in the 1570s and 1580s. His field of correspondence included France, Switzerland, and Germany; his writing against the Jesuits found its way to Beza; and his monument in Magdalen College Chapel may not be over-lavish in eulogy when it declares of him, *'pietatis orbis Christianus testis est'*.[40] He was not only the focus of continental visitors, but was also used by the Queen as an emissary in the affairs of the protestant churches abroad. On 5 April 1578, he told Abraham Musculus that he was being sent as a deputy to the Lutheran synod at Smalcald, where a lengthy controversy about the Lord's Supper had come to a head over the question of Christ's ubiquity.[41]

Humphrey's good name among the German Calvinists was invoked by Hotman in September 1582, when he wrote on behalf of some unnamed young Germans of good family, instructed in the highest arts, who were now drawn to Oxford by its fame and celebrity, its splendid colleges and libraries.[42] Humphrey also maintained a connection with Strasburg. In 1581, Jean Sturm and 'other excellent men' wrote to him commending James Telones who had fled from the city, probably in the wake of the conflict between Lutheran orthodoxy and the reformed tradition which had been raging ever since Johann Marbach had succeeded as chief pastor on the death of

---

[38] *Ecclesiae Londino-Batavae Archivum*, II (Cambridge 1889), 792, Humphrey to de Konink, 9 April 1586.

[39] Clark, *Register*, II, part ii, 119.

[40] Beza to Robert de la Fontaine, 1 July 1584, says that he has received Humphrey's book. *Ecclesiae Londino-Batavae Archivum*, II, 771.

[41] Z.L., II, 301; Lambeth Palace Library, MS 2010, fos. 25, 83, 85; Magdalen College Oxford Archives, Vice-President's Register, fo. 41ʳ, 3 July 1578, Humphrey granted absence *'de mense in mensem'*.

[42] Hotman, *Epistolae*, 293.

Hedio in 1552. By 1580, the position of any who adhered to the faith of Bucer's church had become impossible. Telones became a member of Queen's, where Grindal exercised influence on his behalf. In February 1583 he was allowed to count two terms at Strasburg towards his Oxford degree and received financial help, at Humphrey's bidding, from the Dutch Church in Sandwich.[43] An Oxford contemporary from Strasburg, who had studied in Casimir's academy at Neustadt, was Francis Gomar, who also proceeded MA at Cambridge in 1583.[44]

Oxford could not long avoid involvement in the struggles of her reformed brethren in France and the Low Countries. As a place of refuge throughout the 1570s and 1580s she received into her colleges and halls, sometimes to places of influence as lecturers and catechists, men who were willing to risk life and livelihood in the cause of religion. In the Low Countries, a reign of repression began in August 1567 with the arrival of the Duke of Alva and his Spanish troops. In the following two years thousands of refugees fled, most to Germany, though some to England. The Pacification of Ghent in 1576, followed by the Union of Brussels in 1577, attempted to bring about peaceful coexistence between Catholics and Protestants, but the extreme Calvinist attempt to set up a republic in Ghent finally alienated the Catholics and indirectly brought about the reconciliation of the ten southern provinces with Philip II in the Peace of Arras of 1579.

John Drusius, with his father Clement, were among those who fled from the Low Countries in 1567. John had already been at Cambridge and in London before he incorporated as a BA from Louvain at Oxford in July 1572 at the age of 22.[45] He was the first continental student to open up a new contact with Merton College, after Magdalen and Corpus an obvious focus of attention. Warden Man had not only translated the *Commonplaces* of Musculus, the *summa* of the Berne Professor of Divinity (1549-63) and much favoured by early Elizabethan protestant divines, but had established a further continental

[43] Clark, *Register*, II, part i, 379; Ecclesiae Londino-Batavae Archivum, II, 709.
[44] *Grace Book △, Containing the Records of the University of Cambridge, 1542-89*, ed. J. Venn (Cambridge 1910), 360.
[45] Clark, *Register*, II, part i, 377.

connection as Elizabeth's emissary at the court of Madrid from 1566 to 1569.[46] His successor, Thomas Bickley, once a fiery protestant in his youth at Magdalen, had been an exile in Paris and Orléans, and under his direction from 1569 to 1585 the college welcomed a succession of refugees for religion. Thomas Bodley, who as a child had been an exile in Wesel, Frankfurt, and Geneva had at the age of 12 heard Chevalier lecture on Hebrew, Berealdus on Greek, and Calvin and Beza on divinity. Elected fellow of Merton in 1563, he was constantly abroad as royal emissary in Italy, France, and Spain from 1576 to 1580; and though his activities have been lost to obscurity, he must have maintained contacts with the reformed churches. In 1585 the Queen sent him as ambassador to Frederick, King of Denmark, the Duke of Brunswick, and the Landgrave of Hesse to encourage them to join the English in support of Henry of Navarre, an alliance which, Bodley recorded, 'tended to the advancement not only of the king [Henry] but to all the protestants in France'.[47] Again in 1588, the Queen sent him to conclude a contract with the United Provinces, though he had resigned his fellowship at Merton in marriage two years before. Drusius first appears in the Merton register on 2 August 1572 when, in return for his long service to the college as Hebrew lecturer, he was given a room and a pension of forty shillings a year.[48] Through his teaching, Bodley became an extremely competent Hebraist and they remained in close contact even after Drusius had returned to Flanders.[49] He also lectured in Magdalen at the request of Humphrey, in Syriac and Chaldaic as well as in Hebrew.[50] In October 1574 he was given a salary of twenty marks, at the request of Leicester, to lecture publicly in the Schools in Syriac.[51] He left Oxford two years later, pro-

[46] Z.L., II, 148.

[47] The Life of Sir Thomas Bodley ... written by himselfe (Oxford, 1647), 2, 5.

[48] Registrum Annalium Collegii Mertonensis, 1567-1603, 43. The pension was renewed in 1573 and twice in 1574. Ibid., 54, 64, 66.

[49] See C. Roth, 'Sir Thomas Bodley - Hebraist', in Bodleian Library Record, vii (1966), 242-51; and A. R. Bonner and P. James, 'Two Letters in Hebrew Addressed to Sir Thomas Bodley', in Bodleian Library Record, viii (1971), 258-62.

[50] Wood, Athenae Oxonienses, ed. Philip Bliss, II (London, 1815), cols. 159-62.

[51] OUA/NEP supra/Register KK, fo. 177ᵛ; Wood, Annals, II, 175.

fiting from the Pacification of Ghent to become Professor of Chaldaic at Leiden.[52]

In France, the decade 1563-72 was marked by a series of pacifications which gave the Huguenots liberty of conscience, freedom of worship in one town in each *baillage* and *senechausée*, and, from 1570, four towns of security: La Rochelle, Montauban, La Charité, and Cognac. Between these pacifications, the Catholic party aided by Spanish troops, proceeded against the Huguenots in a campaign which was widely believed to intend their total suppression. Waves of protestant refugees arrived in England in 1567-9, and further parties arrived after the breach of the Treaty of Longjumeau in 1568-9 and following the Massacre of St. Bartholomew in August 1572. There was a short respite in 1576, when some of the exiles were recalled, but later that year an intensification of the wars drove some of them overseas again.

In Oxford, Giles Gautier (Berensarius) arrived from Caen in 1572. He supplicated to proceed BD in 1576, but at this time a letter arrived from the university of Caen asking that their pastor should return, since the city once again enjoyed peace. They were very grateful that Oxford had received him, and had made him one of the *'theologiae professores'*, an error, since he held no university position.[53] Berensarius did not return home, probably because of the rapid change in the political situation. Merton gave him an exhibition in 1576 and 1577. This was clearly not sufficient maintenance and in May 1577 Convocation set up a committee to help those who had been expelled from France on account of their religion, naming Johannes Rhegius, Berensarius, and Bigonius, who were said to have been deprived of all support.[54] Berensarius was still in Oxford in May 1579, when he was catechist at Broadgates Hall. As late as August 1589, Merton gave him an annual exhibition of £3.6s.8d. per term as Hebrew lecturer, but after

---

[52] Four other Flemish refugees are noted in the matriculation registers between 1576 and 1590. Clark, *Register*, II, part ii, 72, 95, 157, 175.

[53] Clark, *Register*, II, part i, 375; Wood, *Annals*, II, 198.

[54] Clark, *Register*, II, part i, 380.

this, he disappears from the records.[55] Another refugee from Caen was Hector Viel (Viellius), who supplicated for incorporation in June 1574.[56]

Two refugees by the name of Rhegius found temporary homes in Oxford. In July 1576 Petrus Rhegius (Pierre le Roy), an MA of Paris of twelve years' standing, was allowed to supplicate for the Oxford BD; he was at that time intending to return to France.[57] In May 1577 Johannes Rhegius was in financial need and it was probably this Rhegius who was granted an exhibition of ten shillings by Merton in October 1576 and forty shillings the following July.[58] In May 1579 he was probably catechist at Magdalen Hall.[59] Philip Bignon (Bigonius) had been Hebrew lecturer in Cambridge from 1572 to 1575. He tried, unsuccessfully, for the Hebrew chair there and shortly after this came to Oxford.[60] He was Hebrew lecturer in Magdalen in succession to Drusius from 1577 to 1580 but continued chronically short of money so that All Souls opened a subscription list for him in July 1581, which raised £20, the only record of a donation for foreign refugees from this college.[61] Magdalen College entertained the Vidame de Chartres, Jean de Ferrières, a Huguenot refugee on a pension from the Queen as early as 1570.[62] Ten years later, two of the young advanced protestants in the college, Smith and Tansye, were appointed to collect money for French refugees.[63] In 1587, Massonius, Fontanus, Castollus, Giles Stevens, Francis Biscope, John Bodley, and others, with the pastors, elders, and

[55] Ibid., 156. Halls of definite protestant sympathy, Magdalen and Broadgates, employed French refugees, Rhegius and Berensarius, as catechists, while Gloucester, St. Mary's, and Hart Halls, all often suspect of harbouring adherents of the old religion, were content with Corro, himself suspect for his religious opinions; *Registrum Annalium Collegii Mertonensis, 1567-1603,* 247.

[56] Clark, *Register,* II, part i, 375.

[57] Ibid., 380.

[58] *Registrum Annalium Collegii Mertonensis, 1567-1603,* 92, 98.

[59] OUA/NEP *supra*/Register, KK, fo. 277ᵛ; Clark, *Register,* II, part i, 156.

[60] In November 1574 the Cambridge heads commended Bignon to Burghley, *Cambridge Transactions during the Puritan Controversies,* collected by J. Heywood and T. Wright, I (Cambridge, 1854), 165-6. C. H. and T. Cooper, *Athenae Cantabrigienses, 1500-1609,* I (Cambridge, 1858), 349.

[61] Macray, *Register,* III, 5; All Souls College Archives, Miscellanea, 293. The Warden and forty-five fellows subscribed, 16 July 1581.

[62] Macray, *Register,* II, 42.

[63] Macray, *Register,* III, 8, 5 April 1580.

deacons of the French church in London, wrote to the Vice-Chancellor asking for financial aid for French refugees. Oxford collected £50 and received a letter of thanks from the French church.[64] Those who were responsible for turning the sympathetic face of Oxford towards the continental exiles for religion cannot have been unaware that they were inviting representatives of churches more fully reformed than their own into the heart of the university society.

Oxford's outlook as a place of refuge may be compared very favourably with that of contemporary Cambridge. In Cambridge, eight foreigners or graduates of foreign universities appear as admitted to degrees or licences to practise in the period 1560-89.[65] Whilst it is true that in Oxford no foreigner attained appointment to a university chair, like Baro in Cambridge, the French refugees were of great value in the implementation of the Catechetical Statute. At the beginning of the seventeenth century, after the refoundation of the University Library in Oxford by Sir Thomas Bodley, the visits of foreign exiles and notables can be charted with higher accuracy from the library records.[66] The twenty-seven foreigners who visited the library in the two years 1603 and 1604 may indicate that more continental visitors came to Oxford at the beginning of the new reign than previously. It is however more likely that many of those who passed through the university in Elizabeth's reign left no record of their visits.

When Convocation decided at its meeting on 20 December 1578 to correct and enlarge the statute *De inquisitione et cautione faciendis contra haereticam pravitatem*, its principal aim was to protect the junior members against the continuing presence in Oxford of many adherents of the old religion and the increasing menace caused by the defection of Oxford students to the seminaries abroad. A secondary objective, outlined by the committee on the new statute which reported in January 1579,

---

[64] OUA/NEP *supra*/Register L, fo. 291ʳ.

[65] For details see *Grace Book △, Containing the Records of the University of Cambridge, 1542-89.*

[66] Clark, *Register*, II, part i, 263-4. Clark's list is compiled chiefly from graces granted by Convocation. The twenty-seven comprise eight Germans, six French, three from Geneva, three Danish, two Dutch, and five unidentified other nations.

was the instruction of youth in piety. The result of this statute was that, perhaps for the first time, the Oxford student of 17 or 18 was brought into contact with the works of continental theology which formed the basis of its prospectus. The new statute with its prescribed texts was framed by a committee of three: Humphrey, Bickley, and Bartholomew Chamberlayne, a former scholar of Trinity and Vicar of Romford from 1578. Humphrey and Bickley had well-established contacts with the churches of the reformed tradition; from his only published work, a 1580 sermon preached before the Privy Council, entitled *The Passion of Christ and the Benefits Thereby*, Chamberlayne emerges as an apologist of the Church of England against papist cavils, and this may explain his presence on the committee.

The works prescribed for catechesis were divided into two sections. In the first, the compulsory reading, were three catechisms, those of Nowell, Calvin, and Heidelberg, together with the *Elementa* of Hyperius. To these works might be added, if desired, Bullinger's catechism, Calvin's *Institutes*, Jewel's *Apology,* and the Articles of Religion of 1563.[67] The bias towards continental works emerges immediately and asserts, at the end of a period of considerable theological development and controversy, the hybrid reformed tradition which was to predominate in the university for the remainder of the reign. The statute also marks the end of an era, for it looks backward to the period when Oxford links with the reformed churches were dominated by the contacts of the exiles with Zurich and Geneva, a time of moderate balance in reformed theology.

Alexander Nowell's *A Catechisme, or First Instruction and Learning of Christian Religion* was not published until 1570, though Nowell probably prepared it for the Convocation of 1563. By 1578, its acceptability in Oxford cannot have been in doubt. In tone, it seems closest to Calvin's catechism and Ponet's catechism of 1552-3. Nowell emphasizes the fundamental place of scripture, as a basic law for life and conduct, for the organization of matters civil and ecclesiastical, and as the sole authority in Christian doctrine. He distinguishes between a true and lively faith, general faith, and dead faith; and though he makes a very clear differentiation between the visible and

[67] Clark, *Register,* II, part i, 155-6.

invisible church, the doctrine of election is never developed in any strict sense, for the church is 'the congregation of those whom God by his secret election hath adopted to himself through Christ: which Church can neither be seen with eyes, nor can continually be known by signs'.[68] Those who are 'chosen and appointed, and (as we term it) predestinated to ... so great felicity, before the foundations of the world were laid ... have a witness within them in their souls, the Spirit of Christ the author, and therewith also the more sure pledge of this confidence. By the instinct of which divine Spirit I do also surely persuade myself that I am also, by God's good gift through Christ, freely made one of this blessed city.'[69] Nowell makes clear the responsibility of the unfaithful in their reprobation, for they 'in refusing the promises offered them by God, shut up the entry against themselves, and go empty away'.[70] Nowell's doctrine of the visible church is also close to that of Calvin. The church is to be discerned by two necessary marks, the sincere preaching of the gospel and the administration of the sacraments. He regretted the decay of ecclesiastical discipline, advocating in all well-ordered churches the choosing of elders 'to hold and keep the discipline of the church', and, in consultation with the pastor, the correction of any who held 'false opinions, or troublesome errors, or vain superstitions, or with corrupt and wicked life, brought publicly any great offence to the church of God'. Such men should be excommunicated until they had 'by public penance satisfied the church'.[71]

Nowell seems to have followed closely the opinions expressed by Calvin in his 1545 Genevan Church catechism. In Calvin, the theocentric emphasis is uppermost: the chief end of men is that they should know God by whom they were created; God 'governs the world by his providence, constitutes all things by his will ... so that nothing is done but through him and by his decree'. The world is 'a kind of mirror, in which we may

[68] The Latin edition printed by Wolff and the English edition by John Daye are both in *A Catechism by Alexander Nowell*, ed. G. E. Corry (Cambridge, Parker Society, 1853), 142-4, 174.
[69] Nowell, op. cit., 171.
[70] Ibid., 208.
[71] Ibid., 218.

observe [God] in so far as it concerns us to know him'.[72] The
work of Christ and the Holy Spirit in redemption and sancifi-
cation are discussed at length before Calvin moves to any
definition of the church, 'the body and society of believers
whom God has predestined to eternal life'. Strictly, however,
the church is 'the company of those who, by secret election,
[God] has adopted for salvation; and this is not always visible
with the eyes nor discernible by signs'.[73] The decree of
reprobation is nowhere discussed and users of this 1545
catechism in Oxford may have been unaware that Calvin's
later 'Articles Concerning Predestination' had made a clearer
analysis of the division between the elect and the reprobate.[74]

The *Elementa Christianae Religionis* of 1563 by Andreas
Gerardus, or Hyperius as he is often known, is at first sight a
surprising companion for the two catechisms of Nowell and
Calvin. Calvin, however, much admired Hyperius, whom he
had commended in 1564 as 'a man of exceptional godliness and
erudition that shines forth in all his writings; they say that the
man is endowed with a peaceable temperament and with great
integrity'. Hyperius's theology is eclectic, a hybrid tradition in
which elements drawn from both Calvin and Luther coexist.
His ideal of the church, as he propounded it for Hesse in 1560,
was of the primitive church revived, rather than the present
church reformed, but his ideas won little acceptance and in the
year before his death in 1564, his influence in the Hessian
church was greatly diminished when he was accused of Calvinist sympathies. Hyperius also admired the writings of
Bucer and there is no doubt that the Melanchthonian spirit of
Marburg was highly coloured by the reformed tradition. It
may have been the practical and analytical approach of the
Elementa, its stress on the Christian life, on Christian exercises,
and the detailed instructions on the duties of magistrates,
ministers, and parents which commended it to the Oxford
theologians. Its method supplemented that of the catechetical

[72] 'The Catechism of the Church of Geneva', in Calvin, *Theological Treatises*, ed.
J. K. S. Reid, *Library of Christian Classics*, xxii (London, 1954), 83-139, esp. 91-3.
[73] Calvin, *Theological Treatises*, 103.
[74] Ibid., 179-80; see also F. Wendel, *Calvin: the Origins and Development of his Religious
Thought* (London, Fontana ed., 1965) 264-5, 269.

stereotype adopted by Calvin and Nowell. Its seven sections deal with penitance from dead works, faith in God, baptism, Christian life (*doctrina*), the laying-on of hands, the resurrection of the dead, and the last judgement.

The final work in the first section of prescribed texts was the Heidelberg Catechism.[75] This was originally drawn up in January 1563 by Ursinus and Olevianus, to replace for use in the Palatinate the conflicting catechisms of Brentz, Luther, and à Lasco then in use, in an attempt to complete the adoption of a moderate reformed theology which Frederick III had initiated in 1560. It rapidly took the place of other local catechisms in German and Dutch reformed churches and not only was it prescribed in Oxford in 1579, but was the only catechism printed in the university. Two editions appeared in 1588, printed by Joseph Barnes, with the arms of the university on the title page and prefaced by a treatise by Thomas Sparke, former fellow of Magdalen. The catechism had been preceded, in 1587, by an English translation, also printed in Oxford, of *The Summe of the Christian Religion: Delivered by Zacharias Ursinus*, his lectures on the Heidelberg Catechism. Ursinus and Olevianus admitted that their catechism owed a great deal to Zurich where both men had been resident when Bullinger was drafting his *Catechesis pro adultoribus*, in 1558-9. Sending a copy of their catechism to the chief minister in Zurich, Ursinus remarked 'If there is any clarity in this work, we owe it in great part to you and the enlightened minds of Switzerland.'[76] The catechism, if close to Zurich, is distant from Calvin's Geneva. Calvin is theocentric; Heidelberg is anthropocentric. Man's misery, man's deliverance, and man's thankfulness are its three principal sections. Election is outlined, but there is no treatment of reprobation. Its doctrine of the Lord's Supper is much nearer to Zwingli than to Calvin. The stress of this catechism on religious feeling and life, and its emphasis on good works done in faith as a sign of man's thankfulness may have commended it to Oxford, as similar in tone to the *Elementa* of Hyperius. For Oxford, as for Zurich, Berne, and later Scotland, the

---

[75] *A catechisme, or short kind of instruction, whereby, to teach children and the ignoraunter sort, the Christian religion* (Oxford, 2 editions, 1588).

[76] E. G. Léonard, *A History of Protestantism*, trans. H. H. Rowley, II (London, 1967), 14.

Heidelberg Catechism embodied 'that mixture of originally conflicting doctrines which was henceforth to constitute "Reformed" theology'.[77]

Despite the preponderant emphasis on the theology of Zurich, Bullinger's own *Catechesis pro adultoribus scripta* of 1559 was listed in the 1579 Oxford statute only as an optional work of study. His catechism would however have restored the theocentric balance which Heidelberg had lost. While Calvin describes faith as 'a firm and sure knowledge of the love of God for us', in Heidelberg this becomes: 'it is not only by sure knowledge that I hold for true what God has revealed to us in his word, it is also by a trusting heart which the Holy Spirit produces in me through the Gospel', and Bullinger swings to the other end of the spectrum with his contention that faith is not knowledge, but the firm assent of the heart. A man's heart confirms what he believes out of the word of God.[78]

Jewel's *Apology* is included in the texts prescribed not only because of the deep respect in which he was held by Humphrey and other Oxford theologians, but also because of its significance as the original Elizabethan defence against Rome. Calvin's *Institutes* had already taken a place on the shelves as a standard manual, both in the libraries and in the collections of individual scholars. Thomas Norton's English translation first appeared in 1561, and was reissued in 1562, 1574, 1578, 1582, 1587, 1599, and 1611. The Catechetical Statute however sees the *Institutes* as an alternative work of the second order, together with the Articles of 1563.

The central theological tradition of mid-Elizabethan Oxford did not confine its sources to Calvin's *Institutes* or the moderate Calvinism of the Articles of Religion. Until the later 1570s, reformers in the university looked to a wider tradition that that of Geneva alone, and the hybrid theology which emerged seems to have given at least as much prominence to the writings of Bullinger, Hyperius, and Ursinus. Even where Calvin's catechism was widely read in the colleges of Oxford,

---

[77] Léonard, op. cit., 15.

[78] Calvin, 'Catechism', in *Library of Christian Classics,* xxii, 105; *A catechisme* (Heidelberg), (Oxford, 1588), 83; Bullinger, *Catechesis* (2nd ed., 1599, Zurich, Wolphius), 29.

many of those who received from it their first insights into Christian theology may have been unaware that the followers of Calvin had begun a movement which was to take them far from their master's careful balance, inspired by the vision of a sovereign God who willed men to come to a knowledge of him through the redeeming love of his Son.

A further index of the balance of continental protestant ideas in mid-Elizabethan Oxford may be obtained from an analysis of the contents of college libraries and the collections of books of individual scholars.[79] These books will be analysed in three periods: from the beginning of the reign to c. 1578, from c.1578 to c.1590, and from 1590 onwards. This is at best a highly speculative index of theological opinion, since many of the books which must have been on the shelves in the 1580s were later replaced when new editions appeared. Libraries do not seem to have attached any sentimental value to books, even when they were the gift of an illustrious alumnus. This could easily be the reason why so few of Calvin's writings survive in Oxford in sixteenth-century editions, for no author was more frequently reprinted, one or more of Calvin's works appearing every year between 1548 and 1643.[80] In many libraries throughout this period the only form of accession was through bequest, though in some colleges, notably the more advanced protestant societies, books were being purchased regularly from the common fund. At the beginning of the 1560s, virtually no library possessed any protestant literature. If Magdalen, Christ Church, or Corpus, for instance, had had any protestant works on the desks in 1553, Cardinal Pole's commissioners would certainly have ordered their destruction. A possible cause of their absence is that the printing houses in Geneva, Zurich, and Basle did not produce folio volumes until the 1550s; the quarto and octavo editions were too small for library desks, though they may have found their way into private collections.[81]

[79] Inventories, made either in wills or in lists of the contents of rooms on a scholar's death, are housed in the University Archives, 'Wills and Inventories', under the name of the deceased.

[80] Cremeans, op. cit., 65.

[81] Ker, *Oxford Libraries in 1556*, 6, 12-13.

In the period up to 1578, three colleges had libraries well stocked with continental authors. All Souls owed its collection almost entirely to one fellow, Andrew Kingsmill. When Kingsmill died at Lausanne in 1569, he bequeathed to the college £5 to be spent on the works of his most favoured authors, Calvin and Peter Martyr.[82] The college did not spend the money until 1575, when it purchased the most important Calvin commentaries, the *Opuscula*, five Peter Martyr commentaries, and his *Defensio doctrinae eucharistiae*. Corpus already had a small number of protestant books which had somehow survived from the collection of John Claymond, the second president, who died in 1537, the most important being the 1532 edition of Bucer's commentary on the Psalms.[83] This collection of reformed literature was augmented through the will of the fifth president, Thomas Greenaway, who left the college a very fine collection in 1571, the bias of which inclined towards Zurich rather than Geneva. Peter Martyr's commentaries, the *Loci Communes* of Musculus, and the commentaries of Gualter on Mark, John, Acts, and the Minor Prophets provided the college with a collection to rival All Souls and Magdalen. Magdalen, however, had been active in buying books since 1536 and pioneered a new venture in 1550, when a fellow was paid to look after the library.[84] John Jewel's very fine collection came to the college in 1572-3 not by bequest, but through the action of the President. Humphrey persuaded the college to pay £100 in 1572 and a further £20 the following year, and eighty books, originally in Jewel's possession, are still in the college library.[85] They demonstrate the same bias as Greenaway's collection at Corpus; there are significant numbers of works by Lavater, Bullinger, Musculus, and Martyr, but no Calvin. This must, however, have been because later editions of Calvin replaced those of Jewel in the Magdalen library, rather than because the Bishop possessed no Calvin. A similar tendency emerges in Merton, which purchased books by Bucer, Musculus, Gualter, and Oecolampadius

[82] All Souls College, Vellum Inventory, fo. 51ʳ, printed by N. R. Ker, *Records of All Souls College Library, 1437-1600* (Oxford Bibliographical Society, xvi, 1971), 33.

[83] Liddell, 'The Library of Corpus Christi College, 1517-1617', 36.

[84] Paul Morgan, *Oxford Libraries Outside the Bodleian*, 64.

[85] N. R. Ker, 'The Library of John Jewel', in *Bodleian Library Record*, ix, 5 (1977), 256-65.

in 1565, possibly under the influence of Warden Man, himself an editor of Musculus; but no Calvin seems to have appeared there until 1584.[86] Christ Church, which generally seems to have been weak in protestant literature until the beginning of the seventeenth century, possessed a Geneva Bible and a Zurich Bible with notes, from the bequest of one of its members, Richard Clyffe, in 1566 and a Musculus commentary and a Peter Martyr commentary from another, William Lant, in 1572.[87]

In the period up to 1578 inventories of individual collections indicate greater variety in book purchases than emerges from college library catalogues, although it seems that very few Oxford men of this generation were in the habit of buying books. Twenty-three of the twenty-seven inventories from this period which list any reformed literature at all contain one or more works by Calvin, generally the *Institutes*, though sometimes his catechism. Roger Charnock of Corpus possessed six volumes of Calvin commentaries and the catechism, but apparently not the *Institutes*. He also owned Beza's New Testament, his treatise *De predestinatione*, and Gualter's commentary on Acts. Richard Clyffe, in his 1566 list, possessed, of Calvin's works, only the *Institutes* in a large library which included works of Bullinger, Musculus, Gualter, Bucer, Brentz, Melanchthon, and Peter Martyr. Thomas Daye, prebendary of Christ Church, seems to have taken a deep interest in Lutheran writings, but his library contained very little from the reformed theologians, apart from Calvin's catechism. As early as 1562, Nicholas Sykes, described as 'late butler of Christ Church', possessed Musculus's *Loci Communes*, Peter Martyr's commentary on Romans, a Zurich Bible, and Calvin's *Institutes*. The Geneva Bible, described by Richard Clyffe as 'the verie treasure of trewe Christianitie' in his will of 1566, had found its way into many collections which contained no other reformed literature. There was also a substantial number of inventories which contained no protestant books at all. A few lists contain some of the works of Beza, or of Hyperius, but virtually no

---

[86] N. R. Ker, 'Oxford Libraries in the Sixteenth Century', in *Bodleian Library Record*, vi (1959), 499-500.

[87] OUA, 'Wills', Richard Clyffe, William Lant.

English authors, except for occasional copies of Jewel's *Apology*.
The dominance of the Swiss writings (Musculus, Bullinger,
Martyr, and Gualter) is demonstrated in the inventories and
wills as much as in the libraries, though the presence of
Calvin's works is more evident in private than in college collec-
tions.

The most important collegiate collection of the period
1578-90 is that of Queen's College. This library probably suffered more than any other during the religious changes and
until Provost Robinson persuaded Grindal to bequeath the college his collection of books, the society seems to have possessed
virtually no reformed literature.[88] Grindal's library contained a
very large number of books from the printing houses of Basle
and Zurich. Very few from Geneva are extant and Calvin's only
surviving work is the *Opuscula*. This must convey a misleading
impression, since if the bequest had contained other writings of
Calvin, these would have been discarded and replaced by later
editions in the seventeenth century. It can safely be asserted
that after 1583, the fellows of Queen's had access to the commentaries of Musculus in nine volumes, some of the works of
Brentz, Peter Martyr, Marloratus, Bullinger, Hemmingsen,
and a little Viret, Bucer, Fagius, and Gualter. Beza's *Icones*,
published in 1580 together with the Latin New Testament containing Beza's marginalia were also there. Like most collections of this date, Grindal's library does not appear to have
contained any of the writings of the English reformers. Almost
all the books are folios, published after 1550. His copy of Zanchius's *De Natura Dei* was joined at the beginning of the seventeenth century by the *Tractatus Theologiae*, the *De Operibus Dei*,
and the commentary on Ephesians, the gifts of a fellow,
William Mitchell, in 1600, confirming the wide circulation of
the writings of Zanchius later in the reign. The library acquired
no reformed writings from the bequests of Reynolds or Robinson,
which may indicate that it was already well stocked. The presence
in Queen's of this great library, rivalling Jewel's at Magdalen,
may in part explain how this college, under Provosts Robinson

---

[88] Queen's College Oxford MS 556, the Library Benefactors' Book lists about 120
books from Grindal's collection. Of these about eighty have been identified as still in
the library today; see Patrick Collinson, *Archbishop Grindal* (London, 1980), 280-1, 314.

and Airay, became the foremost Oxford seminary for the training of godly ministers.

The 1589 library catalogue in Corpus provides evidence that by this time the college had acquired Calvin's *Institutes* and some commentaries. Commentaries by Peter Martyr and Bucer had also been added.[89] In Magdalen, where Jewel's library was now chained, virtually no more reformed writings were added until after the death of Humphrey, despite regular acquisitions, noted in the *computi* between 1586 and 1596. In Merton, the relatively small stock of protestant books was probably not augmented until the 1580s. Calvin's *Opera* together with the fifteen-volume *Opera* of Peter Martyr were purchased in 1584, prompted perhaps by the unusual bequest from William Martiall, who, in 1583, left Calvin's *Institutes*, the 'Stephanus Bible', and Jewel's *Defence of the Apology* among a collection of books which otherwise demonstrated the conservative religious opinions for which he had suffered imprisonment early in the reign.[90]

The number of wills and inventories surviving from the 1580s is much smaller than that from the 1570s. By this time nearly all the private collections contained Calvin's *Institutes* and the works of English theologians and reformers. Thomas Morrey of Christ Church, who died in 1584, possessed some anti-papist writings, but more significantly a copy of *An Admonition to the Parliament* and a work listed as the '*Disciplina ecclesiastica*' which may have been the *Ecclesiasticae disciplinae explicatio* of Walter Travers. He also possessed some Calvin commentaries, and a fine selection of the works of Beza, Zanchius, and Martyr, together with Bullinger's *Decades,* and a few volumes of Mercer, Bucer, Gualter, and Luther. His nine volumes of Danaeus and seven of Hemmingsen must have made him one of the best read men of his day in the reformed tradition. He left to Christ Church library some Calvin commentaries, supplementing the college's tiny collection of reformed literature. If his books accurately reflect his interests, Morrey was a man of advanced protestant sympathies who

[89] Liddell, thesis cit., 61-6.

[90] *Registrum Annalium Collegii Mertonensis, 1567-1603*, 163, 167; for Martiall's imprisonment see SP 13/15/24, n.d.

died on the eve of the revival of radical activity in the university.

Other inventories, like his, demonstrate the increasing currency of the writings of Beza, Zanchius, Danaeus, and Hyperius. The library of Edward Higgins, fellow of Brasenose, is exceptional in size and highlights the tendency of the age: an increasing stress on the later Calvinist writers and English authors. Higgins had at least five versions of the Bible, including Beza's annotations and the Zurich Bible. He had little Calvin, but Zanchius figures prominently, together with Danaeus and Beza. He owned the writings of Frith, Barnes, and Tyndal, Jewel's works, Thomas More, Foxe against Osorius, Kingsmill's *Treatise of Comfort in Affliction* and the sermons of his New College contemporary, John Prime, together with works of Fulke, Reynolds, Latimer, Bilson, and a copy of the *Reformatio legum*.

College libraries were also beginning to stock the works of the later Calvinist tradition. All Souls added by bequest the works of Zanchius, together with the 1539 edition of Zwingli and some volumes of Melanchthon.[91] The library at Brasenose profited from the large bequest of Alexander Nowell in 1602. John Reynolds's massive library of sixteen hundred books was largely left to individual students, which may either illustrate the beneficence of the master towards his pupils, or the fact that the libraries to which Reynolds gave only two hundred books did not desire any of the others. Corpus acquired virtually no new reformed literature from this bequest.[92] In Magdalen, the systematic book-buying from common-fund income continued, and reformed writings were added in considerable numbers during Bond's presidency.[93] Two colleges made major accessions of protestant literature for the first time in this period. At New College, John Garbrand, fellow, gave the college Brentz's *Opera Omnia* and the *Loci Communes* of Musculus in 1590. The following year, Richard Payne gave the Geneva Bible in French, and in 1593 Robert Boxold presented a volume of theological tracts by Beza. The first substantial bequest of reformed authors did not arrive, however, until 1617, when

[91] Ker, *Records of All Souls College Library, 1437-1600,* 103-4.
[92] Bodleian Library, MS Wood D 10. Liddell, thesis cit., 77-83.
[93] Macray, *Register,* III, 25-33.

Arthur Lake, former Warden and Bishop of Bath and Wells, left his large library.[94] The other library which expanded significantly was that of St. John's College. A new library was built in 1596-8, though the real expansion of the collection did not take place until the presidency of William Laud, 1615-21. There were two substantial bequests at the turn of the century, one from Henry Price in 1600; at the same time, eighty volumes of protestant theology were presented by the London merchants Robert Lee and Lawrence Holliday, repairing a gap in a college long noted for its Catholic sympathies.[95] This bequest came at precisely the moment when Laud was beginning to establish himself. One of his contemporaries, John English, a lawyer who died in 1613, possessed 518 volumes and though half of them were theological, only a very few came from the Calvinist school. English owned a few works of Calvin, Beza, Erasmus, Luther, Pellican, and Gualter, and a large number of early seventeenth-century English sermons. Among the controversial literature Danaeus, Jewel, Reynolds, and Perkins figure prominently, but more significant is his breadth of interest in fathers, schoolmen, controversialists, reformers, and Roman Catholic writers.[96] A much more impressive collection is found in the inventory of William Mitchell of Queen's, who died in 1599. He had ten volumes of Calvin, many of Beza's writings, some Zwingli, Lavater, Pellican, and Martyr, as well as a little Zanchius, Danaeus, Hyperius, and some late sixteenth-century English writers. Many Oxford men still possessed a considerable number of Calvin commentaries and nearly all the inventories contain the *Institutes,* but the incidence of works by Beza, Zanchius, and Perkins increases steadily as the century draws to a close. Although the wills and inventories of this period may not provide a very representative sample, taken together with the contents of libraries they suggest the general lines of a theologicial development.

---

[94] New College Archives, Library Benefaction Book, under 1590, 1591, 1593, 1600, 1606, 1607, 1617.

[95] Morgan, op. cit., 126 f.

[96] W. C. Costin, 'The Inventory of John English, BCL, Fellow of St. John's College', *Oxoniensia,* xi and xii (1946-7), 102-31, from OUA.

It is hazardous to trace patterns of theological movement, particularly when no direct reference to authorities is made, but the growing dominance of Beza, Zanchius, and their English popularizer, William Perkins, is as evident in the sermons and treatises of Elizabethan Oxford in the last quarter of the century as in collections of books. The development of Calvin's theology by Beza, so that the process and results of predestination appear in sharper focus is reproduced by his Oxford followers. There is an increasing tendency to the supralapsarian approach: before the Creation, God determined all events in the life of the world and of man, including the fall, the election of some men after the fall, and the reprobation of others. Although, like Calvin, Beza believed that speculation about God's sovereign will in the predestination of mankind should be limited, he later began to suggest that Christ did not die for all men, but only for the elect; while Calvin, realizing the ambiguity of scriptural evidence, advocated preaching the gospel and offering salvation to all.

Oxford theologians and preachers made fewer references to Beza's works than to those of Zanchius, though one prominent Oxford figure, John Harmar, fellow of New College and Regius Professor of Greek, translated from the French *Master Bezaes Sermons upon the Three First Chapters of the Canticle of Canticles,* printed in Oxford by Joseph Barnes in 1587, a controversial work, designed to refute papist arguments about the marks of the true church. In his dedication to Leicester, Harmar described how Beza had shown him courtesy and good will while he had been a visitor to Geneva, and how he had enjoyed the benefit of hearing him lecture and preach.[97] Beza's stricter doctrine of election became one of the fundamental pillars of the Oxford reformed synthesis, reflected in the sermons of George Abbot, Henry Airay, Richard Crakanthorpe, and Sebastian Benefield, though they rarely mention him by name.[98]

Zanchius also produced a detailed treatment of the means by which a man might be assured of his salvation. This was divided into thirteen sections, serving not only to mark the way of final

---

[97] *Master Bezaes Sermons upon the First Three Chapters of the Canticle of Canticles* (Oxford, 1587), sig. ¶ 3.
[98] See below, ch. X.

perseverance, but also to encourage men to good works, the life of faith and daily repentance, despite perennial troubles and the constant tendency to fall into sin.[99] This essentially scholastic approach illustrates how far he and the Oxford theologians who followed him had travelled from the theology of Calvin. The growing influence of Zanchius in Oxford may be charted in the sermons of Sebastian Benefield, fellow of Corpus. In Benefield's early Oxford sermons, preached in the later 1590s, Zanchius was scarcely mentioned. By the end of his second published series, *The Sinne against the Holy Ghost Discovered,* it was to Zanchius that Benefield constantly turned for his distinction between elect and reprobate and for analysis of the eternal decrees.[100] By 1610, when he published his solemn lectures for the DD, Zanchius is described by Benefield as '*clarissimus superioris seculi theologus*', and citing all his authorities—Luther, the Wittenberg Confession, the Helvetic Confession, Bucer, Calvin, Bullinger, Beza, Junius, Lubbert, Polanus, and Whitaker—it is to Zanchius that he habitually returns to define saving faith, to provide rules for the succession of ministers, to differentiate the two creations of God in man, in Christ and through Christ, and to describe how good works are necessary for salvation.[101] Lambert Daneau, one of Beza's Genevan assistants and later professor at Leiden, also figures as a prominent authority for Benefield and Abbot, particularly in the exposition of his doctrine of temporary faith.[102]

When in 1605 Leonard Hutten, Sub-Dean of Christ Church, published *An Answere to a Certaine Treatise of the Crosse in Baptisme,* he had little new to add to the arguments of the past half-century about the use of ecclesiastical ceremonies. Yet his patient analysis meticulously cites the authorities who support

[99] Two of the writings of Zanchius were published in English translation: *H. Zanchius: His Confession of Christian Religion* (Cambridge, 1599), esp. 10-19, and 'A Brief Discourse, Taken out of the Writings of Her. Zanchius...' appended to William Perkins, *A Case of Conscience* (London, 1592); for further discussion see O. Gründler, *Die Gotteslehre Girolamo Zanchis* (Beitrage zur Geschichte und Lehre der Reformierte Kirche, 20, Neukirchen, 1965).

[100] Sebastian Benefield, *The Sinne against the Holy Ghost Discovered* (Oxford, 1615), 113-19, 153.

[101] Sebastian Benefield, *Doctrinae Christianae Sex Capita* (Oxford, 1610), 21.

[102] George Abbot, *An Exposition upon the Prophet Ionah* (London, 1600), 169-70. For further detail on Danaeus, see Olivier Fatio, *Nihil Pulchrius Ordine* (Leiden, 1971), on his contribution to the church in the Low Countries, 1581-3, and *Méthode et Théologie: Lambert Daneau et Les Débuts de la Scholasticisme Reformée* (Geneva, 1976).

his arguments: Beza, twelve times, Zanchius, nine, Bucer, eight, Perkins, six, Peter Martyr, six, Calvin, five, and, perhaps uncharacteristically, Danaeus, once only. Hutten's theological world had changed almost beyond recognition from that of his predecessors in the first two decades of the reign. Calvinist orthodoxy was now the mainstay of Oxford's theology, gently asserted because rarely challenged.

V

THE REFORMED TRADITION
IN CONFLICT

John Reynolds was only 26 when he emerged as leader of the
opposition of the young Oxford divines to the Spanish
preacher, Antonio del Corro, in 1576. Still a relatively junior
member of the society, Reynolds had probably been in Oxford
throughout Elizabeth's reign. His first appointment, as Greek
Reader at Corpus, was made in the autumn of 1572, but his
voice had already been heard in the Schools.[1] The *Oratio in
laudem artis poeticae,* of 1572, provides hints of a formidable
intellectual and controversial force rising in the Oxford firma-
ment and demonstrates in embryo the features which were to
characterize the writing of Reynolds for the next thirty-five
years: immense erudition, massive resources of memory, an
eye for detail, and high seriousness. Reynolds's first lectures at
Corpus contain no surprises. They form a series of studies of
the *Rhetoric* of Aristotle. No Oxford lecturer in the 1570s could
have begun anywhere else, and the strictures of Giordano
Bruno on the narrowness of the Oxford pedants with their
attachment to Aristotle and the forms of rhetoric were not to
resound in the university for another decade.[2] From the opening pages of these lectures, philosophy is subject to godliness
and despite the detailed concentration on method and analysis,
where Reynolds draws a great deal on the example of Ramus
(Pierre de la Ramée), the higher goal is kept prominently in
view. The pagan authors are always to be interpreted through

---

[1] Orations by Reynolds *in Comitiis* in 1568 and 1569 appear in MS Corpus Christi
College Oxford 303, fos. 128-32.
[2] On Bruno, see F. A. Yates, 'Giordano Bruno's Conflict with Oxford', in *Journal of
the Warburg Institute,* ii (1938-9), 227-42; 'The Religious Policy of Giordano Bruno', in
Journal of the Warburg and Courtauld Institutes, iii (1939-40), 181-207; *Giordano Bruno and
the Hermetic Tradition* (London, 1964), 206 ff.; R. McNulty, 'Bruno at Oxford', *Renaissance News,* xiii (1960), 300-5.

the eyes of the Christian scriptures and the fathers, and with a mind and will devoted to godliness.[3]

Reynolds displays the traditional Christian humanist objection to philosophical truth which is not based on the knowledge of God revealed in the universe and in the Scriptures, and admits that Vives, Pico della Mirandola, and Savonarola have argued the case before him. Dr J. K. McConica asserts that the authentic voice of Reynolds from first to last is that of a Christian humanist evoking in his own college the spirit of Bishop Fox, but there is more to it than this.[4] Reynolds reiterates the founder's wish that religion, piety, and godly exercises should flourish, but there is a preciseness, an insistence, and a radical impatience which accords only with difficulty with the more measured tones of the lecture hall. The philosophers, he fears, will 'laugh at my simplicitie, who require Godlinesse, and Christianitie in their Studies. What have wee (say they) with the over-busie godlinesse and Holinesse? Wee leave that to Divines, let them preach Christ devoutly.'[5] This Reynolds will surely do, for 'time posteth away; the arts are difficult, life is short; error is dangerous; trifles are hurtful, truth is precarious. Christ is the Marke.'[6] Here is the paradox which marks the entire career of Reynolds: the respected figure of the Schools became the opponent of the Spanish preacher; later, in 1586, his radical advocacy of discipline and eldership set him apart from the moderate reformers of a previous generation.

In 1576 Reynolds's thought was still developing; it required his work as controversialist against Rome and the radical movements of the 1580s to secure his active godliness, his constant reliance on the churches of the reformed tradition and their teaching, and his demands for further reform in the

---

[3] Queen's College Oxford MS 354, fo. 6. Reynolds's lectures on Aristotle's *Rhetoric* survive in Queen's College Oxford MS 354, and the printed text from which he worked, *Aristotles de arte discendi libri tres* (Paris, Morel, 1562), is Bodleian Library Auct. S.2.29.

[4] See J. K. McConica, 'Humanism and Aristotle in Tudor Oxford', *E.H.R.*, xciv (1979), 303-4. For the influence of Ramus on Reynolds, see Queen's College MS 354, fos. 21ᵛ, 24, 27, 41.

[5] *An excellent oration of the late famously learned John Rainolds ... very usefull for such as affect the studies of logick and philosophie, and admire profane learning*, ET by John Leycester (London, 1638), 79-80.

[6] Ibid., 144.

ministry and discipline of the Church of England. Nevertheless, his objections to Corro were not only grounded in his
conviction that the free-thinking philosophy of the Spanish
preacher would be damaging to the youth of Oxford. The
development of his views on election and reprobation did not
take place until the end of the decade but must already have
been deeply rooted in 1576. The basis of this doctrine is his idea
of a true and lively faith, hammered out in 1583-4 in the conference with the papist, John Hart. To Hart's static doctrine,
that faith is the inheritance which Peter and his successors have
kept soundly within the Church of Rome, Reynolds opposed 'a
lively Christian faith: which imbraceth the promise of the mer-
cie of God; which worketh by love, and bringeth forth the
fruites of faith; which whosoever have, they have assurance of
everlasting life'. Hart on the other hand, according to his
interlocutor, possessed only a dead faith rather than 'the most
holy Faith' of which Jude spoke.[7]

Once he had established that a believer was marked out by a
true and lively faith, Reynolds clearly delineated the process by
which election took place. In his six DD theses, delivered in
1579, he speaks of the eternal goodness and mercy of God,
who, of his free and singular favour, before the foundation of
the world, chose a great number of men he would endue with
everlasting life and make heirs of heavenly glory. These are his
peculiar people, separated by time and distance but gathered
together by the bond of the Spirit. God has called them out and
made a covenant with them. Some men, however, do not yield
themselves to their calling; they may form a part of the visible
church, but only the few who are also chosen, known only to
God, are part of the invisible church. Even the chosen can err,
but their error is curable and cannot lead to everlasting death,
since although they are not totally cleansed in this life, they are
continually renewed by the Holy Ghost.[8] In some anti-papist
sermons, published in 1614 as *The Discovery of the Man of Sinne*,
and probably preached in the 1580s, Reynolds propounds a

---

[7] *The Summe of the Conference betwene J. Rainoldes and J. Hart: Touching the Head and Faith
of the Church* (London, 1584), 284-5; *Haggai*, 50 (sermon of 1584).

[8] Reynolds, *Six Conclusions Touching the Holy Scripture and the Church*, ET of *Sex Theses
de Sacra Scriptura et Ecclesia* (1580), printed at the end of *The Summe of the Conference*, 683,
691-6, 709-11.

starkly supralapsarian doctrine. God chose the elect before he set the world on its pillars; before he framed man, he foresaw the evil that he would do, but chose him despite it. Man's good works were also foreseen by God, but were not the cause of his election, which was solely God's love before the creation of the world and his free will.[9]

Throughout his career, Reynolds demonstrated strong alignment with the churches of the reformed tradition abroad. In his *Sex Theses* he associates the 'Reformed Church' in England, as he calls it, with the reformed churches in Scotland, France, Germany, and other kingdoms and commonwealths, those who have severed themselves from Rome and reformed themselves by God's word. Where such churches are nourished and where ministers preach the word, pure and uncorrupt, there the church may be found to be sound and whole. In a 1584 sermon, he sets up the French church in its adversity as an example to his congregation and warns the English church to prepare for an affliction like the events in France in 1572, when the papists killed 30,000 Frenchmen under pretence of friendship.[10] The example of Huguenots at La Rochelle, where everyone, including the rich women, set about carrying stones to raise the ramparts, he cites as an inspiration to all in England to lend their aid to the building up of the Lord's house.[11]

A clearly-enunciated doctrine of election and a kindred feeling for the continental reformed churches prompted Reynolds to detect in Corro, and perhaps in Francesco Pucci before him, not only intellectual arrogance and assertive pride, which were foreign to those who like him submitted themselves to the word of God as hearers and learners, but also 'a just suspicion of verie great heresies about predestination and justification by faith'.[12] The battle with Corro and Reynolds's coming of age as the leader of the reformed tradition in Oxford were preceded by a skirmish with a disciple of the Spanish preacher, which may have alerted Reynolds to the issues at stake.

Franceso Pucci (1540-?1593) made his earliest contacts with the reformed churches in Lyons. In former generations his

[9] Reynolds, *The Discovery of the Man of Sinne* (Oxford, 1614), 46-7.
[10] Reynolds, *The Prophecie of Obadiah* (Oxford, 1613), 56-7, 95-7.
[11] Reynolds, *Haggai*, 76 (sermon of 8 February 1590).
[12] Reynolds to Humphrey, 7 June 1576, Wood, *Annals*, II, 182.

family had produced three conservative cardinals, but Pucci, encouraged by the commercial links between his native city of Florence and the French centre, and helped, unlike most of his contemporaries, by sufficient financial support to enable him to travel, sought an apprenticeship in one of the mercantile houses there. Here he was probably drawn into the circle of the Calvinist church, founded in 1557, and his growing acquaintance with both reformed and Lutheran writings profited greatly from the large number of printing houses in the city and its strength as a Huguenot centre, attributable in part to the proximity of Geneva. Dissatisfied with provincial society, Pucci soon made his way to Paris, whence he fled with several hundred French refugees in the wake of the massacre on St. Bartholomew's Eve. A stranger in London in the autumn of 1572, he seems to have been attracted to the company of religious refugees of various nationalities, including Antonio del Corro, at this time Reader at the Temple Church.

Pucci's real inclination was to remain outside any organized religious confession and his career in Lyons and Paris has left no evidence that he belonged to any church.[13] In London, he was received into the congregation of the Italian Church in December 1572, a few months after his arrival.[14] Luigi Firpo, Pucci's most recent editor, claims that in his search for truth, a theme in all his writings, Pucci maintained the right to speculate freely. While he refused the obligation to subscribe to the confession of faith of any particular church, he did not hesitate to criticize a church he thought to be in error.[15] After his reception in London, nothing is known of Pucci until his incorporation as an MA at Oxford on 18 May 1574.[16] There is no note of his residence in any college, though Thomas Bodley at Merton was in correspondence with him in 1573-4, and almost nothing would have been recorded of his Oxford career and the

---

[13] Kinder characterizes him as 'a spiritual Quixote', A. G. Kinder, 'Two Unpublished Letters of Jean Cousin, Minister of the Threadneedle Street Church Concerning the Affair of Cassiodoro da Reina', in *Proceedings of the Huguenot Society of London*, xxii (1970-6), 51-9.

[14] BL, Additional MS 48096, fo. 33^r. F. Pucci, *Lettere Documenti e Testimonanze*, ed. Luigi Firpo and Renato Piattoli, II (Documenti e Testimonanze, Florence, 1959), 115 (no. 64).

[15] Luigi Firpo, 'Francesco Pucci in Inghilterra', in *Révue Internationale de Philosophie*, v (1951), 160-1.

[16] Clark, *Register*, II, part i, 379. The foreign university is not named.

controversy it caused had not John Reynolds made reference to it in his attack on Corro.[17]

On 7 June 1576 the young Reynolds wrote to Humphrey in his capacity as Vice-Chancellor, urging him to take more decisive action against Corro. He reminded him of the firm course of action he had taken against Pucci a few years before, and 'sith it pleased God to stirr up your harte with the grace of his holy Spirit, for the removing of Puccius, whose endeavours to represse, the Lord did use you, then of lesse authoritie as a special instrument: God forbid that now having the authority of the Vicechancellor, you should admit him to be a Teacher publickly, who is thought to be a Master to Puccius.'[18] The circumstances surrounding Pucci's expulsion are entirely unknown and no indication survives of the theological opinions which so disturbed the Oxford divines.[19] Pucci's arrogant behaviour and free-thinking inevitably played a part in his downfall. His clash with the London French Church, probably shortly after he was driven from Oxford, reveals him as a man of unyielding obstinacy. He declared that the London French held erroneous opinions and was summoned before its consistory on 15 March 1575 to substantiate his accusations. He questioned the ministers and elders on their right to examine him and refused to debate the theological questions which he himself had raised, concerning the doctrine of the Lord's Supper, original sin, and the sin against the Holy Ghost, declaring the process pointless until they had resolved their disagreement with him on the doctrine of the faith.[20] Eventually, after he had refused a friendly conference, Pucci was suspended from the sacraments, though the elders announced their willingness to readmit him if ordered to do so either by the civil magistrate or by the Bishop of London, their superintendent.[21]

[17] Bodleian Library, MS Bodley 699*, fos. 18-22.

[18] Wood, Annals, II, 182 from Corpus Christi College Oxford MS 303, no. 29. Reynolds is here in error. Pucci must have been expelled from Oxford during Humphrey's Vice-Chancellorship which began in 1571, and he cannot therefore have been 'of lesse authoritie' when dealing with Pucci than in the Corro affair of 1576.

[19] Wood, Athenae Oxonienses, I, col. 587, indicates that the clash between Pucci and the Oxford doctors concerned 'fide in Deum, quae et qualis sit', but this must be based on evidence of later controversies.

[20] Pucci, Lettere Documenti e Testimonanze, II, 116-19 (no. 69).

[21] Ibid., 120.

Pucci's doctrine of faith may be deduced from the debates with the London French from January to May 1575, from a letter of 1578 written from Basle and addressed 'to all lovers of truth', and from the 1577-8 Basle debates with Faustus Sozzini (Socinus). That this was also certainly the central issue in the discussions of Pucci with the Oxford divines is attested in a letter from Socinus to Andreas Dudith in Breslau in 1580. Enclosing a copy of the *De statu primi hominis ante lapsum disputatio* which he conducted with Pucci, Socinus referred to Pucci's residence in London and Oxford and the various disputes with the followers of Calvin (*'Calvini asseclis'*) in the two cities, the content of which may be judged from the book he encloses.[22] In his earliest letter to the London French on the subject of faith in God, dated 22 January 1575, Pucci stated his opinion that faith in God rested on the divine goodwill in general rather than on any specific promise. Promise and covenant are not received except by those who already have faith in God, but such faith is not possible without God's own gift.[23] Here, as elsewhere, Pucci maintained that he did not wish to believe anything which could not be drawn from the Scriptures, but it is difficult to avoid the conclusion that, whether they were biblically based or not, Pucci couched his definitions in deliberately ambiguous terms, capable of a variety of interpretations and difficult to explain. His definition of faith might also have been seen as deviating from the Calvinist opinion that specific covenants and promises were made with the elect before the Creation. The letter 'to all lovers of truth', written on New Year's Day 1578, makes clearer the cause of Calvinist suspicion. Again, Pucci asserted that he maintained nothing contrary to the testimony of the prophets and apostles. His formal thesis, highly complex and devious, stresses that the whole human race (*'totum genus humanum'*) participates in the benefits of Christ's saving work from the womb and from the state of innocence, even before man has the use of reason and discernment. To those who possess the use of reason is given the knowledge of God to salvation, if they believe in him. Men possessing reason who remain contemptuous of this knowledge

[22] Krakow, 3 December 1580. Pucci, op. cit., II, 146-7.
[23] Pucci, op. cit., I, 15-16.

are not immune from the divine wrath.[24] Thus, Pucci makes it clear that although all infants are potentially saved, men are able to accept the divine salvation or reject it by the exercise of reason. Biblical texts are assembled to support this viewpoint which, if defended with Pucci's offensive style in Oxford in 1574-5, would undoubtedly have produced the adverse reaction of Humphrey, described by Reynolds.

Further evidence of Pucci's views on election and regeneration was later provided in the debate with Socinus initiated after Pucci, expelled from Oxford and London, had migrated to Basle, where he matriculated at the university in May 1577.[25] In the discussion, Pucci based his case on the claim that man was by nature immortal, since he was created in the likeness of the immortal God. Death, by which man's mortality was attested, was not part of the natural condition, but a decline from the Creator's intention and came into the world because man neglected divine counsel. If man's original state was mortality, the Messiah in restoring man to his created bliss, would restore mortality, not raise man to the state of immortality. This was clearly contrary to the testimony of scripture.[26] It also accorded badly with the primary stress on the fallenness of man, the divine regeneration and restoration of life to the elect, and the work of Christ in justification, which was basic to the theology of the Oxford divines and the London French Church. Pucci's advent in Oxford in 1574-5 may well have alerted the Calvinist divines to theological tendencies more fully exploited by Corro.

The Oxford debates with Antonio del Corro in the spring and summer of 1576 are inseparable from the quarrel he had been conducting with the Strangers' Churches in London, especially the London French, since the end of the previous decade. Corro is more difficult to characterize than his pupil, Pucci: intellectual, free-thinker, refugee for religion—even contemporaries were not certain how to evaluate his theological

---

[24] Pucci, op. cit., II, 21-3.

[25] H. G. Wackernagel, *Die Matrikel der Universität Basel* (Basle, 1956), II, 248.

[26] F. Socinus, *De statu primi hominis ante lapsum disputatio ... anno 1578* (Racoviae, 1610), '*Francisci Puccii Argumenta*', 2-4. Socinus argued that the animal state was always corruptible, never immortal, and that Christ did not restore man to the state he possessed before the fall, but to a more excellent and incorruptible state.

opinions. While some immediately saw him as a subversive influence, others, Leicester and Burghley among them, were initially prepared to offer him encouragement. Corro was intensely proud of his nation, and in every country he visited, he attempted to gather together a congregation to worship in the Spanish language. Born in 1527, probably in Seville, he became a monk at the house of the Observantine Hieronymites at San Isidro at the age of 20. Here, under the influence of Cypriano de Valera, he came into contact with the ideas of Luther, Melanchthon, and also, it seems, Bullinger.[27] The reformed rather than the Lutheran tradition attracted him and in 1557, disappearing from the monastery with eleven of his fellows, he made his way to Lausanne, arriving at a crucial moment in the history of the reform there.[28] Evidently, he visited Geneva and won the confidence of Calvin, who recommended him to the court of Navarre, where he became tutor in Spanish to the future Henry IV. In the following years, he attempted to found a Spanish church in Bordeaux, was suspect there, probably for personal rather than doctrinal reasons, and moved to Toulouse, where he took the oath as a Calvinist minister in March 1562. Throughout his career, it was his personal bearing and arrogant behaviour rather than any specific doctrinal deviation which initially brought Corro under suspicion. From Périgord at the end of 1563, he wrote to a former monastic contemporary, Cassiodoro da Reina, believing him to be in London. This letter first aroused the suspicions of the French Church and clouded Corro's reception in 1567.[29] Before the arrival of the letter, da Reina had fled from England accused of homosexuality and it fell into the hands of the French consistory; Jean Cousin read the letter and suspected that Corro held unorthodox views about the nature and mission of Christ.

---

[27] For an account of Corro's early career, see P. J. Hauben, *Three Spanish Heretics and the Reformation* (Geneva, 1967), 3-34; W. McFadden, 'The Life and Works of Antonio del Corro, 1527-91', unpub. Ph.D. thesis, Queen's University, Belfast, 1953, chs. i-xviii.

[28] Léonard, *History of Protestantism*, II, 5-6.

[29] The letter from Corro to da Reina from the *Acta Consistorii Ecclesiae Londino Gallicae, cum responsio Antonii Corrani* (1571) is printed in *Bibliotheca Wiffeniana, Spanish Reformers of Two Centuries from 1520*, ed. Edward Boehmer, III (London and Strasburg, 1904), 78-81.

In 1566, Corro migrated to Antwerp where he again attempted to set up a Spanish community. As in the case of
Pucci, his refusal to belong to any definite confession was
revealed when finding that he would be required to condemn
the Anabaptists in adhering to the confession of the Walloon
Church he declined to do so. Like Pucci, he felt free to criticize
a church's polity and doctrine. *An epistle or godlie admonition*,
published in 1567, is the key to understanding Corro's free-
thinking as well as his eirenical intentions. He lamented the
contentions which he had discovered in the church in Antwerp,
where men were denounced from the pulpit, rather than reproved with brotherly admonition. He claimed that fraternal
love should stand as the symbol of a church rather than a
formal confession or catechism.[30] His approach to the eucharist
was naïve and over-simplified, and the London French were
later to accuse him of having accepted Osiander's views on the
reception of the divine nature through faith.[31] Corro was later to
regret deeply his accusation that the Antwerp church behaved
like the Inquisition, which became a favourite taunt of his
opponents.[32] It accorded badly with his final plea for charity
and compassion, that Christians might love all, help all, embrace all, and support the ignorance and infirmity of all.[33]

Corro affiliated himself to the French Church in Threadneedle Street shortly after his arrival in London in April 1567.
His reputation had preceded him, and Grindal, as superintendent of the Strangers' Churches, and 'moved with the desire of
preserving the concord and peace of the church and of defending the good fame of the same master Antonius', conferred
with him and provided him with a testimonial under seal that
he was free from all erroneous opinions and 'embraces the pure
doctrine of the Gospel, which our own and other reformed

---

[30] Corro, *An epistle or godlie admonition of a learned minister of the gospel of our saviour Christ
sent to the pastoures of the Flemish church (who call themselves Confession of Auspurge)*, ET by
Sir Geffray Fenton (London, 1569), 2-4, 9, 12, 18.

[31] Osiander taught not that Christ's righteousness was imputed to sinful men, but
that the actual righteousness of God dwelt in man, the *inhabitatio Christi* in the soul. See
Léonard, op. cit., I, 299-300; F. Lau and E. Bizer, *A History of the Reformation in
Germany to 1555* (London, 1969), 232.

[32] Corro, op. cit., 26.

[33] Ibid., 47.

churches profess'.[34] The French Church however had already enquired of his credentials from Nicholas des Gallars, the minister at Orléans with whom he had had contact in 1564, who was not sufficiently satisfied to allow him to preach in his church, although at this time he was principally concerned with his status as a minister and his conduct, rather than his doctrine. From June 1567 to June 1569, Corro was involved in a protracted quarrel with the London French and was eventually forbidden to preach in March 1569, though again it was for an offence in manner rather than in doctrine.[35]

However, by the summer of 1569, serious doubts had been raised about Corro's beliefs. In London, as elsewhere, he had attempted to gather a group of his countrymen into a church.. In their assembly, Corro expounded the epistle to the Romans and the anti-predestinarian teaching which emerged alarmed Jerlitti, the Italian minister in whose church the Spaniards had formerly worshipped. Corro's intense dislike of confessional and religious tests which led him to heteropraxis also emerged at this time when he was reported to have buried a Jew, conducting the service without any reference to Christ. The publication of the broadsheet, *Tableau de l'Oeuvre de Dieu,* in Norwich on 15 July 1569 cast further doubts over Corro's orthodoxy in the matter of predestination and he was to find himself involved throughout 1570 and 1571 in highly-charged discussions of this doctrine, punctuated by attempts at reconciliation, with the London French. Eventually it became evident even to Corro that his career in England would in the future lie outside the Strangers' Churches.[36]

As early as 1569, Corro had secured the favour of Cecil who used him as preacher to the Spanish prisoners in Bridewell. Cecil may have been more concerned with converting the prisoners than advancing Corro, though when Corro was suspended from preaching in March 1569, the Secretary was

---

[34] *The Remains of Edmund Grindal,* ed. W. Nicholson (Cambridge, Parker Society, 1843), 313, testimonial of 5 June 1567.

[35] For further details see McFadden, thesis cit., chs. xix-xxi; *Bibliotheca Wiffeniana,* III, 83-9; and Collinson, *Archbishop Grindal,* 143-51. Corro's treatise *'Monas theologica'* c.1570, may also have caused alarm with its possible denial of trinitarian doctrine; see *Ecclesiae Londino-Batavae Archivum,* III, part i, 99-101.

[36] For further details see McFadden, thesis cit., chs. xxiii-xxv.

prepared to seek a fresh licence for him, apparently disregard-
ing the decision of Grindal and the other commissioners. A
reconciliation might indeed have been achieved if the *Tableau*
had not been published at the critical moment.[37] Corro's
dependence on Cecil ended here, but he carefully nurtured his
contact with Leicester. To Leicester he owed his appointment
as Reader in divinity to the benchers of the Inner and Middle
Temples. From this time, Leicester was his chief hope of
advancement, a fact Corro willingly acknowledged in his
dedication of the *Dialogus theologicus* in 1575.[38]

Leicester was Corro's chief patron in his attempt to gain a
foothold in one of the universities in 1576. This was prompted
by two dominant concerns: first, to find secure employment,
secondly, to provide a forum in which he could clear himself of
suspicion of doctrinal deviation. However, Corro seems to
have realized that he might not obtain the fair hearing for
which he hoped in the universities: 'I considered howe yee have
very famous Universities, full of excellent lerned men, in which
I know that if any poynt of Christian doctrine require more
diligent opening, it is wont to be inlightned by publike disputations.' This, however, could not be guaranteed, since 'persons
ignorante of holy matters, are oftentimes wont to intermingle
themselves with the learned'.[39] Corro seems not to have realized
that, even in the universities, he might not find the ideal he
sought, 'every man free to his owne judgement'.[40]

Practical considerations may have led Corro to seek this
forum of debate more actively at the beginning of 1576. At the
Temple Church, his position was rapidly becoming untenable;
his theological opinions were probably in disagreement with
those of the Master, Richard Alvey, and the benchers were
discontented with his frequent absences. His first attempt to
find a place in the English universities was at Cambridge.

---

[37] *The Remains of Edmund Grindal*, 309-12; BL, Lansdowne MS 11, fo. 146.

[38] Corro, *A Theological Dialogue: Wherein the Epistle of S. Paul the Apostle to the Romanes is
Expounded* (London, 1575) is an English translation of Corro's Temple lectures on
Romans. In the preface (sig. ¶ iii^v) Corro records that Leicester received him when a
stranger, and stood by him in adversity. He did not always credit the matters alleged
against him. The second preface to the benchers of the Temples (op. cit., sig. A 1^r)
alludes to a third patron, Edwin Sandys, Bishop of London.

[39] Corro, *A Theological Dialogue*, sig. A ii^v.

[40] Ibid., sig. A iii^r.

Corro may have hoped that Burghley, the Chancellor, would act again on his behalf, but difficulties arose when it was discovered that Corro had no degree to incorporate. He claimed later that university degrees were not favoured by the French church in which he had been a minister for ten years. Cambridge could only have overcome the difficulty by conferring a degree by mandate, which required royal approval. Doctrinal objections were not apparently raised; the doubts were purely practical.[41] It was therefore suggested that he should seek the degree at Oxford, where the regulations were less strict, and subsequently apply to incorporate it at Cambridge.

Frustrated in his dealings with Burghley, Corro turned to his other patron, the Oxford Chancellor, Leicester. With Leicester's recommendation, he wrote to Lawrence Humphrey, Vice-Chancellor of Oxford, on 20 March 1576. The letter is a curious mixture of flattery and naïveté. It begins with a eulogy of the university, of whose fame Corro has heard from afar, but he immediately arouses suspicion by asking that he may receive the degree of DD, since his friends have told him that if the university accepts him, this will refute those who doubt his religious purity. Corro has long wished for the honour of an English degree, he claims, but has been deterred by those who argue that the rites and ceremonies associated with it are superstitious and cannot be undertaken with a clear conscience. He struck a further blow to his own cause, apparently unaware of the tactical error of comparing the regulations for the degree in the two universities, in asking that he might be made a doctor at Oxford to incorporate at Cambridge later in the year.[42]

Corro's application, together with the supporting letter, was read at a meeting of Convocation on 2 April. It was a stormy occasion; Humphrey was required to convey the Chancellor's special pleading that 'he is fit for the degree, but has not much

---

[41] None of the papers relating to Corro's Cambridge application survives. It probably took place in the early months of 1576 and is referred to in a letter to Humphrey in March, C.Sepp, *Polemische en Irenische Theologie* (Leiden, 1881), 6-7.

[42] There were debates in Convocation throughout this period on the exact procedure for the incorporation of Cantabrigians. The matter was under discussion at the moment that Corro's case reached its climax, 1 June 1576; see Wood, *Annals*, II, 183, 185; Clark, *Register*, II, part i, 346.

money' and therefore should be excused the expense of taking the lower degrees and paying their fees.[43] Though Humphrey would not have approved the tone of Corro's letter and may have been aware that he was already suspect in London, Leicester's commendation made Humphrey's position as Commissary embarrassing. Leicester's letter inhibited many from speaking their minds and members of the house could not determine whether Humphrey was guided in his support of the application by the Chancellor's letter or by his uncertainty about the cause. One member at least knew that several letters against Corro were circulating and argued that he must come to Oxford to defend his doctrine before the question of conferring a degree could be considered. Few of the doctors, the senior members of Convocation, said anything because of the Chancellor's letter, and the case against Corro was probably presented by the regent masters, men like Reynolds, the junior members of the house. One of these, who does not disclose his identity, writing eight days after the meeting, deplores the fact that Corro had eventually been granted the grace to proceed to the degree, provided that he first came to subscribe to the Articles of the Church of England and performed the other things necessary. This ease of entry, the letter claimed, could never have been permitted in Geneva, Berne, Zurich, or anywhere in Germany.[44] A further indication of the stormy and inconclusive nature of the Convocation debate emerges from the text of the grace in the Convocation register. The application is noted, with the formula '*Concessa est hac gratia simpliciter*', the accustomed form when there were no objections. However, the word '*simpliciter*' is crossed through and the words '*modo purget haereticarum opinionum ante proxima comitia*' inserted to amend the original entry.[45]

Further complications resulted from the fact that Oxford now became the new battleground for the quarrel between the

---

[43] Clark, *Register*, II, part i, 153.

[44] Sepp, op. cit., 11-12. The names of Humphrey and other speakers together with that of the correspondent are omitted, presumably because of the controversial nature of the discussion.

[45] OUA/NEP *supra*/Register KK, fo. 207[v]. The amendment, whether made at the time of the meeting or later, is not noted by McFadden or other commentators. It indicates the dilemma posed by Leicester's support of Corro.

Spanish preacher and the London French Church, and in particular its minister, Pierre L'Oiseleur de Villiers. To the godly
young of Elizabethan Oxford, Villiers probably appeared as
the epitome of the devout protestant gentleman, suffering for
his religion. He had begun his career as a lawyer in the Parle-
ment of Paris, but fled the city under persecution and found a
refuge in Geneva and the friendship of Calvin. Clearly committed to the Genevan reform, he was entrusted with the
translation of some of the annotations of the Geneva Bible, and
in his early days in England in 1569-71 met Laurence Tomson
who was to publish an English translation of Beza's annotations in 1576.[46] Villiers and Corro had first clashed in 1569,
when Villiers was a member of the commission appointed by
Grindal to investigate the complaints of the London French.
In 1570, Villiers attacked Corro's doctrine as set out in
the *Tableau* and a commission of the French Church, set up
to examine the complaint, decided in his favour.[47] The
antagonism which seems to have lain dormant for five years
was now fought out in competition for an Oxford DD. On 20
April 1576, Villiers himself asked to incept in the theology
faculty, that is, to be admitted BD and to be excused the
expenses. In a very cordial reply Humphrey related the events
of the Corro debate, contrasting the stipulations made for
Corro (that he should make a profession of faith and clear
himself of all suspicion before the *Comitia*) with the honour
which the university wished to offer to Villiers '*summa cum assen-
tione et adstipulatione omnium … sine aliquo sumtu sed non sine laude*'.
Humphrey was aware that the pomp of the ceremony might
offend Villiers and it was therefore to be omitted.[48] An unnamed
member of New College made an even clearer statement of the
university's joy at receiving Villiers into the bosom of the
society.[49] This correspondent raises the campaign against
Corro to the level of a crusade for the truth of the gospel.
Corro's application is viewed as the work of Satan and the
writer prays that Villiers will be armed with the power of the

---

[46] Irena Backus, 'Pierre L'Oiseleur's Connections with England in the Sixteenth
Century', in *Proceedings of the Huguenot Society of London*, xxii (1970-6), 441-6.
[47] *Ecclesiae Londino-Batavae Archivum*, III, part i, 108.
[48] Sepp, op. cit., 14-15.
[49] The anonymity was perhaps a cover against the disfavour of the Chancellor.

Spirit against him. No praise is too great for the French minister. The university has been pleased to grant his grace, '*valde probo neque est quod de vestra pietate, prudentia, et gravitate*'. The persecuted state of the French church which Villiers represented only enhanced the fight of faith.[50] Villiers needed all his Oxford support, for Corro launched a fierce attack on him, accusing him of heresy before the university. On 4 July Villiers was summoned before Convocation to rebut the accusations. Nothing is known of the dispute, but Dr Irena Backus speculates that Corro, an exponent of Castellio, probably accused Villiers of excessive adherence to the letter rather than the spirit of Christian faith.[51] Villiers defended himself to the satisfaction of all, and the acclaim which he received in Oxford must have been a severe rebuff to Corro.

The campaign of the London French was not confined to its championship of its minister. During the spring of 1576, its members had been collecting together a corpus of 138 theses, gathered from Corro's writings, speeches, and correspondence, together with their own replies. These 'Theses and Antitheses', principally intended for Grindal and Sandys, were also sent to Oxford, with an accompanying letter, expressing confidence that the university would continue to take the same view of Corro as the London French, Dutch, and Italian Churches.[52] The 'Theses and Antitheses' together with the circulation in Oxford of Corro's *Tableau* crucially altered the university's attitude from that of cautious opposition in March to outright hostility by June. The proposal that Corro be granted a DD may have been raised again after 2 April; it was certainly on the Convocation agenda on 1 June, but was rapidly passed over.[53] On 6 June, the affair took on a new and more disturbing complexion. After Villiers had been granted his DD, it would seem that Leicester redoubled his efforts on Corro's behalf and took a new initiative for him. At the

[50] Sepp, op. cit., 16-17.
[51] Backus, art. cit., 446. Sebastian Castellio (1515-63), converted by Calvin at Strasburg, later parted company with his master and with Beza, advocating unrestricted religious toleration, which would have appealed to Corro. His translation of the Bible (Latin, 1551, French, 1555) contained annotations in direct opposition to those of Beza, which Villiers prized.
[52] Sepp, op. cit., 28-30.
[53] Wood, *Annals*, II, 183.

meeting of Convocation on 6 June, Humphrey, prompted by the Chancellor, raised the question of Corro's being made a reader in the university. The involvement of the Chancellor again threatened to inhibit discussion, but the events of the preceding three months had activated a group of younger members of Convocation, led by John Reynolds, to pursue a more hostile policy than in the early spring. In a letter to Humphrey, written on the day following the Convocation meeting, Reynolds voiced his case: 'the dewtie which I owe unto the Church of God and the common greif of many godly men, whom I do reverence as I ought, have moved me to signifie that which many think, but you perchance shall hear of few'.[54] Reynolds's views were unequivocally opposed to those of Corro and this moment marks his emergence as leader of advanced protestant opinion. 'I beseeche you', he urged Humphrey, 'to take that which I shall write, not as being uttered of any evil affection, but in respect of the truth, and for zeal of the House of God.' First, Reynolds raised the objection that Corro had never been lawfully called to the ministry of any church overseas, nor had he been ordained by any English bishop. Evidently, he feared that the Vice-Chancellor had been unduly influenced by external interference, for 'the letters which are sent from some of the Counsell, and from the high Commissioners, are as from them that are perswaded of him ... I doubte not, I may say of the Privie Counsell and the high Commissioners that these thinges are done *"illis imprudentibus"*, who may be partly misinformed by others, partly deceived by his own fair promises.'[55]

However, it was by now Corro's theological bias which was the principal cause of Reynolds's disquiet and the fear that, if admitted as a public reader, he would subvert the young and influence them towards popery. Reynolds referred to an incident the preceding evening, following the Convocation, when 'a man of sound judgment and verie well learned', only one of 'diverse godlie men [who] suspect the same pointes upon the same places' had delivered to him a copy of the *Tableau*. The notes in this copy had confirmed his view that Corro's 'obscure

---

[54] Wood, *Annals*, II, 180.
[55] Only Leicester's testimonial is extant.

speeches do give just suspicion of verie great heresies about predestination and justification by faith, two of the chiefest points of Christian Religion'.

Reynolds's spur to prompt Humphrey to more decisive action of the sort he had taken against Pucci and against the papists had the desired effect when Convocation met on 13 June.[56] The meeting decided that if Corro be allowed to proceed to DD, it would be prejudicial to the whole university, since he held opinions contrary to true religion. The condemnation was in vehement terms. If he desired to clear himself, he was ordered to produce letters from Grindal and Sandys, declaring that he had held no impious opinions since his arrival in England, and he was to purge himself in front of the Vice-Chancellor and the senior theologians before the next Act.[57] This was a much more extreme demand than that of 2 April and one which Corro was unable to fulfil. The arrival in Oxford of the 'Theses and Antitheses' had ensured that Reynolds, seizing his moment, was able to defy the bidding of the Chancellor and the earlier compliance of the Commissary. On 30 June, Leicester indicated his will to have a new representative and though he praised Humphrey's care for the university and the diligence with which he had discharged his office, his failure to get his way over Corro may have influenced his decision: 'I will not keep any man so long to it, but distribute the travail by yearly change.'[58] Corro, meanwhile, was forced to continue in his increasingly precarious office at the Temple and did not make any further attempt to gain entry to Oxford until the summer of 1578.

Corro's theology, as generally understood in Oxford, was drawn from the *Tableau de l'Oeuvre de Dieu* and the 'Theses and Antitheses', which together present a conspectus of his intellectual outlook, coloured by his arrogant free-thinking and advocacy of universal toleration. The *Tableau*, a broadsheet of twenty articles with four divisions of the faithful and unfaithful,

---

[56] Clark, *Register*, II, part i, 153-4.
[57] Reynolds in his letter of 7 July had objected that it would be improper for Corro to purge himself in Oxford, since it was the London French not the university which had accused him. Wood, *Annals*, II, 181.
[58] OUA/NEP *supra*/Register KK, fo. 216ᵛ; Clark, *Register*, II, part i, 243.

was originally published in Norwich in 1569.[59] It argues that
the state of man in paradise is one where he is persuaded of
God's goodwill towards him, but this is lost at the fall, when
man becomes convinced that God is jealous of him and seeks
his ruin. Since, according to Corro, man fell through disobe-
dience and infidelity, the new promise which God makes after
the fall requires as man's response mortification and obedience. To achieve this, man is sent from paradise.[60] Corro
describes the purpose of God's written word as first, to reassure
men of God's goodwill, and secondly, as a mirror in which
man may view his transgressions and learn the obedience
which is now demanded of him. The process of salvation here
outlined is one of moral improvement and the restoration of
man's knowledge of God through the co-operation of the
human will. The work of Christ follows a similar pattern: it
acts as a further assurance of God's goodness and an example
of the mortification required of those who desire to be saved.[61]
Similarly, the work of the Spirit gives men the power to perform the exercise of obedience. Corro describes the elect as
those who 'receiving the Spirit of adoption, assure themselves
of God's good will towards them, and invoke him and pray to
him with certainty in their needs, afflictions and crosses, and
who, following the guidance of the Holy Spirit who is within
them, occupy themselves with true exercises of faith, mortification and brotherly love'.[62]

It is not difficult to imagine that Reynolds and those like him
detected in the *Tableau* dangerous pelagian and universalist
tendencies in a plan of salvation which had little in common
with that of Calvin, Beza, or Bullinger. The 'Theses and
Antitheses' provided an even more damaging synthesis of
Corro's thought, designed to show how his own words proved
deviation from the mainstream of the reformed tradition, as
received in Oxford and represented by the Strangers' Churches
in London. Corro's adversaries began their attack with illustra-

---

[59] There was a further French edition and a Latin translation in 1570, and a second
Latin edition in 1584. The 1569 French edition is printed in *Ecclesiae Londino-Batavae
Archivum*, III, part i, 75-80.
[60] Corro, *Tableau*, articles 1-12; in *Ecclesiae Londino-Batavae Archivum*, 75-7.
[61] Corro, *Tableau*, articles 15-16; in op. cit., 78.
[62] Corro, *Tableau*, the fourth division; in op. cit., 80.

tions of his free-thought in religious questions. They quoted his willingness to sign, for the sake of peace, a catechism offered him by a Turk and argued that many had heard him say, 'If you are a Jew, you are blessed; if you are a Turk, you are blessed; if you are a Christian, you are blessed and will be saved.' Further evidence of his lack of a confessional discipline was provided by his burial of the Jew.[63] Theses 4 to 8, which deal with the doctrine of God, indicate that in the eyes of his adversaries, Corro's thought tended in a unitarian rather than a trinitarian direction. He was also suspected of Manichaean tendencies, judging that there were two controlling forces in the universe, one good and the other evil.[64] In his desire to preach a universalist doctrine of salvation, Corro was not alone. The Lutheran *Formula of Concord*, issued in the year after his examination in Oxford, taught that God willed all men to be saved and that it was divine foreknowledge of a man's unbelief which was the cause of the reprobation of some, not a fiat of the divine will before the foundation of the world. This view of salvation *ex praevesis meritis* was in accord with the thinking of Melanchthon, the young Augustine, and the early fathers, but contradicted the supralapsarian viewpoint adopted by the later Calvin, Beza, the mature Augustine, and followed by most of the Oxford divines.[65]

In Cambridge, Corro's contemporary and sometime adviser, Peter Baro, held a similar view.[66] Baro's views on predestination were not however aired in public until 1579. In that year, he published his lectures on Jonah which also contained the disputation 'God's purpose and decree taketh not away the liberty of man's corrupt will'.[67] In the Jonah lectures, Baro sees the entire history of the prophet as the merciful work of God, who does not desire the death of a sinner and whose mercy is extended to the whole human race.[68] Lawrence

---

[63] 'Theses and Antitheses', in Sepp, op. cit., 30-1.

[64] Ibid., 31.

[65] Léonard, op. cit., II, 31; T. M. Parker, 'Arminianism and Laudianism in Seventeenth Century England', in *Studies in Church History*, I, ed. C. W. Dugmore and C. Duggan (London, 1964), 20-34.

[66] Baro was incorporated DD at Oxford in July 1576, ironically at the same Act at which Villiers took his DD and at which Corro had hoped to take his. The reason for the Oxford incorporation is unclear.

[67] *Petri Baronis Stempani ... in Jonam Prophetam praelectiones* (London, 1579), 39.

[68] Ibid., 23.

Chaderton and other Cambridge puritans mounted a considerable campaign against Baro accusing him of introducing popish views into the university in his treatment of faith and works in the *De fide* of 1580.[69] Among other points at issue they pointed to his association with Corro.[70]

The Strangers' Churches further alleged that Corro had misunderstood the doctrine of predestination and that he confused it with the divine call to a nation. In fact, Corro appears to have been wrestling with aspects of a doctrine which seemed to him wholly abhorrent. If God predestined men before the creation of the world, then the fall of Adam and man's imputed righteousness after the fall were nothing more than a fiction. Corro's scheme, as the *Tableau* demonstrates, is based rather on the possibility of fallen man regaining knowledge of God through obedience. Further, he regarded as cruel a God who condemned men to eternal reprobation even before their birth. This stress on the eternal decrees of God, he argued, was a misrepresentation of the biblical record. In Romans 8, for example, although St. Paul outlines the election of the Gentiles and the rejection of sinners, he does not make this the foundation of his doctrine of redemption.[71] Corro was anxious to redress false ideas which he believed had crept into the doctrine of assurance. He was concerned at the view that the elect, according to his adversaries, could not forfeit eternal life because of the eternal decrees, even if they sinned and lived badly. On the other hand, he believed that the Jews were rejected on account of their actual unfaithfulness and that those who were faithful and believed in Christ would come to fullness of favour and felicity.[72]

Further extracts from Corro's writings, arranged by the Strangers' Churches under the headings 'The nature of man and the freedom of the will', 'Adam', 'Sin', and 'Law' reinforced the view, already outlined in the *Tableau*, that all men

[69] Baro, *De fide, ejusque ortu & natura, plana ac dilucide explicatio* (London, 1580), 27, 31-33. For Chaderton's reply see *Lawrence Chaderton*, translated from a Latin memoir of Dr Dillingham by E. S. Schuckburgh (Cambridge, 1884), 6; and *DNB*.

[70] For further discussion see P. G. Lake, 'Lawrence Chaderton and the Cambridge Moderate Puritan Tradition, 1570-1604', unpub. Cambridge Ph.D. thesis, 1979, 169-79.

[71] 'Theses and Antitheses', 31-7, in Sepp, op. cit., 36-7.

[72] Ibid., 40-4, in Sepp, op. cit., 38.

have an equal opportunity to come to faith by the path of obedience. Corro protested that his enemies had wrongly attributed to him the view that salvation came partially through faith and partially through obedience. In fact he taught, he said, that justification came only by faith; faith comes from hearing the word of God. Those who believe and obey, like Abel, are placed on the right; those who do not believe are disobedient, like Cain, and are placed on the left.[73]

Corro's thoroughgoing religious toleration can no more have endeared him to the Oxford authorities than to the London French. He opposed the use of the sword against heretics and desired that all should be left to follow the religion of their own choice, since this was not a matter for compulsion.[74] From one of his Temple Church sermons was extracted an injunction to be tolerant of the Roman church, not only because many of its critics had been born and baptized into it, but also in the love which flows from faith.[75]

The circulation of the 'Theses and Antitheses' sealed Corro's fate in Oxford in 1576, though, without the campaign mounted by Reynolds, he might have gained admission to the degree he sought. Corro allowed two years to elapse before he again approached the university. The first indication that he had returned to Oxford is provided in a group of letters in the Convocation register, dated 7 July 1578. The French, Dutch, and Italian Churches were again complaining of his heretical beliefs and of various crimes against him. They requested an examination of his views, since, they said, he had been recommended by the Chancellor and had already delivered some public lectures.[76] A committee was appointed which included both Humphrey and Reynolds. On 10 July, only three days after the committee had been set up, Corro was brought in person before Convocation. He now undertook to stay four, five, or six months in the university, to confer with all who wished to do so, and, if he should be found guilty in any respect to recant. This attitude, so different from that of the assertive and arrogant Corro of 1576, may indicate the anxiety of the

[73] Ibid., 76, 81, in Sepp, op. cit., 45-6.
[74] Ibid., 134-5, in Sepp, op. cit., 57.
[75] Sepp, op. cit., 59.
[76] OUA/NEP supra/Register KK, fo. 260ʳ. Clark, Register, II, part i, 155.

Spanish preacher to take up the work offered in the university as catechist.[77]

It is a testimony to Corro's newly-adopted moderation that when, in the spring of 1582, a rumour reached the ears of the Chancellor that he had been arrested for heresy, the Vice-Chancellor was able to report: 'As regards Corano's doctrine, I never attended his lectures or disputations, and so have nothing to say. As regards his life and conversation, I know of no crime which can be charged against him or any of his family. On the advice of the heads of houses, I called a Convocation, read your letter, and asked any accuser or suspecter to come forward. Neither then nor since has any one appeared.'[78] Corro faded from the public view; in October 1586 at the age of 51 he matriculated, probably in an attempt to retain a last link with the university in which for so long he had struggled to teach and live.[79] His incursion into the society illustrates not so much the beginnings of a new theological current as 'free thought at odds with dogma and discipline'.[80] For one man, John Reynolds, it provided an opportunity to seize the initiative as leader and spokesman of a new generation of Oxford divines, more radical in outlook than the exiles, who were to dominate the university of the 1580s.

---

[77] For a discussion of his activity as catechist, see below, ch. VIII.
[78] Clark, *Register*, II, part i, 157.
[79] Clark, *Register*, II, part ii, 154. By this time Corro had lost all his college appointments.
[80] Collinson, *Archbishop Grindal*, 143.

VI
RADICAL MOVEMENTS AND
THE CHALLENGE OF ROME,
c.1580-*c*.1593

An. Dom. 1580

This year Apr.6, between 5 and 6 of the clock in the afternoon, Oxford was sorely shaken by an Earthquake, being Wednesday in Easter week. All being amazed, left their houses and ran into the open places. The birds that had taken up their nests in the holes and roofs of houses, suddenly fled, and others of the air settled on the earth. The cows and oxen at the sudden alteration lowed, and other cattle were much affrighted. Oxford was not the sole sharer of this Earthquake, but also all England, France, Flanders and other regions.[1]

It was not only the earth which moved in Oxford in the 1580s; from right and left, religious shocks caused great fissures across the established structures. The university in this decade bears all the marks of a vigorous society, full of young scholars and youthful divines. The number graduating was increasing and Leicester noted the growing number of students in divinity with evident pleasure, although his attempts to control the unruly society met with slender success.[2] In January 1583, the Chancellor complained that 'the disorders, not muttered of, but openly cried upon continually and almost in every place, are such, as touch us less than your religion, your lives and conversation, and the whole state of your Universitye, Professions and learning', and, listing particular causes for concern, he reproved the scholars for their over-elaborate apparel, 'like unto, or rather exceeding, both Inns of Courte men and Courtiers', the increasing number of ale-houses and gaming tables, and the 'hauntinge of the towne'.[3] Chief among his concerns in 1583, as in the preceding three years, was the

---

[1] Wood, *Annals*, II, 198-9, paraphrase of the Latin in *Registrum Annalium Collegii Mertonensis, 1567-1603*, 121-2.
[2] OUA/NEP *supra*/Register KK, fo. 350ʳ; Wood, *Annals*, II, 207, 210.
[3] OUA/NEP *supra*/Register L, fos. 231-2; Wood, *Annals*, II, 212-13; for a further discussion of undergraduate life and the complaints of the godly, see below, ch. VIII.

religious state of the society. In the spring of 1580, Convocation had set up a committee to examine the organization of sermons and religious instruction. The report, of 17 July, advocated a Latin sermon at the beginning of each of the four terms and a scheme of sermons at Eastertide, to which were later added sermons for saints' days and the Sundays of the vacations.[4] The Chancellor was scarcely the man to discourage preaching, but as early as 13 October 1580 he had indicated his dilemma:

Complaints have bin made unto me by the space of these two or thre yeares from time to time almost continually, touching disorderlie and uncharitable preachinges among you by sum of the younger sort, which though I have much misliked, yet I have not delt in reprehension or reformation theareof.

The Chancellor had exercised this reserve, he claimed, both because the preachers in question were young men, who in time might be expected to moderate their tongues, and because he did not wish to discourage preaching at a time of severe shortage.[5] Nevertheless, complaints, from the court and from the ecclesiastical commissioners, reached such a level that Leicester was forced to take action. The university, acting on the Chancellor's letters, now provided for the licensing of preachers, after they had been tested in their own colleges, commended by their head of house, examined by the Regius Professor, and had subscribed to the Articles of Religion and the Prayer Book. Privileged persons, presumably visitors, or ministers of the town parishes, were not to be allowed to preach in the university without the Vice-Chancellor's licence and any such person who preached unsoundly or offensively could be convened before the Regius Professor or a DD and forced to revoke his words.[6] The more general problem of providing the university with a supply of moderate and godly preachers had not been solved. In 1584, Leicester, prompted by the Queen's complaints, was forced to write again to the university. On 24 July, Convocation noted the catalogue of complaints

    [4] OUA/NEP *supra*/Register KK, fo. 308^{r-v}; Wood, *Annals*, II, 199-200.
    [5] OUA/NEP *supra*/Register KK, fo. 314^r. Wood, *Annals*, II, 200-1. Wood mistakes the date.
    [6] Wood, *Annals*, II, 202.

concerning apparel, laxity in the observance of lectures and disputations, young ministers playing football on Sundays, and
wandering players in the town. Further provision was made for
the regulation of sermons: 'every Student in Divinity being
Minister, whether he be of College or Haule, shall be com-
pelled to preach in his course according to his seniorite in the
Universitye, being warned thereunto by the Bedle 6 weeks
before his time or to provide sum sufficient person to supply his
place, whome the Vicechanc. shall like of, or to sustaine the
penaltie, which is appointed for those that doe not answer in
their course'.[7]

These provisions for regular preaching may have provided
the advocates of radical reform with a platform. In the longer
term, a more significant development was the loan of £100 in
1584 from Convocation to Joseph Barnes, an Oxford bookseller, to set up a printing press in the university. Now Oxford
doctors and preachers were able to publish their works locally
rather than in London and in the 1590s and in the first decade
of the seventeenth century, many took the opportunity and
sermons poured from the press, some of them bearing the university's imprimatur in the shape of the arms and motto on the
title page.[8]

The middle years of this decade witnessed attempts to force
the pace of change not only in the university, but in the country
at large. Whitgift succeeded Grindal at Canterbury in
September 1583 and at once began a programme for greater
conformity within the church by law established. He first
attempted to deal with nonconforming ministers through the
Three Articles of October 1583. When pressure from the
Council and the court forced the Archbishop to moderate his
demands, allowing a large number of ministers to subscribe
with reservations, he proceeded against the leaders of the
opposition with the more stringent Twenty-Four Articles.[9] In
parliament, the 'puritan campaign' was launched with the

[7] Wood, *Annals*, II, 220.

[8] Oxford may have been inspired by the example of Cambridge, which appointed
John Kingston as its first printer in 1576. OUA/NEP *supra*/Register L, fos. 281-2;
Paul Morgan, *Printing and Publishing at Oxford: the Growth of a Learned Press 1478-1978*
(Oxford, 1978), x, 10-17.

[9] A full discussion of Whitgift's contest with the nonconforming ministers is to be
found in Collinson, *E.P.M.*, 243-72.

intention of providing a learned, resident ministry, and making the church safe for men of reforming zeal. Some members of the new parliament had more radical views, though Dr Peter Turner's 'Bill and Book', introduced on 14 December 1584, which would have made provision for the use of the Genevan *Forme of Prayers and Administration of the Sacraments* and a system of presbyteries, with pastors, elders, consistories, and general assemblies, was shelved after it had met with widespread opposition, from Sir Francis Knollys to Sir Christopher Hatton.[10]

At the same time, a survey of the condition of the ministry, county by county, was in progress. This was devised to demonstrate the falsity of Whitgift's view that those who had refused to subscribe the Three Articles were only a tiny proportion of the ministers of the church. The results were not complete until the new parliament met in 1586, but the 2,537 parishes surveyed, an impressive quarter of the total in England, revealed that there were 472 preachers, 1,773 parishes with no regular preaching ministry, 467 parishes where the minister was a pluralist, and 353 where the minister was non-resident.[11] The campaign in parliament in 1584-5 was effectively quashed by the Queen and privy councillors, but when parliament met again in 1586, the 'Survay' was complete and its proponents better prepared. Sir Anthony Cope, member for Banbury, introduced his extreme 'Bill and Book' on 27 February 1587. The 'Book' was again a version of the Genevan service book. The bill contrasted the corrupt episcopal church with the presbyterian model 'approved by the general judgment and practice of all the best-reformed churches', and proposed the abolition of the ecclesiastical courts, canon law, and the episcopal hierarchy, together with the Acts of Uniformity and Supremacy.[12] Although the Queen acted immediately to prevent further discussion, before the end of the session John Penry's *Supplication* for a preaching ministry in Wales had been laid before the house and Peter Wentworth,

---

[10] For a discussion of this parliament, see J. E. Neale, *Elizabeth I and Her Parliaments*, II (London, 1957), part I, ch. iv; Collinson, *E.P.M.*, 273-88.

[11] For details of the 'Survay' see *The Seconde Parte of a Register*, ed. A. Peel (Cambridge, 1915), II, 88-174.

[12] Neale, op. cit., II, 148-9.

asserting the liberties of the Commons in a speech on 1 March found himself, with a group of his friends, imprisoned in the Tower.[13]

Outside parliament also, radical activity revived. After the Queen's ban on prophesyings in 1577, the exercises of ministers did not cease but now took place unofficially and sometimes, where episcopal supervision was efficient and harsh, in secret. In May 1582, as assembly of sixty ministers, gathered from East Anglia, was held at Cockfield in Suffolk and discussed which parts of the Prayer Book might be tolerated, and what was of necessity to be refused. This, according to Professor Patrick Collinson, may mark the beginning of a new and more active chapter in the Elizabethan puritan movement.[14] In this chapter, the two universities were intimately involved. Oxford and Cambridge, partially protected from episcopal and governmental supervision by their jealously-guarded immunities, were convenient meeting-places, where large companies could assemble at the degree times, the Oxford Act and the Cambridge Commencement, without attracting unwelcome attention. A synod or conference, attended by ministers from a wide area around, was held at Cambridge in July 1582, and with the Cockfield conference marks an important initiative in the new campaign to set up 'a discipline in a discipline, presbytery in episcopacy'.[15] Oxford was first drawn into this movement almost by accident. In the summer of 1584, twenty or more Scottish ministers, with Andrew Melville at their head, retreated into England in the wake of the 'Black Acts' of May, the assertion of the Earl of Arran's anti-presbyterian dictatorship, which banned assemblies to discuss either civil or ecclesiastical matters. The Scottish ministers seem to have secured the sympathy of Leicester and Walsingham and a group of them were present at the Cambridge Commencement and the Oxford Act. Edward Gellibrand told John Field, the national co-ordinator of the synods and *classes,* that 'here have beene a good company of godly brethren this Act. Maister Fen, Wilcox, Axton: the Scot-

[13] Neale, op. cit., II, 145-65; Collinson, *E.P.M.*, 303-16.
[14] Collinson, *E.P.M.*, 218-19, quoting Oliver Pig to John Field, 16 May 1582.
[15] Thomas Fuller, *The Church History of Britain*, ed. J. S. Brewer (Oxford, 1845), V, 7.

tish ministers, and wee, have had some meeting and conference, to our great comfort that are here. One point (which then was moved) I would wish to be throughly debated among you and them, concerning the proceeding of the minister in his duety, without the assistance or tarrying for the Magistrate, etc.'[16]

Gellibrand, whose attraction to extreme courses had already become apparent to Humphrey and his fellows in Magdalen, may well have been influenced to adopt an essentially presbyterian viewpoint through his contacts with Melville at the Act of 1584. Melville, the chief architect of presbytery in Scotland, wished not only to place the supervision of churches in the hands of a committee of ministers, but also to use the revenues from ecclesiastical property to maintain a godly ministry and relieve the poor.[17] In Oxford, radical notions of this kind may have been of some academic interest, though they could scarcely have been implemented in the specialized context of university society. While Gellibrand and other Oxford scholars and fellows were closely involved in the national synods and conferences, especially those held in Oxford itself, it seems unlikely, as R. G. Usher claimed, that there was a *classis* in the university, meeting regularly, like that at Dedham, at least until after the spring of 1587, when the *Discipline* was adopted by an Oxford group.[18] Rather, the university was a convenient and relatively safe place where ministers and laymen, anxious to discuss and encourage the development of an eldership and discipline, could meet.

There is little doubt that Edward Gellibrand was at the centre of this loosely-connected interest. He attended the national conference in London in November 1584 at the time of the parliament. Subsequently, he seems to have been encouraged to take soundings in Oxford about the form of discipline which Oxford radicals might be prepared to adopt. Replying to an enquiry from Field before parliament and the puritan

[16] Richard Bancroft, *Daungerous Positions and Proceedings* (London, 1593), 74.
[17] G. Donaldson, *The Scottish Reformation* (Cambridge, 2nd ed., 1972), 190 ff., esp. 214-16.
[18] R. G. Usher, *The Presbyterian Movement in the Reign of Queen Elizabeth* (Camden Society, 3rd series, viii, London, 1905), xxix.

campaign opened again in February 1585, he was forced to admit that a cautious outlook characterized the university:

I have already entred into the matters, whereof you write, and dealt with three or foure of severall Colleges, concerning those among whom they live. I finde, that men are very dangerous in this point, generally favoring reformation: but when it commeth to the particular point, some have not yet considered of these things, for which others in the Church are so much troubled: others are afraid to testifie any thing with their hands, least it breed danger before the time. And after: many favour the cause of reformation, but they are not Ministers, but young students, of whome there is good hope, if it be not cut off by violent dealing before the time. As I heare you, so I meane to goe forward where there is any hope, and to learn the number, and certifie you thereof.[19]

Gellibrand appears to indicate that the majority of those who favoured the discipline were young scholars, not yet ministers, who, perhaps for fear of losing their places, were wary about making any public commitment such as might have been involved in meeting together. Identification of possible adherents depends almost entirely on Bancroft's two works, the *Survay of the Pretended Holy Discipline* and *Daungerous Positions and Proceedings,* both published anonymously in 1593, intended to discredit the movement and trace its origins, not in the Scriptures, as its proponents claimed, but in the Genevan presbyterian deviations, mediated by the 'consistorian discipline' in Scotland. Bancroft names 'West' and 'Browne' as Oxford scholars sent to the 1586 London synod. Identification could scarcely be more hazardous. 'Browne' may be John Browne, student of Christ Church, proctor in 1582. Gellibrand names 'John Browne of Christ Church', Chaplain of the Earl of Huntingdon, as a favourer of reformation in his 1586 examination before the ecclesiastical commission.[20] 'West' can scarcely be identified either with Henry West expelled from Magdalen in 1578, or with Richard West, a Magdalen contemporary of John Foxe, and Vicar of Woking from 1572. According to Thomas Barber's deposition in the great Star Chamber trial in 1591, 'Mr. Reynoldes of Oxon, Mr. Charke and Mr.

---

[19] Bancroft, *Daungerous Positions and Proceedings,* 74-5.
[20] See below, 139; Stone's deposition, 1591, no longer extant but printed by Fuller, op. cit., V, 163-9.

Travers and others whose names he knoweth not dyd meet together in Oxon about the cause of disciplyne' in 1587.[21] There can be little doubt that John Reynolds would have sympathized with demands for a greater degree of ecclesiastical discipline on the continental model, and there are signs that the increasing emphasis in the later 1580s on curbing non-residence would have appealed more to him than the tone of the *Discipline*. Bancroft was greatly assisted in his task of uncovering the associates of the movement by the discovery of John Field's correspondence. Here three other Oxford sympathizers may be named. 'Gate of Oxford' can perhaps be identified as Anthony Gates, Master of University College 1584-97, the only man of this name recorded in the period. There is, however, no evidence that he was involved with the Oxford radicals.[22] John Hart could be the scholar who matriculated as a member of Magdalen Hall in 1580, and Edward Browne, who questioned Field on whether the godly might hawk or hunt, could be a Christ Church man, *c.*1580, or a member of Broadgates Hall, who matriculated in 1580, or an MA of Brasenose, *c.*1576.[23]

For a brief moment in 1586, radical agitation in Oxford emerges from the shadows. Early in the spring, a fellow of University College described in a letter the 'great adoo about certein sermons preached in Oxford not long since. Wherein were these things handled and discoursed upon. 1. Non residencie. 2. The authority of Bishoppes. 3. Preaching in other mens cure. 4. Excommunication by men having no calling in the churche. 5. The necessity of the eldership. Lastly, the continuance of the Churchgovernement that forme which is prescribed in the woord.'[24] This would seem to represent an advanced and comprehensive radical platform, its demands closely allied to those of the country-wide petitioning and parliamentary movement. The University College letter associates

---

[21] Patrick Collinson, 'The Puritan Classical Movement in the Reign of Elizabeth I', unpub. London Ph.D. thesis, 1957, 582, from PRO Star Chamber 5A 49/31, fo. 3ᵛ.

[22] Richard Bancroft, *A Survay of the Pretended Holy Discipline* (London, 1593), 366 margin.

[23] On Hart, Bancroft, *A Survay of the Pretended Holy Discipline*, 368, 376. On Browne, ibid., 368; Collinson, thesis cit., 1035.

[24] BL, Additional MS 38492, fo. 80. The letter is anonymous and not dated. The date suggested is based on the chronology here proposed.

three Oxford men with this platform, Gellibrand, John Reynolds, and one 'Walford', almost certainly to be identified with John Walward, fellow of Corpus. Walward is otherwise an obscure figure, a Somerset man, a generation younger than Reynolds and possibly his pupil. He was admitted scholar in the same year as Richard Hooker, also sometimes claimed as Reynolds's pupil.[25]

Preaching in All Saints', Oxford on 22 February 1586, Walward launched a fearless attack on the inadequacy of discipline in the Church of England and suggested methods for correcting it. He asserted that:

the order of Jewishe synaguogue, [*sic*] governed by a senate ecclesiasticall or eldershippe...was by Christ in the gospell established to continue forever, to admonishe, to suspend, to interdicte, and to excommunicate in every congregation: That the same was practised by the Apostles, and longe after in the better times of the churche. That those which are put in authoritie accordinge to the lawes of this lande by the BB [bishops] and other ecclesiasticall persons, to see such censures executed, are not sufficiently warranted thereto, but are in danger of gods heavie iudgement therefore, the pastour of the congregation where the offender dwelleth, hath an interest, and oughte to have a dealinge therein.[26]

Further, Walward claimed, 'a necessarie, substantiall, and unalterable platforme of government and discipline to have bene lefte by Christe, for hearinge, orderinge, and determineing of all cases and causes of censures which ... oughte of necessitie to be the ministerie and presbyterye of the congregation where the offender dwelleth'. This would have undermined the jurisdiction of archdeacons and the ecclesiastical government by law established, and, as Walward's accusers later indicated, would have worked 'to the impeaching of her Majesties authoritie in causes ecclesiasticall'.[27]

---

[25] Fowler, *The History of Corpus Christi College Oxford*, 158, 390. Walward was BA 1575, MA 1579, BD 1587. OUA/NEP *supra*/Register L, fo. 86ᵛ, for his BD; Joseph Foster, *Alumni Oxonienses, 1500-1714* (Oxford, 1891-2), IV, 1555, under Walforde.

[26] Dr Williams's Library, Morrice MS 'B', II, fos. 103ᵛ-104 ('Seconde Parte of a Register'). Incomplete transcript in Peel, *The Seconde Parte of a Register*, II, 35.

[27] For a discussion of puritan complaints about the ecclesiastical courts and congregational discipline, see Collinson, *E.P.M.*, 346-55. The radical case was based on a reading of Matthew 18:15-18.

Edward Gellibrand also used the pulpit to propagate this platform, taking as his text Hebrews 2:10, 'It became him, for whom are all things, in bringing many sons to glory, to make the captain of their salvation perfect through suffering.' Perfect through suffering!—this was evidently the phrase which Gellibrand used, buttressing it with Beza's *Annotations,* to indicate his sympathy for the ministers distressed by Whitgift's campaign for ecclesiastical conformity. Though he was later to deny that Christians suffered under the government of Elizabeth, his sermon contained several references which were taken as deeply offensive to the ecclesiastical governors. There was direct criticism of the bishops, and he may specifically have named the Bishop of Winchester. Gellibrand also canvassed the platform for discipline, which he claimed to be a part of the gospel, and compared the non-resident with the Jesuit, since both were responsible for the death of men's souls. He directly attributed the increase in recusants to neglect by non-resident ministers.[28]

At first sight, it is surprising to find John Reynolds as the third member of this radical company. Senior to both Gellibrand and Walward, he was a DD and a frequent member of Convocation delegacies.[29] In 1586, Reynolds's opinions were couched in more guarded academic terms than those of his two associates, but the cause was the same. His view that the government and discipline of the Church of England had diverged both from the Scriptures and from the pattern of the reformed churches abroad had emerged as early as 1579. Debating for his DD, he described 'a sound and whole church, the faculties and powers whereof are not impaired', which he demonstrated had four special functions, according to the Scriptures; to teach the faith, to minister the sacraments, to pray, and to practise discipline according to the word of God.[30] He described the 'warlike discipline' by which the true Catholic church fought against the flesh and the devil, 'to keepe them selves in order, and to gard them safer from their enemies', for God had ordained 'ecclesiasticall societies ... captaines

---

[28] Dr Williams's Library, Morrice MS 'B', II, fo. 109[r-v].
[29] OUA/NEP *supra*/Register L, fos. 14[v], 22[v], 42[v].
[30] Reynolds, *Six Conclusions Touching the Holy Scripture and the Church,* 726.

to teach and souldiers to learne'.[31] This was altogether a more dynamic concept of the church's discipline than the steady state for which the Supreme Governor strove. In June 1584, on the eve of renewed radical agitation in parliament and in the country, Reynolds indicated clearly that while the establishment of true doctrine and discipline was in the hands of the Queen and parliament, all faithful Christians had an important role in the work of building the church. He prayed for 'the increase of true godlinesse by preaching of wholesome doctrine and establishing godly discipline through all the Churches of the Realme according to the prescription of the Lord revealed in his word'.[32] In the closing weeks of 1584, when Whitgift had become seriously alarmed by the strength of the opposition and Waldegrave's press was beginning its run of radical treatises, Reynolds found a treatise of his, title and subject unknown, rejected; and Whitgift explained that 'he could not a low [sic] of it, because of summe glauncing at matters in this tyme'.[33] Later divines seem to have looked back to Reynolds as one of the founding fathers of presbytery. When Edward Leigh published Reynolds's sermons entitled *The Prophesie of Haggai* in 1649, he asserted, with evident pleasure, that the 'Author in this Book seemes to favour the Presbiterian way'.[34]

After the three preachers had struck the first blow in the campaign in February or March 1586, some of the doctors, moved perhaps by the fear that their own position was being undermined by the attack on non-residents, alerted Whitgift to the dangerous developments in the university. Accordingly, the Archbishop sent letters to the Vice-Chancellor, ordering that the preachers be examined.[35] The three men were summoned before a committee of doctors and lawyers who considered in turn the six points raised in the sermons. The doctors agreed with the preachers that non-residence was a great fault, but found Gellibrand's comparison of the non-resident and the

[31] Ibid., 717.

[32] Reynolds, *Haggai*, 49.

[33] Corpus Christi College Oxford MS 318, fo. 139^r, 4 December 1584.

[34] Reynolds, *Haggai*, sig. A 3^r.

[35] There is no reference to this letter or the subsequent proceedings in OUA, Register L, and the only source of the episode here reconstructed is the University College letter, BL, Additional MS 38492, fo. 80.

Jesuit, with his apparent preference for the Jesuit, odious. On the question of the authority of the episcopate, the doctors' position is unclear. The University College letter records that 'the authority that Byshoppes did challenge was thought by the Doctors them selves to be a mere constitution of a man having no ground in the woord', which may indicate that the bishops who claimed *iure divino* authority were considered to have exceeded the warrant of scripture. Preaching in other men's cures was considered lawful by the doctors and Gellibrand himself was prepared to take a moderate line on this, claiming that he 'did not absolutely affirme it unlawfull but did only say that his conscience could not be setled except it was alowed by the work of God and did ther avouche that if any man could bring sufficient ground out of Gods word for it his hand should be foremost then in it'. The Oxford lawyers agreed that lay excommunication was unlawful, suggesting that, provided the Queen allowed, this discipline should be entirely in the hands of ministers. They condemned the procedures of the ecclesiastical courts, advocating that the same practices should be adopted there as in the common law courts. On the eldership, the doctors took a less sympathetic view of the preachers' complaints. While they admitted that both eldership and discipline were frequently mentioned in the Scriptures, this did not induce the belief that they should continue for ever. They were, however, alarmed by the claim made in the sermons that the discipline of the Scriptures had been forbidden by authority. Reynolds seems to have expressed the strongest views on these questions. He 'did prove unto them the necessitye of bothe [eldership and discipline] in these tymes and did also saye that they were authorysed to preach it by the Archb. and BB [bishops] them selves which he proved because they were things putt down by Nowel his catechisme which was commanded by the whole convocation howse to be taught by every scholemaster and then much more by ministers'.[36]

The general impression of the meeting of Oxford doctors and lawyers, even when the biased viewpoint of the University College letter is allowed for, is of a body by no means

---

[36] Reynolds did not defend discipline and eldership from the Scriptures, but from one of the texts prescribed in the 1579 Catechetical Statute; see above, ch. IV.

unsympathetic to the platform raised in the sermons. The letter continues, 'thus the men are for this tyme lett go but what shall hereafter be further said unto them God knoweth'. At this moment, Walward and possibly the other two preachers may have guaranteed to keep the peace. Walward agreed that if he should be allowed to continue his divinity lecture, he would no longer meddle in matters which tended 'to the disturbance of the peace and unitie of the church, or iust offence of anie'. He later admitted that he had been unable to abide by his under-taking: 'I did notwithstandinge shew myselfe the same man I was before, by bitter factiouse speaches and complaneinge that I was troubled (as I thoughte without desert).'[37] Feeling was evidently running very high in Oxford in the spring of 1586 and Gellibrand admitted that he also was unable to hold his tongue. Eventually, the ecclesiastical commissioners were no longer satisfied that the matter could be contained within the university. They may have feared, not only that the preachers were gathering a body of sympathizers there, but that the Vice-Chancellor and Convocation might try to protect them, acting in defence of the university's legal privileges. In April, Gellibrand and Walward were summoned to Lambeth. Reynolds seems to have been excluded from the summons and may have been protected either by his standing in Oxford or by an external patron.

. On 7 April, both the younger men appeared individually before Whitgift, John Aylmer with his Vicar General Edward Stanhope, Thomas Cooper, Bishop of Winchester and Visitor of both their colleges, John Piers, Bishop of Salisbury, and Gabriel Goodman, Dean of Westminster and one of Whitgift's closest supporters. With Piers and Aylmer, he had examined the complaints of the Sussex ministers in the winter of 1583.[38] Also present at Lambeth were the Dean of the Arches, Dr Richard Cosin, a staunch puritan adversary, Dr Valentine Dale, a Master of Requests, and Dr Percy.[39] It was an intimi-dating array of defenders of the status quo. Walward was the first to be examined. His sermon of 22 February was con-sidered in detail and he was ordered to preach again in All

[37] Dr Williams's Library, MS Morrice 'B', II, fo. 104.
[38] See Collinson, *E.P.M.*, 249.
[39] 'Per [ne]' in Peel, op. cit., II, 38.

Saints' with the specific intention that 'he shall not in anye way either covertly or openly impugne any parte of the government ecclesiasticall receaved, and used nowe in this Church of England, but shall stirre upp all his hearers to unitie and peace and to obedience and good likeing of the magistrates lawes and orders, and present government of this churche'.[40]

Whilst Walward was sent out with his keeper into the Lambeth garden, Gellibrand was called before the commissioners. At first, he attempted to claim that the liberties and privileges of the university protected him, maintaining that the Vice-Chancellor, Edmund Lillie, Master of Balliol, had advised him to take this stand; but he was rapidly persuaded that the authority of the commissioners absolved him from his oath to local statutes.[41] His sermon was examined in detail; he denied that he had spoken against the Bishop of Winchester, but 'being pressed' disclosed the name of Mr Browne of Christ Church, the Earl of Huntingdon's chaplain, though it is not clear in what connection. He was also questioned about his speeches 'against the consecration of Archbp. etc.', which may suggest that he raised doubts about the Ordinal.[42]

Walward was then summoned to join Gellibrand. The two men were told that they deserved to be suspended from their ministry, imprisoned, and expelled from their colleges and from the university. Their judges informed them that if they had been in Geneva, they might have been excluded from the city for a whole year, an unkind reminder for those who had been earlier advocating the Genevan discipline. The commissioners bound over each of them in the sum of £100 and ordered them to make public submissions in Oxford before Whitsunday, and an order was sent to the Vice-Chancellor instructing him to arrange for this, providing four 'discrete and strait Men' of the university to witness it.

[40] Dr Williams's Library, Morrice MS 'B', II, fo. 103ᵛ., incomplete transcript in Peel, op. cit., II, 35.

[41] The claim to maintain the statutes was also made by Gellibrand and other members of the militant party in Magdalen in 1585 and 1589; see above, ch. III. Peel, op. cit., II, 36-8.

[42] The 'Browne' here is probably John Browne, see above, 132. For puritan doubts about the ordinal, see Collinson, E.P.M., 264-5.

While his associates were scarcely free of the proceedings at Lambeth, Reynolds seems to have taken the opportunity of a sermon on 19 April to declare in more forthright terms his views on eldership and discipline. The second sermon in the collection *The Prophesie of Haggai* is an attempt to establish the place of ecclesiastical discipline as essentially moderate in character, founded by the Jews, commanded by Christ to the apostles, adopted by the primitive church and restored by the reformed churches, and even commended by a papist, Bodin. Reynolds desired to establish a 'learned Pastor joyned to a sufficient number of grave and sober elders' to have oversight of a congregation. The biblical pattern was to be their *modus operandi*, 'first, to admonish privately offenders; then if they amend not, to proceed forward'.[43] As supporting evidence, Reynolds cited Nowell's catechism, where it was clearly maintained that 'every Church well grounded ought to have a sufficient number of Elders, who, together with the Pastors should exercise Church-discipline, and so avoid all those offences and faults which happen in the congregation'.[44] In addition to Nowell, Reynolds buttressed his case by reference to the Ordinal where 'there is granted unto the Minister authority to preach the Word, minister the Sacraments, exercise Discipline', and to the work of the thirty-two commissioners appointed by Edward VI to consider the *Reformatio Legum*, who appointed 'this order, that the Minister with others according to Christs commandement should first deale by brotherly admonition, and so to proceed according to Christs rule in this case'.[45] While the establishment of discipline was Reynolds's principal concern in this sermon, he also complained that in some places the foundations of the church had not been laid and pleaded for more catechizing and preaching. Further, he argued that none with cure of souls elsewhere should be permitted to remain in residence and any who did so should be denied graces to proceed to higher degrees. Reynolds's bitter sarcasm breaks out against his non-resident fellows, for 'better were it for you to return again to the teaching of Schollars, than

---

[43] Reynolds, *Haggai*, 16.
[44] Reynolds, *Haggai*, 17; *A Catechism by Alexander Nowell*, 218-19. The Heidelberg and Genevan Church catechisms would also have supported this view of discipline.
[45] Reynolds, *Haggai*, 17.

to provide for your selves by such meanes, though I hope you shall not need to do that neither'.[46]

Given this lead by Reynolds, Walward and Gellibrand can scarcely have remained silent. Recorder William Fleetwood, now evidently called in to supplement the commission, reported to Burghley on Whitsunday, 22 May 1586 that on the previous Friday afternoon 'I satt in commission at Lambeth with my L. grace, Where three Oxford preachers were charged for that they woold have all temporall causes to be decided by the Seniors of the Church and that her Majestie had not to deall in causes ecclesiasticall, with such licke matters. My Lord Almener did bear much with them.'[47] It would appear from this report that Gellibrand and Walward had failed to make their submissions before Whitsunday and that now Reynolds was summoned to Lambeth with them to explain his sermon of 19 April. However, nothing more is known of the case.

Further proceedings, if they took place, did not long impede the activity of Gellibrand. While there is no reason to associate his name with the English translation of the *Disciplina Ecclesiae,* he was certainly once again in active contact with Cartwright and with Field.[48] A 'Book of Discipline', a constitution to which ministers could subscribe, modelled on the confessions of the continental reformed churches, had been under consideration as early as the beginning of 1585. Cartwright's return from eleven years' exile in the Low Countries and Geneva in April 1585 may have quickened interest, and he and Walter Travers were principally responsible for framing the *Discipline.*[49] By the end of 1585, Gellibrand, who had already sounded opinion in Oxford, was impatient to have the document in his

---

[46] Ibid., 20.

[47] BL, Lansdowne MS 49, fo. 1.

[48] A. F. Scott Pearson, *Thomas Cartwright and Elizabethan Puritanism* (Cambridge, 1925), 259, claimed that Gellibrand was involved with writing the *Discipline,* on a reading of BL, Harleian MS 7029, 128. Collinson, thesis cit., 536, argues that the sentence in question refers to Cartwright's reply to Whitgift and not to the *Discipline.* Gellibrand was certainly in contact with Cartwright; see Bancroft, *Survay of the Pretended Holy Discipline,* 375 (n.d.), where he asks Field if he may come to London to see Cartwright.

[49] Collinson, *E.P.M.,* 295. The Latin text of the *Disciplina Ecclesiae* is appendix III of F. Paget, *An Introduction to the Fifth Book of Hooker's Treatise of the Laws of Ecclesiastical Polity* (Oxford, 1899), 238-51. There are two Oxford manuscripts, MS Corpus Christi College, 294, 1-11 (Latin) and MS Queen's College 280, fos. 163-9 (English). On the manuscripts see Collinson, *E.P.M.,* 297, 490-1.

hands: 'I pray you hasten the forme of Discipline and send it', he wrote to Field in November 1585. Three months later, he wrote again: 'I pray you remember the forme of Discipline, which Master Travers promised to make perfect, and send it to me when it is finished. We will put it in practise, and trie mens minds therein, as we may.'[50]

When the *Discipline* eventually arrived in Oxford, probably in the spring of 1587, Gellibrand indeed needed to 'trie mens minds therein', for it posed difficult problems of adaptation to the collegiate context. Repeated revisions had probably delayed its dispersal and those who now received it were invited to subscribe an appended form of confession, if necessary leaving doubtful points for discussion and putting it into effect as far as the law of the land would allow and the present state of the church would suffer.[51] Chapters I and II would have caused little dissent in Oxford circles, though the reference in Chapter II to a legitimate calling of the minister, expanded in Chapter III to '*Vocationis Ineundae et Definiendae Ratio, contra Ministerium Indefinitum et Deserto [sic] Ecclesiae*', made it clear that no man was to be called, except to an established ministry of a definite church or congregation. This was reiterated in Chapter V, which outlined the congregational election of a minister and disallowed an indefinite, free, or vague ministry. Chapter XVII, '*De Studiosis Theologiae et Eorum Exercitiis*', expounded the method of exercise in the congregation, a discipline strictly for ministers where the more learned could offer correction to their brethren. In theory at least, this could have provided a tiny local seminary for the training of godly ministers which in the minds of some of the more radical brethren would have surpassed any training available in the universities. A Warwickshire meeting in 1588 evidently considered the university pattern inadequate, since it prescribed that students in divinity should be present at the *classis,* so that their judgement in handling the affairs of the church could be tried and sharpened.[52] They were not alone in questioning the role of the universities. 'The humble petition of the Commonaltie'

[50] Bancroft, *Daungerous Positions and Proceedings,* 76.

[51] A copy of the *Discipline,* with signatures of Gellibrand, Lord, Cartwright, and others is BL, Harleian MS 6849, fo. 222; Collinson, thesis cit., 564.

[52] Bancroft, *Daungerous Positions and Proceedings,* 107.

addressed to the Queen, pleaded, 'wee pray you to vouchsafe to understande, howe many hundreths of worthie men are shut up and incloistered in the two Univesities of Cambridge and Oxford, by most injurious patrons, and otherwise'.[53]

In Oxford, the discussion of the *Discipline* seems to have initiated a new phase in the activity of which Gellibrand was again the centre. 'The discipline we have received', he wrote to Field, 'and we give you and the brethren heartie thanks for it. As yet we are not resolved in all points of it: having had but small time to peruse it, nor the commoditie of often meeting about it. But we have taken order for our monthly assembly, and after our owne consents yeelded unto it, for associating other into our companie, whom we shall thinke approved.'[54] Some adaptation of the plan for the local *classis* in the *Discipline,* which is described as the meeting of the representatives of a few churches, for example twelve, composed of one minister and one elder from each congregation, would have been needed in the context of the university and its colleges. The *classis* was at one and the same time an administrative body and a preaching exercise. In Oxford, it was presumably the young men named by Gellibrand in his letter of 1585, who would have been foremost in putting their names to the *Discipline*. Chapter III posed a particular difficulty, and they requested Gellibrand to discuss this with the national organization. Writing to Field, Gellibrand commented, 'I left with you a paper, conteining certaine question about entring into the Ministerie ... The iudgment of the godly learned brethren would much prevaile with them either one way or other etc. Your assembly is more travailed and practised in such difficulties then in other places.' According to Bancroft the chief point at issue was: 'Whether fellowes of Colleges might enter into the ministry, being thereunto bound by their statutes.'[55] Many colleges were bound by statute to oblige their fellows to take orders within a term of years from election, and in Magdalen this had been a major cause of controversy in 1575.[56] These Oxford men,

---

[53] *A parte of a register* (1593), 314.
[54] Bancroft, *Daungerous Positions and Proceedings*, 76. Collinson, *E.P.M.,* 323 takes Gellibrand's remarks to imply that Oxford had devised its own local order for meetings.
[55] Bancroft, *Survay of the Pretended Holy Discipline*, 365.
[56] See above, ch. III.

fellows in orders, were clearly in a different category from those who, though they had a cure of souls elsewhere, remained resident in the university, leaving their parishes unattended or in the hands of a badly-paid and inadequate stipendiary. Many moderate men in Oxford, though fierce critics of non-residence, would not have objected to those bound by their college statutes taking orders, and only the most radical proponents of the *Discipline* would have insisted that a man must, in all circumstances, be called to a definite congregation.

Favourers of the *Discipline* in Oxford had strong links with centres of the *classis* in other parts of the country and in particular with neighbouring Northamptonshire. Gellibrand and John Barebon, one-time Magdalen contemporaries, restored the link broken when Barebon was thrust out of the college in the autumn of 1578. The two men met at the 1584 London assembly. In his capacity as Oxford correspondent, Gellibrand wrote to Daventry in 1586, reporting the Oxford discussions. Barebon in turn informed Field, 'I receaved from our faithful brother Maister Gellibrand a direction of the brethren, concerninge the observation of the Sabaoth, and convertinge the Churchwardens into Elders and Collectors into Deacons etc.'[57] Under examination in 1591, Snape admitted that the Daventry *classis* was in regular correspondence with Gellibrand in Oxford, as well as with Cambridge and with Travers in London.[58] In the Warwickshire *classis,* where John Oxenbridge, a Christ Church man in the 1560s, was, after Cartwright, the leading figure, Gellibrand had another and more permanent connection. In August 1587, he married the daughter of the Vicar of Southam and after that stayed frequently with Oxenbridge and his family. Gellibrand subscribed the *Discipline* in Southam in 1588.[59] Edward Lord, another

---

[57] Bancroft, *Survay of the Pretended Holy Discipline,* 366.

[58] Bancroft, *Daungerous Positions and Proceedings,* 79-80. George Wilton describes a fast he attended in 1582 at which Barebon was *concionator.* Puritan activity of this kind reached a peak in 1581-2 and may have been a foretaste of the *classes* and conferences. Magdalen College Oxford MS 617, 53; Collinson, *E.P.M.,* 214-16. Unfortunately Wilton's letter-book contains no information on the period between 1585 when he left Magdalen and the 1590s when he had settled as a schoolmaster in Crediton. On Northamptonshire, see W. J. Shiels, *The Puritans in the Diocese of Peterborough, 1558-1610* (Northants. Record Society, xxx, 1979), esp. 96-8, for links with Oxford.

[59] BL, Harleian MS 6849, fo. 222, cited Collinson, *E.P.M.,* 327, 492.

of Gellibrand's Magdalen contemporaries, by this time Vicar of Wolston, six miles from Coventry, was another of the signatories, as was Daniel Wight, late of Alban Hall and St. John's and two years later to be deprived of his curacy at Stretton for nonconformity.

While few of the resident Oxford divines would have supported as radical courses as Gellibrand, Lord, or Wight, many younger members of the university may have been encouraged by the sermon campaign of 1586 to re-examine the place of the Church of England within the reformed tradition and to find it wanting, not only in respect of discipline, but in its defective view of the work of the godly parish minister as pastor, preacher, and prophet. Such a view had been heightened in the preceding years not only by the remaining crypto-papists but, in the early 1580s, by the new incursions of Jesuits and seminary priests. Great vigilance was now required to ensure that the university and its ministers aligned themselves with the example provided by the continental reformed churches.[60]

Protestant leaders in Oxford had been aware of the presence in the university of crypto-papists since the beginning of the reign. Despite the early attempts to impose a settlement, through royal and episcopal visitation, thereafter the Council or crown rarely intervened directly in the affairs of the university or of its colleges and halls, except in the matter of elections; though, from time to time, Chancellors were prompted by agitation at court to issue orders to Convocation to undertake reforms. Generally, however, the regime preferred to work 'by persuasion, arbitration, patronage, and advice rather than by diktat' in the gradual establishment of religious uniformity.[61] In colleges where active visitors, like Robert Horne, were at work, attempts were made to root out crypto-papists and in some cases, practising papists, but where visitors or patrons were inactive, or even favourably disposed towards the old religion, an enclave of reaction could be preserved.[62] In

---

[60] For a discussion of the parallel movements in Cambridge and the distinguishing features of the 'moderate puritan tradition' as defined by Dr Lake, see P. G. Lake, *Moderate Puritans and the Elizabethan Church* (Cambridge, 1982).

[61] P. H. Williams, *The Tudor Regime,* (Oxford, 1979), 305.

[62] For example, Balliol College, SP 12/146/10, n.d.; Exeter College, Strype, *Annals,* II, part ii, 196; St. John's College, W. H. Stevenson and H. E. Salter, *The Early History of St. John's College, Oxford* (Oxford Historical Society, new series, i. 1939), where papist influences remained, at least until the late 1570s.

Lincoln College, Leicester, often considered a friend and promoter of only advanced protestants, appointed John Bridgewater as Rector in succession to Francis Babington in 1563, and until his flight to Douai in 1574 the college was a safe refuge for papists.[63] The halls remained a haven for those who had been expelled or had withdrawn from the colleges because of their religious opinions. Their principals were private proprietors, often holding leases from sympathetic colleges, and intervention was difficult, though the Chancellor's court made sporadic attempts to enforce conformity.[64] In the 1570s, an increasing number of members of the university were denied the graces necessary to proceed to degrees, because their religion was suspect. All of these were crypto-papists; no radical protestant seems to have been challenged in this way.[65]

The intensification of Jesuit activities in the early 1580s, which heralded a new era in papist initiatives in England and in government repression of them, was brought home to the doctors and masters in Oxford when they assembled in St. Mary's for the Act on 27 June 1581. In their seats, they found copies of a slim volume by one of their own alumni, daringly placed there by a young Derbyshire priest, William Hartley, once a member of St. John's, but recently ordained at Reims.[66] Edmund Campion's *Decem Rationes,* by a scholar for scholars, set out ten ways in which the protestants had undermined the intellectual foundations of the church, spurning the Scriptures, fathers, councils, and history, and resorting to violent means rather than rational argument to defend their position. Campion was already much more than an Oxford preoccupation. After his capture in July 1581, the Privy Council wrote to the Vice-Chancellor, reporting that most of the seminary priests at that time disturbing the peace of the church were Oxford scholars, and requesting enquiry in the university and its colleges and halls after suspected persons, whose names

---

[63] Green, *The Commonwealth of Lincoln College, 1427-1977,* 127-32, 139-43.

[64] OUA/Hyp/B/1/ Chancellor's Court Deposition Book, 1566-78, 65, 68, 70, 71.

[65] Clark, *Register,* II, part i, 152, case of Ralph Swinburne of Trinity; ibid., 154-5, case of Hugo Weston; there were at least six other cases in 1573-4, ibid., 152-4.

[66] Campion was elected a fellow of St. John's in 1557. He disputed before the Queen on her visit to Oxford in 1566 (Wood, *Annals,* II, 159), but in 1571 became a member of the Roman Catholic Church at Douai, and a Jesuit in 1573.

were to be sent to the Council.[67]   From this time a greater vigilance was applied. In October 1581, Leicester wrote to the university, complaining that the old matriculation order, enforced by the statute of 1565, was frequently omitted. This was the source of many difficulties. Large numbers of junior members had remained unmatriculated, especially in the halls. Here, with little control over tutors, a crypto-papist might almost imperceptibly, and with the encouragement of family and friends, draw pupils away to the Roman communion. No student over the age of 16 was to remain unmatriculated in any college or hall longer than the Friday week after his admission to the society. Matriculation now included subscription to the Articles and the first subscription book appears in this year. Further control, particularly in the halls, was provided by the licensing of all tutors and readers, who were to be allowed to continue in their duties only with the consent of the Vice-Chancellor, their head of house, and two DDs, BDs, or at the least, two licensed preachers.[68] However, by the beginning of 1583, the new statute seems to have had limited effect, for Leicester complained again of neglect by tutors and 'the suffering of secret and lurking Papists among you'.[69]

Statutory control, imperfect as it clearly was, was matched by the steady increase in the provision of apologetic sermons, lectures, and treatises. Lawrence Humphrey and John Reynolds, different in age and temper, were the two principal spokesmen for the university. Here protestants of all complexions saw the immediate need to present a united front. Humphrey's particular concern was with the Jesuit influx. Two parts of a single work, his *Iesuitismi*, appeared in 1582 and 1584. The first part, *Iesuitismi pars prima, sive de praxi Romanae Curiae*, dedicated to Leicester, attempts to counter the charge that Campion and other Jesuits died as martyrs without any

---

[67] *Acts of the Privy Council*, ed. A. S. Dasent, xiii (1581-2) (London, 1896), 170, 14 August 1581. See also 350, 399-400. Unfortunately, the Privy Council register for June 1582 to February 1586 is not extant. For other examples of government intervention in the university against papists, see SP 12/60/4, SP 12/119/55, and Historical Manuscripts Commission, *Report on the Pepys Manuscripts*, 166 (= 'Papers of State', II, 345).

[68] Clark, *Register*, II, part i, 163-9; Wood, *Annals*, II, 205-8; OUA/NEP *supra*/Register KK, fos. 338^r-341^r.

[69] Wood, *Annals*, II, 212.

charge being proven against them. Humphrey sets against the Oxonian, Campion, the heroes of Oxford's protestant history, from Chaucer to Colet, Tyndal, and the Oxford martyrs. He praises Leicester in fulsome terms as the advocate of religious truth in the university, and defends the Queen against the papal bull and the Jesuit mission, demonstrating that obedience is due to princes and magistrates.[70] The volume, conceived as an Oxford apologia, ends with a sermon preached before the university on Ash Wednesday 1582 and entitled *'Pharisaismus Vetus et Novus'* in which Humphrey alerted the university, explaining that since the Jesuits conformed in many practical ways to the Church of England, it was difficult to distinguish the true and false servants of Christ. Humphrey then listed seven methods of distinction, and enumerating the Oxford scholars who had defected to the Society of Jesus when they could have been ornaments of the university, he called on his hearers to beware.[71] Humphrey returned to this theme in a series of sermons preached in Oxford and other parts of the country and published in the year of the Armada under the title *The Romish Hydra and Monster.*

By 1586, John Reynolds had already made a reputation as a defender of the Church of England in his conference with Hart. In the summer of that year Walsingham announced his intention to set up a special lectureship. In his letter to Sir Thomas Bromley, acting Chancellor of Oxford in the absence of Leicester in the Low Countries, he lamented the growth of seminaries abroad and the seeming indifference of the universities in England: 'I cannot but marvaile and much mislike, that in our Universities here at home as great care is not had for advancement of trewe Religion of God here professed by some more Lectures of Divinity to be read, especially the handling of the principale parts of our Religion, whereby no doubt but that the Ministrie of the Churches of this Realme, which should spring from the Universitie, would be not onlye better to deliver all trewe doctrines, but also to confute upon every occasion the contrary.'[72] The university had no hesitation in

[70] E. Rosenberg, *Leicester, Patron of Letters* (New York, 1955), 261 ff.

[71] Humphrey, *Jesuitismi Pars Prima* (London, 1582), 163 ff., esp. 170-2, 181.

[72] OUA/NEP *supra*/Register L, fo. 288ʳ, Walsingham to Bromley, 30 July 1586; Wood, *Annals*, II, 227.

appointing Reynolds to the lectureship and the financial assistance allowed him to leave Corpus where 'dissentions and factions ... did make me so weary' and migrate as a pensioner to Queen's where he quickly found companionship in Provost Robinson.[73] The chief product of the Walsingham lectureship was a refutation of Bellarmine's *Controversies,* the three volumes of which appeared between 1586 and 1593. Reynolds worked with painstaking slowness, producing one general work, the *De Romana Ecclesia Idolalatria* [*sic*] in 1596, and a series of 250 lectures on the Apocrypha, published posthumously in 1611 as the *Censura Librorum Apocryphorum,* though anti-papist apologetic was his constant preoccupation throughout the last twenty years of his life. He also established himself as a preacher in the defence of England against Rome in both town and university.[74]

Even while it was essential to preserve a united course of action against the papists, in print and from the pulpit, younger radical divines continued to press for reforms within the Church of England, though the attack on Rome may have moderated some more extreme courses. At the end of the decade, William Hubbock, a Durham man, matriculated at Magdalen Hall and later a fellow of Corpus, produced an English translation of the *Ad Rationes Decem Edmundi Campiani* of 1581 from the Cambridge apologist, William Whitaker.[75] Later, he was to enjoy a settled ministry as James VI and I's Chaplain at the Tower of London, but in 1589 he did not seek the favour of men. Preaching at Oxford on 15 March 1589, he lamented the insufficiency of so many, particularly the non-resident and non-preaching ministry. He complained at the

---

[73] OUA/NEP *supra*/Register L, fo. 286, Reynolds's appointment. For the difficulties of Reynolds in Corpus, see Corpus Christi College Oxford MS 303, fos. 170-80, 192. For copies of correspondence between Walsingham and Bromley over the establishment of the lectureship, see Corpus Christi College Oxford MS 303, fos. 136ʳ-138ᵛ. In January 1590, Reynolds, who had failed to obtain the Regius chair on Humphrey's death, wrote to ask Walsingham for a continuation of the lectureship; ibid., fo. 140. In April 1590, Walsingham died and Essex became patron of the lecture.

[74] As well as the *Censura,* Corpus Christi College Oxford MSS 330-1 contain lecture notes on this subject. Bodleian Library, MS Cherry 33 is a lecture against Nicholas Sander and BL, Additional MS 30498 contains an English translation of some lectures against Bellarmine. The sermons were published as *A Sermon upon Part of the Eighteenth Psalm* (Oxford, 1586) and *The Discovery of the Man of Sinne.*

[75] Bodleian Library, MS Crynes 837, item 3.

abuses of patrons of livings, and the want of maintenance which caused so many godly ministers to suffer. Where he saw men forsaking the ministry, he blamed poverty and subscription, and found himself imprisoned for twenty-six weeks and eventually thrust out of his fellowship by Cole.[76] In the following year a member of Christ Church was summoned before the Vice-Chancellor, Nicholas Bond, for speaking against the use of the Apocrypha in church, and subscription. Complaints were made, possibly to the Privy Council, and the Vice-Chancellor tendered him a form of submission prepared by the Lord Chancellor, at the same time maintaining his own case that the apocryphal books, though they were not 'canonica', were 'hagiographa' and that if anyone taught to the contrary, he himself would confute him.[77] Radical dissent continued however. In June 1591, John Barfolde of All Souls and Bernard Robinson of Queen's were ordered to deliver to the Vice-Chancellor copies of sermons which they had preached in St. Mary's and, though no evidence of their content survives, there is little doubt that they were enunciating advanced protestant views.[78]

In the university and in the country at large, an era of more strict supervision was beginning. Extreme courses were now out of the question for most, and only a very small number of ministers and laymen took the path of separation; Oxford supplied at least one of the leaders, the Welshman, John Penry. In the university, the death of Leicester in 1588 and the appointment of the Lord Chancellor, Sir Christopher Hatton, as his successor marks a tightening of control. Hatton wrote on 22 August 1589 enjoining on the university observation of regulations concerning matriculation, subscription, sermons, exercises, lectures, the taking of degrees, the use of Latin, and dress.[79] On 8 July 1590, Hatton complained to Bond 'I am now again enformed that the same disorders do still continue',

[76] BL, Additional MS 48064, fos. 148-50. Hubbock set down notes of his Oxford sermon and a pathetic account of the proceedings against him; fo. 150 is a form of subscription, though there is no evidence he subscribed. On 29 March 1590, Sir Francis Knollys petitioned on his behalf, see BL, Lansdowne MS 68, fo. 173. Essex may also have supported him, see Collinson, *E.P.M.*, 446.

[77] BL, Lansdowne MS 61, fo. 58.

[78] OUA/NEP *supra*/Register L, fo. 255ᵛ, 5 June 1591.

[79] OUA/NEP *supra*/Register L, fo. 297ʳ; Wood, *Annals*, II, 237-40.

listing the slackness in lectures, disputations, subscription, apparel, and the other matters raised in the previous year.[80] Bond was grieved and perhaps embarrassed by the renewal of the Chancellor's complaints and in a bold move returned the letter to Hatton, indicating that he had not read it to Convocation, having consulted two or three friends who agreed with him that it would cause grief. He also wrote to Bancroft, asking him to intercede with Hatton 'so that his Lordship may not be offended, nor I discredited', and in further notes he defended himself point by point against the Chancellor's charges.[81]

On 20 November 1591 Hatton died. The advanced protestant party in the university attempted to secure the election of Essex to succeed him, but the intervention of the court and of Whitgift and the machinations of Bond on their behalf secured the election of Thomas Sackville, Lord Buckhurst.[82] When the members of the university presented themselves before him to install him as Chancellor, he made a long speech, lamenting the disorder and faction in their society and stressing his determination to have good government in the university.[83] On 13 April 1592, and again in 1594, he tried to reiterate the injunctions of Hatton in 1589 and 1590, and also repeated the warnings against Jesuits, seminarians, and notorious recusants.[84] Outside the university, the jaws of ecclesiastical repression closed around the more extreme designs of puritan ministers and gentlemen, discredit was cast on their aspirations by the writings of Martin Marprelate, and Richard Bancroft set out to expose the true motives of the upholders of the 'consistorian discipline' in his *Survay* and *Daungerous Positions*. In Oxford, as elsewhere, men of moderate views turned their attention to the preaching of godliness and righteousness, the state of their souls, and the state of their colleges.[85]

[80] BL, Harleian MS 4240, fo. 60; Magdalen College Oxford MS 280, item 49; Wood, *Annals*, II, 241-3.

[81] BL, Harleian MS 4240, fos. 69-70; Magdalen College Oxford MS 280, items 50-1; Wood, *Annals*, II, 243-5 (incomplete).

[82] Historical Manuscripts Commission, *Calendar of the Manuscripts of the Marquis of Salisbury at Hatfield House*, IV (London, 1892), 162-5. Lambeth Palace Library, MS 2004, fo. 7, letter of Francis Holliock to Mr Moore at Banbury, dated 21 November ?1591, records Whitgift's opposition to Essex.

[83] Lambeth Palace Library, MS 178, fo. 146.

[84] OUA/NEP *supra*/Register L, fo. 253^v; ibid., fo. 272; Wood, *Annals*, II, 258-9.

[85] See below, chs. VIII and IX.

VII

THE UNIVERSITY AND THE CHURCH OF ENGLAND: OXFORD AND THE PROVISION OF A GODLY, LEARNED, AND RESIDENT MINISTRY

When Elizabeth came to the throne, 10-15 per cent of the livings in the country were vacant and many who might have sought ordination were deterred by political, social, and financial insecurity. Emergency recruitment was necessary which often took little account of the education and moral quality of candidates. Few, however, would have expected the majority of parochial clergy to be graduates, although later in the reign university men were increasingly in demand from patrons of distinctly protestant persuasion, some of them educated at the universities themselves, to fill the role of parish preacher, pastor, and educator.[1] Among those who sought to bring the Church of England into closer conformity with the ministry and discipline of the continental reformed churches, broad agreement emerged on the need of the universities to provide larger numbers of godly and learned ministers. This was the theme of the paper 'Means for the Establishing of a Learned Ministry', written in 1585-6, which calculated that Oxford would be able to provide 194 ministers and 'if it be reformed, non-residents being removed, bad Heads displaced, and the young fruit cherished, it would yield great plenty in a short time'.[2] Another paper 'Certeine Points Concerninge the Pollicie and Government of the Ecclesiastical State' petitions for the universities to send lists of suitable candidates to the Lord Keeper and the Lord Chancellor so that the Queen might bestow benefices in her gift upon them.[3] 'Articles for the Refor-

[1] For further discussion see H. F. Kearney, *Scholars and Gentlemen* (London, 1970) ch. 1; R. O'Day, 'The Reformation of the Ministry, 1585-1642', in *Continuity and Change,* ed. F. Heal and R. O'Day (Leicester, 1976), 55-9.

[2] Dr Williams's Library, Morrice MS 'B', I, fo. 545; Peel, *The Seconde Parte of a Register,* II, 198-9. It was estimated that Cambridge could provide 140 suitable men at this time.

[3] Dr Williams's Library, Morrice MS 'B', I, fo. 221; Peel, op. cit., II, 21-2. See also Inner Temple, Petyt MS 538, vol. 38, fos. 137ᵛ-138ᵛ for details of the scheme.

mation of the Mynisterie', probably of the same date, indicates a projected survey of colleges to gauge their capacity to provide godly ministers, and requires that 'the universities render up yeerly a just note unto her majesties counsell of such learned mynisters as thei shall have yielded to the common wealth and Church'.[4]

However, not all advanced protestants adopted such a favourable attitude towards the universities. The most harsh criticisms came from those who were later to separate altogether from the ministry of the Church of England. John Penry, graduate of Peterhouse, Cambridge and an MA of Alban Hall, Oxford, complained of decay, so few men applying themselves to divinity because they could see no purpose in it, the small number of ministers the universities had provided for his native Wales, and Welsh livings occupied by non-residents who spent their time in the universities and never came to their parishes.[5] A violent attack also emerges in the Marprelate tracts and Henry Barrow, educated at Clare Hall, Cambridge rejected the universities after his conversion and constantly advocated the abolition of the 'munkish dennes'.[6] Barrow and his fellow separatist, John Greenwood, were advocating the suppression of Oxford and Cambridge in favour of 'gathered seminaries' at the same time that the Queen was attempting to gain greater control over the training of ministers.

This was, however, an extreme and minority view and the majority of advanced protestants would have been well content with the statutes provided by Sir Walter Mildmay for his new college of Emmanuel in 1585: 'in establishing this College we have set before us this one aim, of rendering as many persons as possible fit for the sacred ministry of the word and sacraments; so that from this seminary the Church of England might have men whom it may call forth to instruct the people

[4] Dr Williams's Library, Morrice MS 'B', I, fos. 435-6; Peel, op, cit., II, 199-202.

[5] John Penry, *A treatise containing the aequity of an humble supplication* reprinted in *Three Treatises Concerning Wales,* ed. D. Williams (Cardiff, 1960), 37-40.

[6] *The Epitome* (1588), sig. F. 3^v; *Hay any work for Cooper* (1589), 47; *The Protestatyon* (1589), 25. Henry Barrow, 'A Brief Discovery of the False Church', in *The Writings of Henry Barrow,* 1587-90 ed. L. H. Carlson (Elizabethan Nonconformist Texts, III, London, 1962), 344-5, 350, 539.

and undertake the duty of pastors.'[7] Oxford had no Emmanuel but preachers and godly tutors were constantly encouraging their undergraduate hearers to exercise a painful and zealous ministry of pastoral care and self-sacrifice. John Chardon, fellow of Exeter, preaching in St. Mary's, Oxford on 11 December 1586 prompted his congregation 'carefullie and painfullie to walke in their vocations and callings' and warned 'how daungerous a thing it is for men to behave themselves coldly or deceitfully in that charge whereunto God hath called them'. He deplored the 'divelish and damnable carelessnes which ... is to bee seene in the ministers of the Church, magistrates of the common wealth, parents ... [because] the greater part thinke and believe that they are seated in the rooms they are not of God, but either of Fortune, or of their own industry'. The world, he believed, was in such a bad state, because 'it is thought a fault ... to be zealous and fervent in the Lordes cause: especially in the beating downe sinne and iniquitie'.[8] Henry Airay, preaching a decade later, provided his students with guidance and warning. Not only was continual residence demanded, but utter dedication to the people's need. He caricatured the congregation which desired 'such a Pastor as neither can, nor will teach us the wholesome word of truth, one that will suffer us to go on in our sinnes, and never wake us out of our dead sleepe of securitie: one that will sowe pillowes under our elbowes, and crie, peace, peace, where there is no peace, one that will sort himselfe unto our manners, and apply himselfe unto our humors, he is a man fit for us'.[9] The true pastor was unlikely to gain the affection and praise of his people, for 'generally if the Minister be such a one as makes a conscience of his waies amongst them, as carefully feedes them with the bread of life, and painfully leades them forth ... such a one as will religiously call them unto the sanctification of the Lord his Sabboth, and restraine them of their meriment, and sports, and pleasures, and wanton dalliances ... if he be sicke unto death wee will reioyce and be glad at his death'.[10]

[7] H. C. Porter, *Puritanism in Tudor England* (London, 1970), 186.

[8] John Chardon, *A Second sermon upon the ix. chapter of the holy gospel of Iesus Christ according to St. John* (Oxford, 1586), sigs. A. iiii[v], A vi[r], A viii[v], B i[r].

[9] Airay, *Philippians*, 232; see also 10-11, 212-13, 232, 508, 738.

[10] Ibid., 545.

This then was the ideal: a godly, resident, preaching ministry. However, even godly patrons and diligent bishops were often unable to provide ministers of the quality desired because of inadequate maintenance. In March 1573, William Bradbridge, Bishop of Exeter, wrote to Lawrence Humphrey and Convocation imploring the university's help for a certain Mr Corynton, who held a university living near Penzance. The Bishop argued that the university should improve the maintenance, since 'the better the vicarage is, the more your commendation, and the sooner you shall retain a learned man to serve the cure'.[11] He added that people were eager to provide for their own financial advantage to the detriment of their parson. In 1585, Whitgift estimated that half the benefices in the country with cure of souls were worth less than £10, most of them less than £8. William Harrison reckoned that £30 was necessary for the support of a learned minister and, at the beginning of the seventeenth century, Ralph Josselin expected £80 from his people at Earl's Colne. Only one quarter to one third of the livings in the country would have been able to provide this maintenance and so support a graduate minister but a number of these livings were in the hands of pluralists.[12]

As early as 1560, Lawrence Humphrey had attacked the 'vain and counterfeit nobility' who took the revenues of benefices and then bestowed the basest part on a 'toylinge, sweating and swinking minister'.[13] John Reynolds perpetually reminded his Oxford congregation of the need for sufficient maintenance and training for ministers: 'When we had gotten *Calice* from the Frenchmen, there was one appointed to put them in remembrance from time to time of *Calice* in all their solemne meetings for State consultations, till they had regained it... Wherefore, to put you in minde even now also of our Spirituale *Calice*, I beseech you fathers and brethren ... now at length to regard the state of the Soules, the precious Soules of men committed to your charge.'[14] Reynolds sought to inspire

[11] Bodleian Library, MS Rawlinson D 837, fo. 43ᵛ.
[12] J. E. C. Hill, *Economic Problems of the Church from Archbishop Whitgift to the Long Parliament* (Oxford, 1956), 202; F. Heal, 'Economic Problems of the Clergy', in *Church and Society in England: Henry VIII to James I*, ed. F. Heal and R. O'Day (London, 1977), 117-18.
[13] Humphrey, *The Nobles or of Nobilitye*, sig. h iiʳ.
[14] Reynolds, *The Prophecie of Obadiah*, 36.

his hearers with the example of their ancestors, who had furnished houses, glebeland, and tithes to provide for the dwelling
and maintenance of pastors, but now 'the livings appointed for
their maintenance, are so impaired and minished: that, being
not able therewith to find themselves in souldiourlike state,
they refuse the calling; or if they undertake it, they are
distracted from it with cares how to supply their need'.[15] James
Bisse, fellow of Magdalen, preacher at Oxford and at Paul's
Cross, complained in a 1581 sermon that preachers of God's
word were neglected, that 'livinges are not geven, they are
solde as common oysters at Byllingesgate. This is the cause that
Ministers are not, nor cannot be so liberal as their predecessors
... why doltes, ignorant Asses, idle and idole Shepheardes have
the livings.' He contrasted with these men the good scholar and
honest, godly minister who would rather beg than buy his
living.[16]

The covetousness of patrons and the miserable state of
benefices, vacant because of lack of maintenance, became one
of the burning themes in the preaching of John Reynolds. In a
sermon of April 1586, he described his ideal of the reformed
pastor, bringing up his people by sound doctrine and true
discipline, and lamented the 'beggarly creatures' being sent
out into parishes by patrons. He admitted that the universities,
however, could not supply sufficient learned ministers and
hoped that the cathedral churches and bishops' households
could also join in this task, so that a learned minister could be
settled in every parish in the country.[17] He also recognized that
'a great cause hereof are Patrons of Benefices ... the interest of
choosing the Pastour belonging of old time to the Congregation, is
now conveyed to them, because their predecessors did benefit the
Church some way, and therefore were put in trust as Patrones of
it'. He complained of those who had turned their patronage into
pillage and warned them that the church's goods which they had
taken were sacred not profane and that those who had purloined
them were guilty of sacrilege. Turning to his student congregation, he continued: 'I hartily beseech the young Gentlemen
that be here present, and al that are or shalbe Patrones

---

[15] Ibid., 42.
[16] James Bisse, *Two Sermons* (London, 1581), sig. E 1r.
[17] Reynolds, *Haggai*, 21 (sermon of 19 April 1586).

hereafter, in a religious reverence and fear of the Lord, to keep themselves pure from this abomination.'[18] The problem had not been solved by the 1590s, when Henry Airay lamented that, while in times of ignorance, men had given plenteously to their massing-priests, they now took away all that they could from their preaching minister. Hinting at the enhanced status which the post-Reformation godly minister might hope to enjoy, he argued that such men should be given enough maintenance for their livelihood and reverence for their persons.[19]

One of the principal methods advocated by reformers for the improvement of livings was the restoration of impropriated tithes. In 1603, the bishops estimated that 3,849 of the 9,250 livings in the country were impropriated and as early as 1588, Whitgift had calculated that the financial loss to the church through impropriation was £100,000 per annum. Colleges depended on these tithes and Oxford and Cambridge and other corporate bodies together held 107 livings in this way. The New College living at Hornchurch, for example, part of the founder's gift in Essex, a large rural parish where the parishioners maintained two chapels, was worth £800 per annum to the college, but the vicar received only £55 from the small tithes.[20] Reynolds, among others in Oxford, realized that the restoration of tithes to provide more adequate livings would be detrimental to the colleges. While he hoped that the university would make better provision for ministers where it held the impropriation, he did not intend it to give away the money by which its Schools and scholars were maintained: 'God hath ordained Ecclesiasticall goods to finde, not only Priests and Levites, but their offspring, even them who are to be brought up to be Priests and Levites, and them who bring them up.'[21] He hoped, therefore, that where there was sufficient money from impropriation to provide for the maintenance of both the pastor and the college, that the rents should be reserved to the college and the rest of the living to the pastor. Other impropria-

---

[18] Reynolds, *The Prophecie of Obadiah*, 43-4; see also *Haggai*, 82-3.

[19] Airay, *Philippians*, 509-10; see also 86, 920.

[20] Hill, *Economic Problems of the Church*, 150-1 [estimates of impropriated livings from H. Grove, *Alienated Tithes* (London, 1896)].

[21] Reynolds, *The Prophecie of Obadiah*, 47-8.

tions not used for educational purposes were deemed by Reynolds to be intolerable.[22] For him, as for many of his contemporaries, where new justification had to be found for inherited wealth, it was to be discovered in the provision which the church needed to make for the training of a preaching ministry. Reynolds believed that if the impropriated tithes were restored to a parish, it would have the obligation to support students in training for the ministry. He also advocated that a parish should maintain its own pastor by freewill offering, as in the primitive church.[23] In 1603, the King himself urged the universities to follow his example and surrender their impropriated tithes, thereby providing benefices with sufficient maintenance for learned men. He admitted that he did not wish colleges to be deprived of the necessary means for their own continuance, but hoped that they would be able to provide better livings for their own graduates.[24]

John Howson, Canon of Christ Church, preaching at Paul's Cross on 4 December 1597, condemned the buying and selling of spiritual promotion. This was intolerable, since it not only destroyed the fellowship of mankind, but 'will make barren and like desolate and forsaken widdowes the two Universities, the two fruitfull Mothers and full of Children, though now readie to give up the ghost, and powre out their soules into their Mothers bosomes'. He claimed that those who had been members of the universities had spent £500 on maintenance, books, and their degrees and 'if by this price of the expence of our time, our bodies and spirites, our substance and patrimonies, wee cannot purchase those smal rewards which are ours by law and right of inheritance, a poore Parsonage or a Poore Vicarage', but must pay for a lease, none would tolerate it.[25] Howson argued that the buying and selling of benefices would produce an insufficient and unlearned ministry, because ignorant men would buy the right of entry, while university graduates, already impoverished, would be unable to afford them.

---

[22] Ibid., 46.

[23] Corpus Christi College Oxford MS 294, 378. See Simon Pett's request about Magdalen impropriations, 1585, above, 65.

[24] Bodleian Library, MS Tanner 75, fo. 67^{r-v}.

[25] John Howson, *A Sermon Preached at Paules Crosse ... the 4 of December 1597* (London, 1597), 28-31. See also *Epistolae Academicae, 1508-1596*, 354-5.

Some men refused the offer of a benefice on grounds of cons-cience. Jeremy Corderoy, one of the chaplains of Merton for nearly twenty years from 1590, would not accept a living. His *Warning for Worldlings* of 1608 is a dialogue between a traveller and an Oxford student, who would seem to be Corderoy himself. The traveller finds the scholar pale and thin and understands from other Oxford men that he has not yet been preferred to a living. This surprises him, since he knows that the scholar has studied divinity for many years, has preached often, and conforms to the church's discipline; and that his life and conversation have been unexceptionable. The scholar replies that he has been offered a living 'without sute and also upon sute', but that he has been unable to accept because of his conscience. He had resolved never to use any indirect means to preferment and patrons were not so simple as to give their livings freely.[26]

When preaching became an equal focus in parochial ministry with the administration of the sacraments, a pastor of higher calibre and stability was demanded. Sometimes, patrons appealed to the university to provide a man' of the quality they desired. Leicester wrote in March 1573, lamenting that Jersey and Guernsey had for so long been impoverished of ministers. He asked if the university would find places for four scholars, two from each of the islands, to be trained for the ministry and the university agreed, provided that a college could be found whose statutes permitted it.[27] In 1584, Henry Hastings, Earl of Huntingdon, unconvinced by the arguments that the universities could not provide the ministers he required for the market towns of the north-west, requested a larger number of suitable men.[28]

Occasionally, the university or its colleges were able to secure definite improvement by direct action. In October 1572, the ecclesiastical commissioners for the northern province wrote to the university voicing the complaint of the par-ishioners of Holme Cultram that they lacked a good pastor

---

[26] Jeremy Corderoy, *A Warning for Worldlings* (London, 1608), 2-5.
[27] Bodleian Library, MS Rawlinson D 837, fos. 45ᵛ-46ʳ.
[28] Huntingdon to William Chaderton, Bishop of Chester, 27 June 1584, in F. Peck, *Desiderata Curiosa*, I (London, 1779), 151.

because of the lowly income of the living. The university immediately agreed to pay the annual stipend, a modest £8, over a period of six months so that an honest man could be found to serve the cure.[29] The chapter of Christ Church, painfully aware of the lack of preaching ministers even in the villages around Oxford, made special provision, on 19 December 1577, that those admitted to the charge of the parishes of St. Thomas's, Oxford and of Cowley were not only to administer the sacraments and conduct public prayer, but also to preach the word. Further, the chapter provided for quarterly sermons in sixteen villages of which the college was patron. Four appointed preachers were to give an account to the treasurer of the four sermons they had preached each quarter before receiving payment, and each was to deliver to the dean 'a note in his own hand' with the name of the vicar or curate of the living where he had preached that quarter, his ability in learning, life, and conversation, and what superstitious monuments in the church needed removal.[30] This appears as a very serious attempt to supervise the college livings and improve the standards of the resident ministers, as well as providing a temporary supply of preachers.

This scheme can have met with only limited success. When the puritan 'Survay' was conducted in 1585-6, the surveyors for the county of Oxford noted not only the conditions of the livings but also their patronage. Christ Church was patron of eight of the livings listed. In all but one the tithes were impropriate, that is, the right of collection had been annexed to a lay proprietor for a term of years. In only one of the eight Christ Church livings was the parson, Richard Brent, described as 'resident and a preacher'. Three had no preacher, two had little preaching, at Chalgrove the curate preached sometimes, and at Berrick there were quarterly sermons. The Berrick parson was non-resident and the curate of 'mean ability'. Although the survey demanded impossible standards, where a resident, learned parson, preaching weekly, was the only acceptable norm, its results show the colleges of Oxford in a bad light. New College had at least five livings in the county. At three,

---

[29] Bodleian Library, MS Rawlinson D 837, fo. 42, 12 October 1572. The university's reply, dated 27 November 1572, is on fo. 43[r].
[30] Christ Church Archives, Chapter Act Book, 229.

there was no preaching. At Adderbury, where the incumbent was both resident and a preacher, the acceptable minimum was provided, that is a quarterly sermon. At Swalcliffe, an impropriate living, the vicar, a non-resident, yielded the profits of the living to provide the parish with a resident and preaching curate. This was evidently exceptional. Protestant Queen's, now flourishing under Provost Robinson, possessed a non-impropriate living, Baldwin, St. Lawrence (Baldon in the survey) where the incumbent, a preacher, was resident; but elsewhere the picture was gloomy. Corpus had two livings, one at Wayborough, where the curate was of 'mean ability' but where, nevertheless, quarterly sermons were preached; and another at Lower Heyford, where the incumbent was the President, William Cole, who had placed there as his curate one John Boulton, who was no preacher. The Heyfords fared badly, since Upper Heyford, a New College living, was in the hands of Martin Culpepper, Warden of the college, also a non-resident. Thomas Glasier, presumably the Rector of Exeter, held the Lincoln living of Kidlington, where he is noted as 'non resident a lawier and no preacher'. In general, the personal example of heads of houses was poor. Two Merton livings, Easington (Esinden in the survey) and Cuxham, had quarterly sermons and resident vicars, though one was of 'mean ability'. A general picture emerges, even in the countryside surrounding the university, of impropriate livings as the norm, frequent non-residence, and little preaching, at most a quarterly sermon. Even committed protestant colleges seem to have been at fault, though in many cases impropriations may have been of long standing and outside their immediate control.[31]

Pluralism was almost universally condemned by clergy and laity alike and frequent legislative efforts were made to curb it, but the average income of a benefice was so low that it was practically impossible to ameliorate the situation. By the 1571 Canons, no minister was allowed to hold more than two benefices, which were to be not more than twenty-six miles distant from one another, though later this was extended to thirty miles. In some dioceses, Norwich, Oxford, and Worcester, for

---

[31] This analysis is based on the survey in Peel, *The Seconde Parte of a Register*, II, 130-42. In the 'Survay' as a whole, 565 parsons held 1,933 livings as non-residents.

instance, the canon seems to have been observed, though even at the end of the reign, the situation in the country generally remained acute.[32] Radical Oxford preachers frequently inveighed against non-resident pluralists. This was one of the principal points at issue in the 1586 sermon campaign.[33] John Reynolds warned his congregation not to send others to their parishes as vicars or deputies, but to work in them themselves. He refused to countenance the occupation of a living with cure of souls by a resident member of the university. A benefice, he protested, was not to be regarded as a supplementary source of income and fellows who had insufficient maintenance were urged to leave their colleges and return to their benefices, rather than leave their people without a pastor.[34]

Whilst Oxford opinion was divided between outright condemnation of plurality and limited defence of it as providing a means of maintaining resident members, puritan demands in the country grew in force. One of the puritan replies to the 1583 Articles demanded that the Archbishop should look into the carelessness of those pampered in universities and colleges, as well as in cathedrals and bishops' houses, and as chaplains to noblemen.[35] Throughout the latter part of the reign, bills were introduced to abolish plurality. In 1584, the bill passed the Commons, but was turned out in the Lords. A similar fate met bills introduced in 1589, 1601, 1604, 1610, 1621, and 1625. In 1589 a more detailed defence of the universities and of learning in general was mounted. An anonymous paper, after discussing the impairment which would be suffered by the cathedral churches and scholars, moves on to 'Hinderance of Learninge and the Universities'. Learning, it asserts, would decay if pluralities were totally abolished, rich men would not send their children to school because of the limited rewards of education, and poor men would be deprived of the help in education given by the clergy, particularly in the grammar schools. Secondly, the public readers in the universities and colleges would lack maintenance, unless they were able to

---

[32] Hill, *Economic Problems of the Church,* 226-7.
[33] See above, ch. VI.
[34] Reynolds, *Haggai,* 95!, 105!, 115! (= 103, 114, 124).
[35] Peel, *The Seconde Parte of a Register,* I, 182.

obtain the very small number of livings *sine cura*.[36] A further defence, probably of the same date, entitled 'Inconvenience to the Universities' protested, 'Who will bring up his child twenty years in divinity for the hope of one benefice and that small? This is the right way to an unlearned ministry.' Scholars, it argued, would not be able to proceed to higher degrees if forced to be resident in their benefices, since they would have no time for study, nor would they have the money to pay the fees for their degrees. The result would not only be undesirable; it would be socially dangerous. Here a new note sounded: 'grave men will be driven out of the universities and young men will come in, who are apt for innovations and contentions, and being unfurnished in livings are ready to supply their want by spoil of their colleges and making merchandise of scholarships and fellowships'.[37]

The Millenary Petition of 1603 raised the questions of a learned and resident ministry in a more acute form. The petitioners did not dismiss the universities, as radicals had done in the 1580s, but pleaded for sufficient ministers to be admitted to cures, for the removal of those who could not preach, and for an end to all non-residence. Those who held plurality of livings were to leave them.[38] University pluralists are not mentioned, but the framers of the Oxford *Answere*, the Vice-Chancellor, doctors, and proctors, realized that they were implicitly threatened by the proposals. They assured the petitioners that they desired nothing more than sufficient ministers and weekly sermons, though they would not agree that non-preaching ministers were in general insufficient. They agreed that the abolition of non-residents would be 'a matter of wise and sound deliberation', but indicated that it would adversely affect the universities, colleges, and cathedrals. The plan to abolish impropriations would also impoverish the university and make it contemptible. It would extinguish all future hope of that learned ministry which the petitioners claimed they desired for

---

[36] Inner Temple, Petyt MS 538, vol. 52, fo. 38ʳ.

[37] Inner Temple, Petyt MS 538, vol. 52, fo. 40ᵛ. For a further discussion of corruption in collegiate elections, see below, 193-6.

[38] *The Answere of the Vice Chancelour, the Doctors, both the Proctors and other the Heads of Houses in the University of Oxford* (Oxford, 1603), 3 (the *Answere's* reprint of the 'Humble Petition').

'do we not see ... where due reward of learning and liberal maintenance of Ministery is fraudulently impaired, or iniuriously taken away, there Religion and learning come to decay? There Atheisme Barbarisme and Confusion must needes ensue? In fact, the Oxford doctors replied, it was because there was sufficient maintenance, honour, and encouragement in the English universities, that there were more learned men in England than among all the ministers of religion in France, Flanders, Germany, Poland, Denmark, Scotland, and even Geneva—a thrust at those who were always comparing the English church with the superior state of the continental reformed churches.[39]

The two surviving puritan manuscript replies to the Oxford *Answere* refute these arguments and claim that the university was motivated in its opposition to the petitioners solely by consideration of its own financial disadvantage if their demands were implemented. They attacked the heads of houses, maintained in pomp and dignity, as drones who kept young students out of the university. The life-style of the Oxford heads required non-residence and plurality, but their founders had intended otherwise and had supposed that they would be examples to their students in sobriety and temperance, so that the young could be weaned from ambition and covetousness.[40] University men who complained that after twenty years of study they could not get a living should look to their learning, because some men in the church had more learning and experience in the things which belonged to the gospel.[41] Though they honoured the university, and some of them were university men, the preaching ministry could not be wronged in order to provide for the university, and in such a plentiful land which the Lord had blessed there could be room for both.[42]

Some of these issues were again raised at the Hampton Court Conference. The King maintained that the question of providing a resident, learned minister for every parish could

[39] Ibid., 14, 28-9, 31.
[40] BL, Additional MS 8978, fos. 54, 63. Bodleian Library, MS Bodley 124,143.
[41] MS Bodley 124, 29, 219.
[42] Ibid., 217.

not be resolved, because the universities could not yet provide a sufficient number.[43] In an anonymous account of the conference, written to favour the puritan cause, Reynolds's request for a preaching minister in every parish is met with the King's answer that he had already consulted with the bishops about the provision of preachers in those parishes where the minister could not preach; the doubly beneficed were to be resident in one of their cures and to maintain a preacher in the other.[44] However, Lord Chancellor Buckhurst seems to have taken the view that although there were livings which lacked men, there were also bachelors and masters in the universities pining for a living, while some men had two.[45]

Despite the social, economic, and ecclesiastical considerations which inhibited the placing of godly, resident, preaching ministers in the parishes, there are definite signs that by the end of the century the standard of education of the clergy, at least in some parts of the country, was improving. Oxford made its contribution. Other factors also played a part: the crown and diligent bishops made real efforts to improve the standard of those presented and ordained; and patrons, particularly those who had themselves received a university education, insisted on higher attainments. In London, by the 1590s, very few non-graduates were being instituted to a cure of souls, and this also applied to the university dioceses, Oxford and Ely. Increasingly, only graduates could escape from the requirement that men must be ordained in the diocese in which they were born or had been long resident, unless they had the bishop's letters dimissory, which were rarely granted.[46]

In the university itself, the number of those remaining to proceed to the higher degrees in divinity rose from 46 BDs and 23 DDs in 1571-80 to 169 BDs and 49 DDs in 1591-1600. Though no Oxford college had a statute like Mildmay's Emmanuel, forcing a fellow's withdrawal within a year of proceeding DD,

[43] W. Barlow, *The Summe and Substance of the Conference,* printed in Edward Cardwell, *A History of Conferences* (Oxford, 1849), 190.

[44] R. G. Usher, *The Reconstruction of the English Church* (New York, 1910), II, 346, from BL, Harleian MS 828, fo. 32.

[45] Usher, op. cit., II, 337, from Cambridge University Library, MS Mm.I.45., fos. 155-7.

[46] O'Day, *The English Clergy,* 5, 50, 52, 57.

some of the Oxford BDs and DDs must have found their way into the parishes.[47] Not all who proceeded from the universities had such high intellectual attainments, however. On 10 January 1589, Herbert Westphaling, Bishop of Hereford and once Canon of Christ Church, wrote to complain that some ignorant and unlearned men had been allowed to graduate to the disgrace of the university. Convocation set up a committee immediately and ruled that no undergraduate was to be made BA, and no BA was to incept, unless he could recite the Articles from memory and show them to be according to the sense of scripture.[48]

In the last two decades of the reign, there was definite advance in which some members of the university took pride and pleasure. Robert Wakeman of Balliol, put up by the Vice-Chancellor to preach on Act Sunday 1604, encouraged his hearers with these words: 'The Lord hath blessed our Church of *England* ... her maintenance although not so good as in former times (and I wish that it were bettered) yet farre exceeding the mercenary state of stipendiary churches. Her Temples glorious, her professors infinite, her ministers in numbers more, in knowledge more abundant.'[49] Godly Robert Bolton, of Brasenose, who had been converted as a member of the college, was not so easily convinced: 'I looked above me in this famous Universitie where I have lived, and saw many reverend and learned men, full of light of divine truth, and of the water of life, able glorioulie and comfortablie to illighten many darke places and drie soules in this land, readie to expire and powre out their souls in the bosome of their famous Nurce ... but if they might have honest and lawfull passage, readie and resolute to enlarge Christs kingdome abroad.'[50] While Bolton declared himself disinclined to accept preferment in the church, other Oxford men faced the perennial dilemma, whether to heed the allurements of learning, or bring light to the dark corners of the land. In the late sixteenth century, it was difficult to do both.

[47] These figures are based on the tables in Clark, *Register,* II, part ii, 410-14; Porter, *Puritanism in Tudor England,* 192-3.
[48] Clark, *Register,* II, part i, 169.
[49] R. Wakeman, *The Christian Practise* (Oxford, 1605), 63.
[50] Robert Bolton, *A Discourse about the State of True Happinesse* (London, 1611), sig. ¶ 3ᵛ.

Three nurseries: Brasenose, Queen's, and Exeter

Oxford could boast no seminaries like Mildmay's Emmanuel, but it was not without its nurseries for godly preachers. Three colleges in particular made an outstanding contribution to the provision of godly, learned, and resident ministers in the last two decades of the century. Each had its own catchment area: Brasenose, where many of the members were drawn from Lancashire and Cheshire, Queen's with interests in Cumberland and Westmorland, and Exeter with its links with the diocese of Exeter and the south-west in general.

Throughout Elizabeth's reign, the King's College and Hall of Brasenose was growing steadily in size. Between 1565 and 1612, its membership doubled from 102 to 227. In 1612, 145 of the members were commoners, indicative of the general growth in the fee-paying members of colleges.[51] Its strong connection with the north-west through the founder, William Smyth, a native of Lancashire, was reinforced by Alexander Nowell, a fellow of the college in Henry VIII's reign, who placed his grammar school at Middleton under the college's protection on its foundation in July 1572 and provided thirteen places at Brasenose for poor scholars. Earlier in the reign, the college had produced a substantial number of Jesuits and Catholic priests, many of them drawn from the religiously conservative Palatinate of Durham. The society seems to have flourished despite the neglect of the fourth principal, Richard Harris, who held office from 1574-95. At the end of his reign in 1590, seven of the fellows wrote to complain to the Bishop of Lincoln, the Visitor, about the disorders in 'your little commonwealth'. The college was in debt and disordered, but Harris maintained his place until 1595 when Alexander Nowell, then nearly 90, held the office for three months.[52]

In 1590, probably as a result of the complaints against Harris, the Bishop of Lincoln's commissary conducted a visitation. During this visitation, a letter, probably addressed to Sir Christopher Hatton, Chancellor of Oxford, urged the need for reform in the college. Its author, clearly a north-countryman, was principally concerned with the effect of the college on the

[51] J. Gutch, *Collectanea Curiosa*, I (Oxford, 1781), 197.
[52] Inner Temple, Petyt MS 538, vol. 10, fos. 10^v, 47^v.

ministry 'for that there is no other nourserie in the universitie to breed preachers and learned men for the service of that Cuntrey wherein the chief state of my Lyvinge lieth'.[53]. Dr R. C. Richardson, in his study of the diocese of Chester from the accession of Elizabeth to the Civil War, has convincingly demonstrated the importance of Brasenose in providing godly ministers for Lancashire and Cheshire. While the college furnished men who would return home to improve the state of their local ministry, it was, paradoxically, only graduates, through patronage and a wider field of influence, who were able to move outside their local areas.[54] According to Dr Richardson's survey between 1558 and 1642, there were 160 known puritan ministers in the diocese of Chester, though in this count, he includes many who were in no sense nonconformists, but were concerned principally with preaching the gospel and with the pastoral care of their parishes. Ninety-five of his total, that is, three-fifths, had been educated at the two universities, fifty-three in Cambridge and thirty-nine in Oxford.[55] Of the Oxford total, fourteen had been members of Brasenose, a much higher tally than any other college. Middleton Grammar School and Farnworth Grammar School furnished the college with a steady stream of candidates. Among the ministers trained in this nursery who returned to evangelize their own people were Christopher Harvey (BA 1581, MA 1585), minister at Bunbury in Cheshire, a parish later served by William Hinde of Queen's; Anthony Calcott (BA 1576, MA 1581), minister at Astbury, Cheshire; Robert Eaton (BA 1577, MA 1587), Rector of Mobberly, Cheshire from 1595 to 1621; and, in a slightly later generation, Nicholas Hulme (BA 1583, MA 1585), minister at Kirkham.[56]

Most of these ministers remain obscure local figures, but one or two emerge from the shadows. One such was William Massie, fellow from 1573, Vice-Principal 1582-3, and BD in 1586, two years before he forfeited his fellowship through marriage. Massie had been maintained at Brasenose by Sir Edward

[53] Inner Temple, Petyt MS 538, vol. 10, fo. 61.
[54] See O'Day, *The English Clergy*, 5.
[55] In the case of three, their university is uncertain.
[56] R. C. Richardson, *Puritanism in North-West England* (Manchester, 1972), 58-63, 186-7.

Trafford, and in September 1586 his patron summoned him to his Lancashire home to officiate at the marriage of his daughter. In an address encouraging the newly-married couple to adhere to the sound protestant religion and perform their religious duties, the preacher also turned to the task of the godly minister. Ministers, he maintained, were to preach by feeding, by hospitality, and by godliness of life. Preaching was their first priority and here John Jewel was his model. Massie was not above flattering his godly patron and encouraging others to be like him, for, he reminds the guests 'it is a great matter and of great importance, when princes, nobles and men of great worship be religious and geven to prayer and the holy service of God'.[57]

One of his contemporaries in Brasenose was William Leigh, who entered the college in 1571, was a fellow from 1573 to 1587, and Vice-Principal from 1584 to 1587. In 1587, he resigned to become Rector of Standish in Lancashire. He was one of the moderators in the Lancashire exercises but was evidently no nonconformist, since in October 1580, during the Archbishop of York's visitation of the northern province, he was one of those who certified that he used the Book of Common Prayer for divine service and no other.[58] At least seven of Leigh's sermons survive in print and an early one, published in 1608 under the title *The First Step towards Heaven, or Anna the Prophetesse*, was preached at Christmas for his parishioners in Standish. Leigh's godliness was not universally popular. 'Many a Sabboth have we sanctified with a double solemnity of prayer, praise and prophesie', he told them, but complained of the 'paucitie of professors, barenness of faith and the narrow way ... temporising with all', and warned them that 'our zeale is cold, our spirits are dumpish', while 'godliness is great gain, both in this life and in the life to come'. He admonished his parish 'go not into the streets, to haunt the Theaters', but rather make 'right use of prayer and fasting to refresh and inflame' their faith.[59] Not all Brasenose men returned to the

[57] W. Massie, *A sermon preached at Trafford in Lancashire at the marriage of a daughter of the right worshipfull Sir Edmund Trafforde* (Oxford, 1586), sigs. A 4ʳ, A 6ʳ, A 8ʳ, B 7ʳ.

[58] Strype, *Annals*, II, part ii, 547; Historical Manuscripts Commission, *14th Report*, Appendix, Part IV, 'The Manuscripts of Lord Kenyon' (London, 1894), 597-8.

[59] W. Leigh, *The First Step towards Heaven, or Anna the Prophetesse* (London, 1608), sig. A 6ʳ⁻ᵛ; pp. 14, 17, 24, 26, 42, 74, 80.

north-west. William Fletcher (or Fleshware), a Cheshire man, who matriculated in 1576, remained as a fellow until 1594, but also held several Northamptonshire livings. He was a member of the Northamptonshire *classis* and is at least one example of a puritan minister remaining in the university while he held a parochial cure of souls.[60]

In a later generation, a man of great religious fervour became the director of young divines in the college. Thomas Peacock was born in Cheshire in 1571, went up to Brasenose in 1589, was elected fellow in 1594, and served as Vice-Principal from 1608, resigning the year before his death in 1611. More is known of him in his dying than in his living, since one of his pupils, Robert Bolton, set down *The Last Conflicts and Death of Mr. Thomas Peacock*. On his death-bed John Dod from Hanwell, Henry Airay, and some of the fellows of the college tried to solace Peacock in his spiritual trials, pointing to the good effect he had had upon his scholars and his diligence as a teacher: 'Consider what would have become of many of them if you had not taken them.' But Peacock was not to be consoled and replied, 'Better, farre, better.'[61] Edward Bagshawe, who published Peacock's *Conflicts* in 1646, also wrote the life of his pupil, Robert Bolton, published in 1632. He describes his humble parentage, his aptness as a scholar, and consequent entry into the grammar school in his native Blackburn. At the age of 20 in 1592, he went up to Lincoln College, but later removed to Brasenose, drawn by the fellowships there for Lancashire and Cheshire men. He was, says Bagshawe, 'very learned, yet he was not good, he was a very meane scholler in the schoole of Christ, he drew no religious breath from the soyle he came'. He dabbled with papism, and 'he could not abide their company that were of a strict and holy conversation, such he would fetch within the compasse of puritans, thinking by that lawlesse name he had deprived them *ipso facto* both of learning and of good religion'. He heard Perkins at Cambridge, but called him 'a barren empty fellow and passing mean scholar'. No doubt Bagshawe emphasized the profligacy

---

[60] PRO Star Chamber 5A 49/34; H. I. Longden, *Northamptonshire and Rutland Clergy from 1500*, V (Northampton, 1940), 57.

[61] Edward Bagshawe, *The Last Conflicts and Death of Mr. Thomas Peacock* (London, 1646), 17, 21-4, sig. A 2^{r-v}.

of his subject before his conversion in 1608 through Peacock's agency. In 1609, at the age of 37, he became a minister and was presented by Sir Augustine Nicholls to the living of Broughton in Northamptonshire. He wore himself out in study and service of the distressed, and refused all preferment. He prayed six times a day, preached twice on Sunday, and catechized in the afternoon, sparing the sins of none, small or great. Here indeed is the model.[62]

'Invenit destructum, reliquit extructum et instructum.' So runs the tribute to Henry Robinson inscribed upon the walls of his college in the memorial brass in Queen's College Chapel. Robinson, Provost from 1581 until 1599, and his successor, Henry Airay, Elijah and Elisha as contemporaries conceived them, rebuilt the college so that, from being in a state of decay and emptiness, it was able to assume from Magdalen the mantle of principal nursery for godly ministers. Professor Patrick Collinson has argued that Robinson has not attracted the attention he deserves, as a moderate puritan, bearing the same relationship to the cause as Reynolds in Oxford and Whitaker and Some in Cambridge.[63] While there is no doubt that radical protestants looked to Robinson for support, his chief concerns were with the regularization of collegiate and later of diocesan discipline and administration, and with evangelization, pastoral care, and the placing of godly ministers. The Queen's memorial shows him in rochet and chimere, in his left hand his pastoral staff, its crook enclosing an eye and bearing the motto *'Corrigendo, sustenando'*. Three sheep-folds to his right represent his flock as chief pastor. They are illuminated by a candle, held in his right hand, whose rays diffuse the legend, 'To give light to them that sit in darkness.' The sheep are under the control of three dogs, one of which is held by a leash bearing the inscription', 'As bound, yet free.' Here we have the most important clue to Robinson's character and achievement.

Henry Robinson was elected a fellow of Queen's in 1575 and became Provost on 5 May 1581.[64] As Principal of St. Edmund

---

[62] *Mr. Boltons last and learned worke. Of the last four things. With his life* [by E. Bagshawe], 5-9, 12-20.

[63] Collinson, thesis cit., 1081.

[64] He was confirmed in office four days later by the Visitor, Archbishop Sandys of York. Queen's College Oxford, Muniments, Register H, p. 31.

Hall, then in the college's gift, from 1576, he had already established himself as administrator and reformer. In Queen's, the financial fortunes of the college were placed on a firmer foundation when Robinson restored the copyholds, previously in the hands of the provosts, to the common fund. Through the agency of Walsingham, whose help he had first engaged in 1582, he obtained a new royal charter for the college in 1585, which freed the society from the anxiety of earlier years, providing greater security to resist challenges to the college's title to lands.[65] Robinson also improved the buildings, in particular, refurbishing the library with Grindal's collection.[66] As early as 1573, Grindal had encouraged the college to reform its tutorial arrangements and the 'Liber Sponsorum' was begun, which provided a formal personal and financial arrangement between a tutor and his students by which the fellow made himself responsible for his pupil's battels.[67] In 1583, Grindal made the college a substantial endowment for scholarships and forged a link with his new school at St. Bees in Cumberland. From this year, the college was to elect a Grindal fellow, 'born or sprung' from Cumberland or Westmorland, who was to receive twenty shillings annually over and above the normal fellows' portion. Grindal also provided two closed scholarships from St. Bees, or, failing a supply, from the two counties.[68] This additional local connection ensured a continuing tradition of godly ministers for the north-west.

Robinson's concern, as provost and bishop, was with the evangelization of the dark corners of the land through the provision of a resident, pastoral, preaching ministry. Shortly after his consecration as Bishop of Carlisle, he wrote to Burghley, reporting that 'the moste part of the gentlemen of the Countrey gave good tokens of soundness in religion and the poorer sort were generally willing to hear but pitifully ignorant of the foun-

---

[65] SP 12/156/31 December 1582. Provost and fellows to Walsingham, seeking the charter, January 1585, SP 12/176/17.

[66] See above, 96-7.

[67] Part of the 'Liber Sponsorum' is to be found in Queen's College Oxford, Muniments, Register G, 289-316.

[68] Queen's College Oxford, Muniments, G. 1, a late sixteenth century copy of the agreement between Grindal and Robinson, 30 June 1583. See also Muniments, G. 2a, G. 2b, G. 3, G. 4.

dations of Christianity'. The fundamental difficulty was 'weaknes and carlesnes of the Ministry ... some few verie commendable both for knowledge and conscience, but the number verie small'. Most, he complained, were unlearned and careless, hampered by the very large number of impropriate livings served by stipendiary curates and the distance of many homes from the parish church. Superstition and popery abounded.[69] Robinson also maintained a continual correspondence with his successor, frequently lamenting the state of his diocese. In May 1601, probably during a progress around the parishes, he wrote 'I come now from Crosthwate where the sight of so great a people hath made my heart heavy, that they should by a sacrilegious lease be kept without a shepheard that can feede them.'[70] Here was a root cause of much frustration, not only in the diocese of Carlisle, but throughout the Elizabethan church.

Airay had been Robinson's trusted lieutenant for many years before he succeeded him as Provost in 1599. One of the unfortunate results of the new royal charter was that the Queen now claimed the right to appoint the Provost and only after lengthy negotiations was the right of the fellows reasserted.[71] Airay's memorial brass in the chapel, a companion piece to Robinson's, also gives a clear impression of his character and achievement. Foremost among its rich symbolism is Elisha assuming the mantle of Elijah and praying for a double portion of his spirit. Airay himself is pictured kneeling on an altar tomb. At his right hand is a scroll on which are inscribed the words, 'Abuse brings judgment after it', perhaps a vindication of Airay against the accusations brought against him for his 'preciseness'. Christopher Potter, Airay's successor but one, describes, him, in his preface to the *Lectures on Philippians,* as a man who 'condemned himselfe to obscuritie and affected a private and retired life, yet he could not hide himself from the eyes of the world'. It is Airay's pastoral qualities he stresses: his holiness, integrity, learning, and gravity and his 'indefatigable paines in the discharge of his ministeriall function'. He praises

[69] F. O. White, *The Lives of the Elizabethan Bishops* (London, 1898), 387-8.
[70] Queen's College Oxford, Muniments, G. 15, 5 May 1601.
[71] Queen's College Oxford, Muniments, 2.T.43, 8 October 1598.

his 'singular wisdom and dexterity in the government of our college which ... hath sent forth many learned Ministers into the Church, many worthy Gentlemen into the Commonwealth'. He defends Airay against the charge of 'preciseness', claiming that he was 'zealous and fervent, not turbulent and contentious', seeking only to condemn the separatists and oppose all faction and superstition.[72]

To this succession of provosts, a third figure must be added. John Reynolds took up residence in the college, as a fee-paying guest, in 1586 and remained there until he became President of Corpus in 1598. He seems to have been a tutor and retained many friends and pupils, to judge by the list of the Queen's men in his bequest of books in 1607.[73] His friendship with Airay is attested by William Hinde, who matriculated in the year that Reynolds came to the college. In his preface to Reynolds's *The Discovery of the Man of Sinne*, dedicated to Airay and published in 1614, Hinde wrote, 'I know, Sir, you are no stranger, neither to the Tree, nor fruit, having formerly dwelt together under one roofe, drank togither of one Cisterne, and mutually reioiced togither in all offices of duty and love.'[74]

Hinde himself was one of the most important of the godly preachers produced by the college in this period. Reynolds probably exerted a greater influence over him than Robinson and Hinde published his sermons on *The Prophecie of Obadiah* as well as *The Discovery of the Man of Sinne*. He was elected fellow in 1594 and remained in Queen's until about 1603, when he became minister at Bunbury in Cheshire, where he stayed until his death twenty years later. His chief concern seems to have been the moral and spiritual life of his small community; for their benefit he wrote *A Path to Pietie, Leading to the Way, the Truth, the Life Christ Jesus,*[75] a catechism with a lengthy concluding section on prayer. His *A Briefe and Plaine Catechism ... for the good of both young and olde*[76] is more polemical in tone, as is *The Office and Use of the Moral Law*[77] which confutes antinomian views. Not only

---

[72] Airay, *Philippians*, sig. A 3.
[73] Bodleian Library, MS Wood D 10. Wood, *Annals*, II, 294-5. The longest lists of recipients are significantly in Magdalen, Corpus, Brasenose, and Queen's.
[74] Reynolds, *The Discovery of the Man of Sinne*, sig. ¶ 2[r-v].
[75] Oxford, 1613.
[76] London, 1620.
[77] London, 1623.

did Hinde himself typify the godly minister; he wrote a blueprint for the godly layman in his *A Faithfull Remonstrance, the Holy Life and Happy Death of John Bruen.*[78]

Some of Hinde's contemporaries in Queen's also represent the model of the resident, preaching, and pastorally-minded minister. George Benson from Westmorland, who matriculated in 1585, eventually forsook his native north-west to become Rector of Rock in Worcestershire in 1607. His only published work, a 1609 Paul's Cross sermon, shows his pastoral zeal, his desire that men should hold fast to a godly minister, 'the man whose prayers and preachings are countermines for your defence against the enemy'.[79] John Aglionby, who came up to Queen's from Cumberland in 1583, was appointed by the college as Principal of St. Edmund Hall. He was later a royal chaplain and one of the translators of the New Testament for the Authorized Version. Richard Crakanthorpe was his exact contemporary, fell under the influence of Reynolds and returned his master's loyalty after his death, defending him against the charges of nonconformity in ecclesiastical ceremonies.[80]

Not all Crakanthorpe's contemporaries could have been so successfully defended. Bernard Robinson, fellow from 1582 to 1593, was in trouble before the Vice-Chancellor in 1591 for preaching a disorderly sermon.[81] He eventually returned to his native Cumberland to become Vicar of Torpenhoe and a canon in Robinson's cathedral. John Shaw, matriculated in 1579, was deprived of his living at Woking for some unspecified nonconformity in 1596. Simon Wastel, Shaw's contemporary in Queen's, who became master of the free school at Northampton about 1592 and gained a considerable reputation as a teacher, translated and published Shaw's *Bibliorum Summula* in 1623, commemorating his school friend of fifty years before in Westmorland and his contemporary in Queen's by 'this book I saw much applauded by the godly learned ministers and many other scholars'.[82] His translation, entitled, *The True Christians*

---

[78] London, 1641; on Bruen, see below, 199-200.

[79] G. Benson, *A Sermon Preached at Paules Cross* (London, 1609), 17.

[80] R. Crakanthorpe, *Defensio Ecclesiae Anglicanae* (1625), reprinted in *The Library of Anglo-Catholic Theology* (Oxford, 1847), 458-9.

[81] See above, 150.

[82] S. Wastell, *The True Christians Daily Delight* (London, 1623), sig. A 4^r.

Daily Delight is a summary in verse of every chapter of the Bible, devised for easy memorizing, presumably for children. Another contemporary was Thomas Wilson, who matriculated in 1581 and for whom Robinson seems to have obtained the living of St. George the Martyr, Canterbury, in 1586. He remained there for the rest of his life, preaching, it was said, three or four sermons a week. He was in particular demand among the godly of his parish and was more than once in trouble with the Archbishop for his nonconformity.[83] Wilson was a rigid double predestinarian. His 1611 treatise, *Jacobs Ladder,* is a practical outline of the process by which the elect and the reprobate respond to God's eternal and unchanging purpose.[84] Wilson was probably more famous for his *Christian Dictionary,* first published in 1612, which ran to several editions and was the first attempt in English to provide a concordance of the Scriptures.

Under Henry Airay's provostship, the college continued to provide a steady stream of ministers for the north-west. David Hechstetter, who supported Airay in his troubles with Vice-Chancellor Howson in 1603, became Vicar of Brough-under-Stainmore in 1611. Thomas Jackson, later Bishop of Winchester, began his parish ministry at St. Thomas's, Newcastle. Lancelot Dawes, son of poor parents from Barton Kirk in Westmorland, came, like so many of his contemporaries, as a servitor and rose up through the ranks as tabarder and scholar to a fellowship in 1605. In 1608, he was presented to the living of his home village and eventually became a canon of Carlisle in 1619. His sermon *God Mercies and Ierusalems Miseries,* preached at Paul's Cross in June 1609, was published with a dedication to Robinson. Dawes claims that the small flock of Christ can be distinguished by the preaching of the word and the right use of the sacraments, but encourages individuals to examine themselves further to see if they belong to the elect.[85] Thomas Sutton followed a similar route to Dawes. Born at Bampton in Westmorland, he became *pauper puer serviens* at Queen's in 1602, successively

---

[83] *DNB.*

[84] T. Wilson, *Jacobs Ladder, or a short treatise laying forth distinctly the several degrees of Gods eternall purpose, whereby his grace descends upon the elect, and the elect ascend to the predestinate glory* (London, 1611), 4-5.

[85] L. Dawes, *Gods Mercies and Ierusalems Miseries* (London, 1609), sig. E 2^{r-v}.

tabarder and fellow, then lecturer at St. Helen's, Abingdon, minister of Culham, and lecturer at St. Mary Overie in Southwark. His sermons, *Englands Summons* and *Englands Second Summons,* which frequently quote Zanchius, warn that 'the profession of religion without zeale and forwardnesse is odious and loathsome to God'.[86]

Most significant perhaps among all the godly preachers from Queen's in this period is Robert Mandevil. Another Cumberland man, he retired into St. Edmund Hall on taking his BA in 1600 and eventually became Vicar of the university's living at Holme Cultram in 1607. His most famous writing, entitled *Timothies Task, or a Christian Sea-Card,*[87] consists of two addresses given to the diocesan synod at Carlisle, where Mandevil seems to have been used by Robinson to address the godly ministers. He stresses the quality of life required if a minister is to be an example to his people: his faithfulness in affliction, the profit he may reap through the faithful discharge of his duties, his self-forgetfulness, his patience in adversity, his triumph against the wiles of Rome, and his care for the eternal safety of his flock. No better model could have been supplied of the type of minister which for over thirty years two provosts of Queen's had laboured to produced.

The transformation of Exeter College from a religiously conservative society in the first two decades of the reign into a seminary for godly ministers for the West Country may be dated from the election of Thomas Glasier as Rector in October 1578. Glasier and his successor, Thomas Holland, built up the membership of the college and gave it a wider territorial interest. In this, they were assisted by the new fellowships founded by Sir William Petre in 1566, so that the old West Country catholics gradually found themselves overtaken by new fellows from Somerset, Dorset, Oxfordshire, and Essex. The college grew rapidly in size; in 1541 there were only four MAs, and in 1572 only twenty-four. By the time that John Prideaux became Rector in 1612, the college had come to occupy fifth place in numerical order in the university, after

---

[86] T. Sutton, *Englands Second Summons* (London, 1615), 41.
[87] Oxford, 1619.

Christ Church, Magdalen, Queen's, and Brasenose, all of them staunchly protestant colleges.[88]

Even during its most conservative days at the beginning of the reign, the college had nourished some zealous preachers. John Chardon, elected in 1565, eventually became a canon of Exeter and Bishop of Down and Connor in 1596. It was not until the last decade of the century, however, that Exeter produced a series of distinguished preachers. Daniel Price, who had moved to Exeter from St. Mary's Hall before taking his BA in 1601, was well known as a champion of the anti-papist cause, and as royal chaplain to Prince Henry and James I was much favoured as a court preacher. Edward Chetwynd, sojourner in the college from 1592, became public preacher at Abingdon and was well known in the surrounding area. On the recommendation of Reynolds and Airay, he became public preacher at Bristol in 1607 and in 1612 published *The Strait Gate and Narrow Way to Life*, which is particularly critical of those who allow their assurance of election to 'belch out that damned poison, drawn by the Atheistical Spider, from the most fragant flower of Gods eternall Predestination'.[89] On the reputation of his preaching, he was advanced to be Chaplain to Queen Anne in 1613, and in 1616, the year he proceeded DD, he became Dean of Bristol. Another exceptional preacher was Nicholas Byfield, who came to the college at the age of 17 in 1596. He became a public preacher at Chester and was a strong proponent of the cause of Sabbath observance. His treatise *The Signes, or an Essay Concerning the Assurance of Gods Love and Man Salvation* lists sixteen infallible signs to distinguish the true child of God.

Preaching at the dedication of the new college chapel of St. James in 1624, Rector Prideaux looked back on the generation of alumni of the college in Holland's day. He speaks of his eminent predecessor as the father of so many bishops and doctors and a 'knot of noted scholars', among whom he names Chetwynd and Price. The sermon is dedicated to Dr George Hakewell, who came to Exeter in 1595, subsequently spent four years at Heidelberg, and was Archdeacon of Surrey before succeeding Prideaux as Rector in 1642. Hakewell and his con-

---

[88] Gutch, *Collectanea Curiosa*, I, 199.
[89] E. Chetwynd, *The Strait Gate* (London, 1612), 126.

temporaries, Prideaux reflects, lived 'under the moderation especially of that painfull and judicious Director, Mr William Helme ... ever with thankfulness of me to be remembered', with whom he joins in 'godly emulation of industrious study and joynt care for the Colledge good ... those two religious and constant Preachers, M. William Orford and M. Isaiah Farrington'.[90] Orford proceeded BD in 1594 and retired to the Devon rectory of Clyst Hedon; Farrington, a Devon man, remained until 1604, when he became Rector of Lympstone.

This golden era provided the diocese of Exeter with many preachers. From 1600, Thomas Denys was for thirty-seven years Rector of Menheniot. He had been preceded in the living by the Marian exile, Richard Tremayne, and Reginald Bellot, both graduates of the college. Anthony Lampthorne, elected from Devon in 1593, became Rector of Lanrake, Cornwall in 1600 and was deprived of a Herefordshire living in 1634, presumably for puritan sympathies, since the Westminster Assembly named him Rector of Sedgefield, Durham. William Wylshman, matriculated in 1587, became Vicar of Dartmouth in 1606. Three sermons which he preached there were published in 1616 under the title *The Sincere Preacher*. They complain of impropriations, unlearned ministers, and those who do not have the wit to reprove their people, or those parishes which secure preachers who please them by paying them voluntary contributions. He also warns against the dangers of avarice and ambition in a preacher.[91] His senior contemporary, Robert Wolcombe, who matriculated in 1584, became Vicar of Chudleigh, Devon in 1600. His principal work, *A Glasse for the Godly*, contains a series of treatises which combine exhortation, moral encouragement, and assurance.[92] The college also produced a number of nonconformists. Edward Birdall, matriculated 1585, Vicar of Abbots Kerswell, Devon, Thomas Deane, matriculated 1575, Rector of Milton Damerel, Devon, and William Huish, matriculated 1575 or 1578, Rector of Kilkhampton, Cornwall, all appear in the list of 'resolute

[90] John Prideaux, *Certaine Sermons* (Oxford, 1637), sermon of 5 October 1624, sigs. T 8ᵛ, V 1ʳ.
[91] W. Wylshman, *The Sincere Preacher* (London, 1616), 23, 35, 61.
[92] London, 1612.

Puritane ministers' which Melancthon Jewel brought up to London in December 1604.[93]

These three colleges, largely by reason of long-standing territorial interests, were, by the end of Elizabeth's reign, producing a steady stream of ministers for the remoter parts of the realm. The majority were marked out less by ecclesiastical nonconformity than by devotion to their parishes, reproving and nourishing their flocks, teaching by example and family life as much as by word.

[93] SP 14/10A/81.

VIII

A NURSERY FOR THE GODLY: VIRTUE AND VICE IN UNDERGRADUATE SOCIETY

Your Colleges they are seminaries of pietie, nurseries of Religion and vertue, and like the house of Bethel, or the garden of Eden, they are the verie houses of God, and pleasant gardens of the Lord, the trees of knowledge and the trees of life...And I pray God to blesse and multiplie such blessed plants in your Colleges.[1]

The preacher nominated by the Vice-Chancellor to address the assembled university on Act Sunday would have failed in his duty had he omitted the customary eulogy of his Alma Mater. On 12 July 1607, Richard Crakanthorpe, once fellow of Queen's, returning to Oxford from his Essex rectory of Black Notley, did not disappoint. His sermon contains more than kindly words of praise, the establishment of an ideal. It is a call to the sanctification of mind and understanding, of will and affections, such as must be found in the elect of God, lest weeds grow up in the university. Yet even Crakanthorpe is forced to admit that 'the onely perfection of men in this life [is] to know and acknowledge their owne imperfection'.[2] Imperfection is the constant refrain of these years: the failure of colleges to fulfil the intentions of their godly founders, a prevailing sense of decline from a more virtuous past, and the zeal of a few marked men who judged their contemporaries by the unrelenting standards of their tender consciences and found them wanting.

In January 1583, when Leicester wrote to his university, all was far from well. 'In your Conversation and Life', remarked the Chancellor, 'are these things noted. Excesse in apparell, as silke and velvet, and cutt dubletts, hose, deepe ruffs and such like, like unto or rather exceeding, both Inns of Courte men and Courtiers. The Haunting of the Towne, that the streets are every daye and all day longe more full of Schollers then

---

[1] Richard Crakanthorpe, *A Sermon of Sanctification* (London, 1608), 18-19.
[2] Ibid., 25.

Townsmen. That Ordinary Tables and Ale-houses, growen to great number, are not yet so many as they be full fraight all daye and much of the night, with Schollers tipling, dicing, carding, tabling and I will not saye worse occupied.'[3] Excessive display in dress seems to have been one of the endemic problems of the age; complaints had been made in 1576 and Hatton was reiterating them in 1590.[4] One vociferous critic, the author of the 1584 letter known as *Leycesters Commonwealth*, blamed the Chancellor himself for the destruction of the university, the breakdown of its discipline, and the spoliation of its farms, woods, and benefices.[5]

Leicester was by no means the only member of the society to complain about its state of life; the last two decades of the century are replete with cries for reform of the university and of individual colleges. John Reynolds, preaching in the mid-1580s, compared the state of Oxford unfavourably with the school of Christ in Geneva. No whoring, dancing, drunkenness, or beggars, he protested, should be found in any city, but in Oxford all was not well. How could it be hoped that 'we should find no dancing; when there are dancing-schooles in the chief Cities? ... no gamesters, while there are divers publiquely permitted not onely in houses in the Towne, but also in Halls and Colledges of the University.'[6] Sebastian Benefield reminded his congregation in January 1598 of Oxford's need for repentance, for 'were shee so fruitfull in good works, as shee ought to be, there could be no such report of her as there is; of *ignorance* in her Citizens, of *corruption* of her Colleges, of *idlenes* and *loosenes* of life in her seniors, of *wilfull, impudent* and *contemptuous behaviour* in her juniors'.[7]

Other men interpreted the disasters of the natural world as signs of God's wrath against the university. James Bisse, fellow of Magdalen, preaching at Paul's Cross on 8 January 1580, reflected on the evils of the time: 'Never more supplanting ...

---

[3] Leicester to the university, 25 January 1583, OUA/NEP *supra*/Register L, fos. 232-3; Wood, *Annals*, II, 213.

[4] Wood, *Annals*, II, 184-5, 242; C. E. Mallet, *A History of the University of Oxford*, II (London, 1924), 120.

[5] *The copie of a leter* (= *Leycesters Commonwealth*) (London, 1584), 78-80.

[6] Reynolds, *Haggai*, 5.

[7] Benefield, *The Sinne against the Holy Ghost Discovered*, 43. See also Airay, *Philippians*, 833-4.

never more whoring, never more building, I meane not the building of Colledges, or almes houses or schooles, there was never lesse ... never more building of private houses which wee think shall continue for ever.'[8] England, Bisse continued, was ripe in hypocrisy, and the university was not spared: 'Whom did the Lord smite down in that terrible plague in Oxford, not mockers of Gods servantes ... but the most religious, zealous, the godliest, the strongest, the best learned ... the chosen men that were in Oxford.' Plague struck Oxford in 1571 and in October 1575.[9] In July 1577, during the Assizes, 'there arose such an infectious damp or breath among the people' that in five weeks in July and August, 510 people died, including one of the Assize judges and 100 scholars. Every college and hall was affected and nearly all the heads of houses and doctors fled.[10] There was another outbreak of plague in April 1579, and on 6 April 1580 an earthquake rocked the university.[11] *Memento mori* was still a watchword. A contemporary versifier wrote of these distracted times. Death speaks:

> Thinke you that I dare not come to Schooles,
>   Where all the cunning Clerks be most;
> Take not I away both Clerks and fooles?
>   And am I not in every coast?
> Assure your selves no creature can
>   Make death afraid of any man,
> Or know my coming where or when.[12]

Not all the young men were utterly given over to god-lessness. In Magdalen, young George Wilton could write of 'many both faythfull and paynefull laborers in the lords harvest in our colledge', yet they were an oasis in a parched land, for, Wilton admitted, there was a famine 'not of bread and water, nor of riches and possessions, of pearls and pretiouse stones, but a famine and scarcity of the word of God, of that heavenly

[8] Bisse, *Two Sermons*, sig. A 4ᵛ, B 7ᵛ. See also Thomas Brasbridge, fellow of Magdalen, 1561-75, *The Poore Mans Iewell, that is to say, a treatise of pestilence* (London, 1578), sig. B iiiiʳ.

[9] Wood, *Annals*, II, 170, 179.

[10] Wood, *Annals*, II, 188-91; on plague in general, see L. F. Hirst, *The Conquest of Plague* (Oxford, 1953).

[11] Wood, *Annals*, II, 195, 198-9

[12] Ibid., 189.

Manna, the food of our soules, the want of the iewell and treasure'.[13] Wilton's spiritual notions are conventional enough, but they demonstrate his hope that the small and ordered collegiate societies might still provide an example of that higher standard of Christian practice and discipline for which they were so well adapted in theory and by statute.

The statutory curriculum provided little scope for training in godliness, since divines and laymen were all brought up together in the Arts faculty, some staying the minimum of four years to proceed to the BA, others remaining a further three years for the MA. Formally, at least, the inculcation of godly living was based on the catechetical lectures and on attendance at sermons, and only those proceeding to the higher degrees in divinity attended the theological disputations. The religious upbringing of an undergraduate depended, therefore, in large measure on the careful choice of a college and a tutor, often made by local contact before a young man came up to Oxford. John Reynolds was evidently one of the body of trusted tutors. His *Letter to his Friend* resembles the master plan for a godly young man, in this case one seeking ordination. At the outset, Reynolds makes it clear that true divinity is to be carefully distinguished from formal study: 'God forbid you should thinke divinity consists of words, as wood doth of trees, divinity without godlinesse doth but condemne consciences against the day of vengeance.' True divinity is rather a matter of the disposition of the heart and mind, for 'shall he ever perswade others to embrace godlinesse, that hath not perswaded himselfe that it is a pearle to be redeemed with all treasures?'. Prayer and meditation are the principal ways to knowledge of God, but linguistic skills can also be of use. The study of Hebrew and Greek is encouraged, but examination of the Scriptures, with the aid of Calvin's *Institutes* and the writings of Peter Martyr is to lead to meditation, not speculation. Above all, persistence will be needed. Reynolds does not hesitate to repove his protégé: 'You have bin too much carried away by means of company, from earnest travaile to your study, to sweet inticements of the flesh, seeing of vain spectacles, overmuch eating and drinking, banqueting, frequenting of the town, deliting to

---

[13] Magdalen College Oxford MS 617, 41-2.

vanity, resorting to tavernes, forgetting the word of God ...
they have made you to neglect your profit in study, they have
hurt your wit, weakened your memory, corrupted your good
desire, stained your manners ... but yet I thank God that they
have not put out the lively sparks of Gods spirit in you.'[14]

A later sermon from Reynolds draws a distinction between
the performance of outward ceremonies and the offering of the
soul and body: 'How many of us are there that do not come to
the outward service of God, so as they ought? I refer it to every
mans conscience to consider how they frequent the assemblies
for prayer and divine service in their private Colleges, but for
the comming at the beginning of tearms, when as we are by
oath and conscience bound thereto, how slackly is that done, if
done at all?'[15] Sebastian Benefield offers more practical advice,
for since 'God would not have us be idle and carelesse, he hath
appointed certaine exercises for us as good helpes for our deny-
ing our selves'. These he lists as prayer, daily and serious
meditation of our professions and vocations, contrasting the
state of this world with things celestial and eternal, and the
careful breeding of a man from childhood. He laments that the
university does not always encourage this growth, for many
scholars and young gentlemen come 'well nurtured full of
tokens of sobrietie and modesty; which staying here a short
time ... their manners are lost'.[16]

Apart from the sermon, the most important fixed element
in the religious upbringing of an undergraduate was the
catechetical lecture. The principal intention of the 1579
Catechetical Statute was to extirpate heresy and fence off the
young from its dangers. Its stated secondary aim was to instruct
the young in true piety.[17] Unfortunately, the office of catechist
seems to have been regarded as a lowly occupation and frequently colleges and halls employed an outsider, rather than
assigning one of their own number. Merton was an exception; a

[14] Reynolds, *A Letter of Dr. Reinolds to his Friend, Concerning his Advice for the Studie of
Divinitie* (London, 1613), sig. A 4^{r-v}, A 5^{r-v}, A 7^{r-v}, A 8^v, A 9^r, A 10^{r-v}, A 11^{r-v}.
[15] Reynolds, *Haggai*, 151! (= 161).
[16] Sebastian Benefield, *Eight Sermons* (Oxford, 1614), 15-17. See also Airay, *Philippians*, 110-11, 120-3. For the regulation of sermons in the university, see above,
ch. VI; and for a discussion of the place of the sermon in later Elizabethan Oxford,
see below Ch. IX.
[17] Clark, *Register*, II, part i, 155.

fellow was appointed at the annual stipend of £3. Thomas
Bryzenden was catechist in October 1589, Thomas White in
October 1591, and the later celebrated Francis Mason, while
still a junior fellow, was appointed in 1593.[18] Earlier in the
reign, Edmund Bunny, who was elected fellow in 1565 and
became Grindal's chaplain at York in 1570, is recorded as
visiting Oxford from time to time, to preach and catechize the
young, especially in All Saints' Church, where many came and
took notes and were induced to take orders by his holiness of
life and soundness of doctrine.[19] In the halls, the foreign protestant refugees filled the posts of catechists, at least for the early
years after the passing of the statute.[20]

Little is known of the method of the catechists, though some
evidence can be gathered from the Heidelberg Catechism, one
of the works prescribed in 1579. The popularity of this
catechism in the university is attested by the many editions, in
1587, 1589, 1591, 1595, and 1601 of *The Summe of Christian
Religion,* the English translation by Henry Parry, fellow of
Corpus and Jacobean Bishop of Gloucester, of Ursinus's lectures on the catechism, designed to resolve controversial questions. This volume, so frequently reprinted, bears all the marks
of a standard Oxford textbook. There was no lack of other
catechetical material available. Over eighteen printed and
seventeen manuscript catechisms are known to have been circulating in Elizabeth's reign, of which the most popular was
that of Alexander Nowell, also among those prescribed in
1579.[21]

The 1579 Statute ordered that these catechisms were to be
used by all juniors in the university and those without degrees,
and instruction was to be provided privately by tutors and
publicly in halls and colleges by the appointed catechists.
Annual examination was ordered and anyone negligent of the
rudiments, in the opinion of the head of his house, was to
be sent up for punishment by the Vice-Chancellor. A unique

---

[18] *Registrum Annalium Collegii Mertonensis, 1567-1603,* 249, 264, 280, 285, 297, 313, 316, 320.

[19] Wood, *Athenae Oxonienses,* II, cols. 219-24.

[20] For further details, see above, 85-7.

[21] For an analysis of the theological content of the catechism and other works prescribed in 1579, see above, ch. IV.

insight into the methods and content of the catechetical lectures of one of the catechists is revealed in the *Epistola Beati Pauli* which Antonio del Corro published in 1581. Corro was catechist in Gloucester Hall, Hart Hall, and St. Mary's Hall, all three religiously conservative. Leicester seems to have provided him with help again, and Corro's new-found willingness to conform, without involvement in theological wrangles, may have helped him to secure appointment as Censor Theologiae at Christ Church, a post which he took over from Lawrence Humphrey at Michaelmas 1578.[22] Corro's *Epistola Beati Pauli* is a summary in dialogue form of the lectures which he had originally delivered as Reader at the Temple Church in 1574, and published as the *Dialogus Theologicus*. According to its author, it is to be used in conjunction with the Prayer Book catechism. In the first of the two prefaces, addressed to the Vice-Chancellor and heads, Corro explains his wish that the young should be brought up in the knowledge of Christ and the pure understanding of the gospel, while at the same time studying languages, humane disciplines, and liberal arts. His dialogue, he continues, has been so devised that it can be recited alternately by the juniors and so memorized. He requests the heads to commend it to their students.[23] A second preface, addressed to the young men of the university themselves, states Corro's three-fold aim, the deep understanding of the pure and sincere doctrine of Christianity, civility and probity of morals, and learning and justice.[24] We do not know how much Corro's catechism was used in Oxford, but opinions of him continued to differ. Robert Batt, a Brasenose undergraduate, wrote of his haughtiness but Thomas Pye, who translated his *Solomons Sermon: of Mans Chief Felicitie* in 1586, speaks high praise of him.[25]

Though the formal exercise of catechism may have been nothing more than the fulfilment of a university regulation in

---

[22] Merton and St. John's made Corro grants for this work, and from 1580 Christ Church paid him an annuity of £2. *Registrum Annalium Collegii Mertonensis, 1567-1603*, 128; McFadden, thesis cit., 496-500.

[23] Corro, *Epistola Beati Pauli* (London, 1581), sigs. a 2-4.

[24] Ibid., sigs. a 6-7; pp. 1-3.

[25] Bodleian Library, MS Rawlinson D 985, fo. 52ᵛ, 18 December 1583. Corro, *Solomons Sermon: of Mans Chief Felicite* (Oxford, 1586), sig. * iiiʳ.

some colleges, in the hands of a godly catechist it could have become, in university and parish, a daily form of exercise for the zealous and an occupation for Sunday afternoon, when it was intended not only for the young, but to be joined together with prayer, psalm-singing, questions, and a sermon.[26] Puritan divines certainly favoured the exercises of catechism provided in the universities. A 1584 reply to Whitgift's Articles IV and IX, which ordered that no man might preach unless he was in orders, enquired whether, if this was effected, 'the exercises of commonplaces and catechising enjoined on graduates in the Universities for their better training in divinity' were to be restrained? These exercises had often encouraged men to take orders. Other replies indicated that the articles might prevent men who were not qualified to minister the sacraments from reading divinity lectures in the university.[27] The nursery for the godly was threatened, from within by those who by laxity propagated the spirit of worldliness, and from without by those who wished to exercise firmer control over the ministry.

The godly faced many temptations: plays, gaming, dancing, drinking, excess in dress, and 'haunting the town'. Drama seems to have presented the greatest threat in the minds of their tutors. Before 1577, however, no attack on the stage by men of any shade of opinion seems to have been launched. Peter Martyr, much admired in Oxford, praised honest plays in his 1564 commentary on Judges; the Privy Council licensed companies of players to entertain the court; and when, in 1574, some restriction was introduced in London it was prompted by dangers to health and order rather than by moral or religious scruples.[28] Although travelling players had been controlled in Cambridge as early as 1575, it was not until 14 July 1584, in response to a request from the Chancellor, that the Oxford Convocation decreed that it should not be lawful for travelling

---

[26] For a further discussion of catechesis, see *Cartwrightiana*, ed. A. Peel and L. H. Carlson (Elizabethan Nonconformist Texts, I, London, 1951), 156-8, and Collinson, thesis cit., 749-52.

[27] *The Seconde Part of a Register*, I, 177, 192.

[28] For discussion of the general background, see Williams, *The Tudor Regime*, 305-10; and William Ringler, 'The First Phase of the Elizabethan Attack on the Stage, 1558-1579', in *Huntington Library Quarterly*, V (1941-2), 391-418.

players to act within the precincts of the university without express permission.[29] This however was not intended to restrict the performance of comedies and tragedies by members of the university. University drama was regarded in a different light from that performed by the professional companies.[30]

By the end of the 1570s, the puritan attack on the stage in general was beginning to gain ground. Stephen Gosson, a younger contemporary of Reynolds in Corpus, where he had been elected a scholar in 1572, and one of a circle of celebrated men which included Richard Hooker, Edwin Sandys the younger, George Cranmer, John Barefoot, later Archdeacon of Lincoln, and Henry Parry, launched a forthright attack on drama in *The Shoole of Abuse* of 1579.[31] The treatise is directed to his friends in Oxford, for he comments, 'I have been matriculated my selfe in the Schoole, where so many abuses florish'; yet, he continues, men who will not 'steppe from the university for love of knowledge, seeing but slender offences and small abuses within their own walles, never beleeve such rocks are abrode nor such horrible monsters in playing places'. He blames those who 'sit concluding of sillogismes in a corner, which in a close studye in the Universitye, who coope themselves up xl yeres together studying al things and professe nothing'. The university, rather, should be an example for, says Gosson, 'I speake not this to preferre Botley to Oxeford ... let out your springs, geve us drink of your water, light of your torches, and season us a little with the salt of your knowledge.'[32]

As a young scholar of Corpus, Reynolds had appeared in *Palamon and Arcyte,* performed before the Queen in 1566. In

---

[29] Wood, *Annals,* II, 219.

[30] See, for example, the support for academic plays in John Case, *Speculum Moralium Quaestionum in Universalem Ethicen Aristotelis* (Oxford, 1586). See F. S. Boas, *University Drama in the Tudor Age* (Oxford, 1914), 227-30.

[31] Stephen Gosson, *The Shoole of Abuse, Conteining a Pleasaunt Invective against Poets, Pipers, Plaiers, Iesters, and such like Caterpillers of a Commonwelth ...* (London, 1579). Gosson attended the lectures of Reynolds, who greatly influenced him. He had himself written plays before his conversion in 1579. W. Ringler, *Stephen Gosson* (Princeton, 1942).

[32] Gosson, op. cit., 6, 11, 33-4. See also the attack on stage plays in Philip Stubbes, *The Anatomie of Abuses* (London, 1583). Stubbes, a Cambridge man, lodged in Gloucester Hall in the 1570s.

maturity, his views changed. In his DD theses of 1579, he saw
the university assailed by *'ludos illiberales, symposia intempestiva,
pestes scenicorum, Theatralia spectacula'*.[33] Thomas Thornton,
Canon of Christ Church, who invited Reynolds to attend the
Christ Church Shrovetide play, William Gager's *Ulysses Redux*
on Sunday, 5 February 1592, can scarcely have anticipated the
vehement reply he received. Reynolds first refused verbally,
but when pressed to attend, penned a spirited apologia. He
presented three arguments: that men appeared on the stage in
women's costume; that changes in times and circumstances in
plays are condemned by both the pagan writers and the fathers;
and that plays should not be performed on Sundays.[34] These
arguments were expanded in an address to the play's author,
dated 10 July 1592, occasioned by the publication of *Ulysses*.
An exchange of correspondence followed, which was partially
printed in 1599 in *Th'overthrow of Stage-Playes*. Reynolds
broadens his attack on men playing women's parts, and the
defilement caused by 'immodest speeches and wanton deeds',
into a more general attack on time-wasting. He admits that
recreation is as necessary for scholars as for other men, yet
'it were not fit for them to play at stoole ball among wenches;
nor to Mum-chance or Maw with idle loose companions, nor
at trunkes in Guile-hals, nor to danse about Maypoles, nor
to rifle in Alehouses, nor to carowse in tavernes, nor to steale
deere, nor to robbe orchardes'. Here we may have a picture of
undergraduate recreation for, adds Reynolds, 'who can deny,
but they may do theese thinges, yea worse'. He protests that on
the stage, young men are permitted to see amorousness,
lewdness, and violence, and attacks football, not on the ground
put forward by the Chancellor in 1584, that it was played even
by ministers on the Sabbath, but because of its 'beastly fury
and extreme violence'.[35]

    Gager, defending his play, contrasts the unruly bands of
professional actors with the scholars who produce plays 'to

---

[33] Reynolds, *Sex Theses de Sacra Scriptura et Ecclesia*, 30; preface to the heads and
members of Colleges, 2 February 1580.

[34] Corpus Christi College Oxford MS 352, 11-14.

[35] Reynolds, *Th'overthrow of Stage-Playes* (Middleburg, 1599), 22-3. Wood, *Annals*,
II, 220. The entire Reynolds-Gager-Gentilis controversy is in Corpus Christi College
Oxford MS 352, 11-316.

recreate owre selves, owre House, and the better parte of the *Universitye* ... to trye their voyces and confirme their memoryes; to frame their speeche; to conforme them to convenient action; to trye what mettel is in evrye one, and what disposition they are of; whereby never any one amongst us, that I knowe was made the worse, many have byn muche the better, as I dare reporte me to all the Universitye'.[36] Reynolds agreed that preachers must be taught their craft through the use of logic and rhetoric, but, he warned Gager, 'Behold the great difference between a heathen mans conceit of instructing of oratours for civill causes: and yours, of Christian Preachers or what soever place your Studentes shall be called to in Church or Common weale, at least of honest men and Christians.'[37]

After the stage, the most intolerable temptation for undergraduates was 'the horrible vice of pestiferous dancing'. Philip Stubbes had written of the allurements of dancing and its corrosive nature. He refuted the suggestion that it was good exercise for the body and recreation for the mind, and maintained narrowly that 'the only thing in which a true Christian delights is meditation of the passion of Christ, the remission of sins and the contemplation of joys after this life'.[38] Even Gager, though he protested at Reynolds's inclusion of dancing among the recreations unfit for scholars, thought it an exercise more fitting for the meaner sort than for university men.[39] George Abbot condemned both stage plays and dancing masters, though not all honest recreation.[40]

Most of the offences in manners arose from too much contact with the town. Reynolds was not alone when he warned his protégé against this course of idleness. Enclosure within collegiate walls and insistence on medieval apparel must have been the last vestiges of an order which was breaking down under pressure from the newly-arrived commoners and from greater social mobility. Lawrence Humphrey, preaching before

[36] Gager to Reynolds, 31 July 1592, quoted by Boas, *University Drama in the Tudor Age,* 235-6.
[37] Reynolds, *Th'overthrow,* 121. For a general discussion of the puritan criticism of university drama, see Boas, op. cit., 220-51, and E. K. Chambers, *The Elizabethan Stage,* I (Oxford, 1923), 236-68.
[38] Stubbes, op. cit., sigs. M vii-viii.
[39] Boas, op. cit., 238-9.
[40] Abbot, *An Exposition upon the Prophet Ionah,* 92-3.

the university in St. Mary's, reminded the young that they must obey their masters, 'for where youth rules, there is headiness'. He required humility, expressed in diligence and obedience. He insisted on enclosure, for 'as it is dethe for a fish to be out of water, so it ought to scholers to be dethe to walke the streates and to leave their studie and go out of their chambers, but theie cleane contrary have great delite to walke streats and leve their studie'.[41] In 1598, Simon Paddye, a Magdalen demy, was deprived of commons for two weeks because he had spent a night in the town without leave or reasonable cause. One week of his deprivation was remitted on account of his poverty, but he was ordered instead to make a public declamation in the hall against the haunting of taverns by scholars.[42] Paddye's case is one of hundreds recorded in college registers. Though the university held a monopoly of licences to sell wine or keep an inn within the precincts and also issued all licences to keep taverns to sell ale, undergraduate drunkenness was endemic, if we are to credit the constant message of the pulpits.[43] Reynolds allowed the moderate use of wine, but excessive drinking brought weakness to the body, danger to the soul, and drew on all manner of diseases.[44] George Abbot warned those who frequented taverns when they should have been in bed, at their studies, or on Sunday at service. He seems to have been less concerned with the danger to health than with the fact that time wasted through drunkenness could never be recalled.[45]

In the mid-1580s, mindful of the corruption in his college which was soon to be the cause of his exile from it, John Reynolds, like Jewel before him in Corpus, reminded heads and members of the ways in which they had fallen away from the original intentions of their founders. In an address 'to you my brethren in the university', he admits that in many places the commons of fellows are very slender, and short of the founders' allowances, because of the lack of faithful stewards: 'We may thanke God for our sumptuous palaces ready

[41] Humphrey, sermon on I Peter. 5:5., n.d., BL, Sloane MS 2987, fos. 64-8.
[42] Macray, *Register*, III, 33.
[43] Clark, *Register*, II, part i, 322, 324. An Act of Edward VI had limited taverns to three, but was not enforced. Mallet, op. cit., II, 108.
[44] Reynolds, *The Prophecie of Obadiah*, 115-16.
[45] Abbot, op. cit., 94.

prepared for us, I would to God that we were like them in other things,' In particular, he mentions the behaviour of heads who have devoured for themselves what was intended for the whole college.[46] Lawrence Humphrey in Magdalen had been accused of taking into his own hands and those of members of his family, lands and rents which belonged to the common fund; Henry Robinson, when he became Provost of Queen's in 1581, immediately restored to the general use rents which had been appropriated by earlier provosts.[47] Another member of Corpus, Sebastian Benefield, preaching in 1599, devoted an entire sermon to the state of the colleges, 'that those who live within goodly buildings might keep the laws'. Heads, he continued, should not grieve their companies by withdrawing from them their statutory and ordinary maintenance; members should not complain too much when they were restrained by heads according to the statutes. He indicated that frequent mention had been made in Oxford pulpits of a particular departure from the will of founders, the wicked sale of college places, intended by founders for the most worthy men. Benefield reported that the sale of such a place could raise £20 to £30 or more.[48]

Election to scholars' places in most colleges was restricted to particular schools or counties. For example, the entire fellowship of New College was drawn from those who had attended the founder's school at Winchester; in Exeter College, places were restricted to the diocese of Exeter and the counties within which Sir William Petre had given lands to the college in 1565.[49] In many cases, fellowships were limited to those who were already members of the foundation, though there were constant complaints of the breach of this rule.[50] Some colleges seem to have been frequently in breach of their statutes, 'salving their conscience by the statement that "though they did this county an injustice on this occasion to favour another county,

[46] Reynolds, *The Discovery of the Man of Sinne*, 40-1.
[47] On Humphrey, see above 48; on Robinson, see above 172.
[48] Benefield, *The Sinne against the Holy Ghost Discovered*, 73-4.
[49] G. D. Squibb, *Founders' Kin* (Oxford, 1972), ch. 1.
[50] For an examination of this question in Corpus Christi College, see J. K. McConica, 'The Social Relations of Tudor Oxford', in *Transactions of the Royal Historical Society*, 5th series, 27 (1977), 128-30.

they would give it a turn belonging to the unduly-favoured county on another occasion''—which seldom came'.[51]

Control of corrupt elections must have been potentially one of the most important ways in which the standard of the body of scholars and fellows in a college could be improved. In 1576, a bill was introduced in parliament to prevent the buying and selling of college places; it passed the Lords and the Commons, but was vetoed by the Queen, Burghley having advised her that such legislation would risk perpetual ignomy being cast on the universities.[52] It is difficult to resist the conclusion that the court exercised strong pressure against the bill, since, throughout this period, colleges found themselves overruled in elections by the Chancellor, the court, and sometimes the crown itself. In Magdalen, for instance, the protests of the more scrupulous did not prevent, on five occasions at least, one of them the nomination of a president, the intrusion of men at the Queen's command.[53] It was not until 1589 that 'An Act against abuses in election of schollers and presentation to benefices' finally reached the statute book.[54] Henceforward, the taking of bribes, gifts, or rewards in order to place a man in a college, or elect him to office, would result in automatic disqualification of the person proposed and the exclusion from the college of the member or members who had received bribes. Nevertheless, the procedure at elections and the corruption of collegiate life continued to trouble the more sensitive.

In 1611 the scruples of the godly about the manipulation of elections, contrary to the statutes which they desired to uphold, found classic expression in the writing of a fellow of Brasenose, Robert Bolton. Bolton had been a member of Lincoln College before his removal to Brasenose in 1596, and although he did not become a fellow there until 1602, his *A Discourse about the State of True Happinesse,* the 'first fruits of my employment and business in the ministry' as he calls it, may reflect his experience in both colleges in the last decade of the sixteenth and first

[51] Clark, *Register,* II, part i, 6.
[52] See M. Dewar, *Sir Thomas Smith: A Tudor Intellectual in Office* (London, 1964), 185-6; J. B. Mullinger, *The University of Cambridge from the Royal Injunctions of 1535 to the Accession of Charles I* (Cambridge, 1884), 268-70.
[53] See above, ch. III.
[54] 31 Eliz. c.6.; *House of Lords Journals,* II, 150, 156, 161, 164.

decade of the seventeenth centuries. Towards the end of this volume, he contrasts the 'notorious sinner', who would have no care for oath or statute, conscience or honesty, the honour of his college, or the good of the church, with the godly man to whom enemies have given the title 'puritan'.

First, in Bolton's account, appears the sinner, who

would most carefully cast about with himselfe by all meanes, to defeate and prevent the purposes, and to stoppe the passage especially of all Puritanes. You must know by the way, that these are a very dangerous kind of men, able to blow up whole Houses, by their too fierie zeale against idlenesse, drunkennesse, and other shamefull corruptions, close and politike cariages of many rotten and unconscionable causes and the like.

Against such a man, Bolton opposes the true model of the 'puritan', a description which he must have drawn from his own conscience and experience:

By Puritanes in this place I only understand them, (for even such are so branded) who make conscience of studie, and religious education of Schollers, who are readie ever, and resolute to uphold goodnesse in a House, though they be crusht, disgraced and disoffic'd; when out of a gracious and ingenuous freedom of Spirit, wil be their own men in Elections, and other Collegiate services; and not suffer their consciences to be led hood-winkt to serve other mens humours and private ends.[55]

Such a man, 'a puritan' if he must be so called, is contrasted with a member of the college who would exercise 'grosse hypocrisie in the weighty businesse of Elections', who first 'would commune with his own covetous heart, then cast an eye over the competitors for the place, assessing their gifts and bribes. Only having done this would he adopt a 'vizard of piety'.

Adherence to the founders' statutes was the most important argument advanced by the precise in college government and elections. The hypocrite, for his part, claimed that 'some liberty and dispensation must be given to statute discretion, against the bare letter and strict meaning of the statute'. At all costs, the hypocrite sought to avoid the election of one 'of knowne,

---

[55] Bolton, *A Discourse about the State of True Happinesse,* 131-2.

professed and practised forwardnesse in religion', for, he reasoned,

> if such a fellow come in amongst us, we shall have all moulded anew after the strict modell of his irregular conscience: we should be troubled with new tricks and erections, for the encreasement of study and reformation of manners; he would be stil standing and striving for an Ideall and abstractive purity in Elections, and other affaires of the Colledge, so that our former quietnesse and peace would be much dissweetened by his tartnesse, and too much precisenesse.[56]

The consequences of corrupt elections spread into the whole life of the college and beyond, and Bolton lamented those who were

> thornes in the sides, and pricks in the eyes of all that love grace and goodnesse; they either turn idle, truly factious, or notoriously scandalous, by misspending the unvaluable pretiousnesse of their golden houres, in Taverns, Ale-houses, or some other course of good-fellowship to the inexpiable and externall dishonour of those *Houses,* of which they should be ornaments: and when they have done much hurt and mischiefe here, they are the onely men to bargain for, buy, or compasse by indirect and sinister dealing, Benefices, and spiritual promotions abroad: of which being possest, they either by unconscionable and cruell negligence, and Non-residence in their charge, betray the soules of their people to wildnesse and barbarisme to ignorance, prophanenesse, or poperie.[57]

As the reign advanced, those colleges which had emerged as 'seminaries' for the training of godly ministers, also turned their attention to the formation of godly laymen. Dr McConica has distinguished two principal groups in the Arts faculty, which he sees as the most significant point of growth in the Tudor university;[58] first, fellows and scholars, still bound by their collegiate statutes to proceed to holy orders and to the higher degrees in the theology faculty, though most colleges had a limited number of places for those proceeding to the higher degrees in law and medicine who did not take orders;

---

[56] Bolton, op. cit., 135.
[57] Ibid., 137-8.
[58] McConica, art. cit., 122-32.

secondly, commoners, increasing rapidly in the more advanced protestant colleges, in particular Brasenose, Magdalen, Queen's, and Corpus, and paying for the privilege of living in college and receiving tuition. Recent research has suggested that, in the last two decades of the century, wealthy commoners did not merely use the university as part of a finishing school as formerly, but were prepared to fulfil the statutory requirements to proceed to the BA degree.[59] Some of the gentry families seem to have been fired by genuine religious enthusiasm in sending their sons to the universities and this may account for the growth in the number of commoners in some colleges, for example, at Magdalen under Humphrey and Corpus under Cole. Mr More of Losely sent his son to Corpus in 1570, before the President was discredited. Cole evidently took the assignment seriously, giving the boy a place in his lodgings and writing to his father, 'I will take upon me to be his corrector alone, and you shal know, that I will be no harde maister to him ... thogh I have appointed him a teacher, yet doe I meane to be half a teacher to him myself.'[60]

In Oxford, and in particular in Humphrey's Magdalen, a new blueprint for the education of the godly gentleman had been drawn up at the beginning of the reign, though its author and his college lapsed sadly in later years. In his *Optimates*, published in Basle in 1560, Humphrey contrasts true and false nobility. He rejects those who live carelessly and do not devote themselves to study, government, or the public good, and those who live idly around the court, giving themselves over to pleasure, display, and magnificence. Godliness and learning are the keys of this new nobility. The model is not the successful courtier, as in Elyot or Castiglione, but Christ himself. Humphrey provides three signs by which true nobility can be discerned: 'yf they honoure theyr stocke and Nobylytie wyth inwarde ornamentes'; secondly, 'then yf the same they accomplyshe more copiouslye and plentifully than the dreggs

[59] See McConica, art. cit., 122-31; Kearney, *Scholars and Gentlemen*, ch. 1, *passim;* Elizabeth Russell, 'The Influx of Commoners into the University of Oxford before 1581: an Optical Illusion?' in *English Historical Review*, ccclxv (Oct. 1977), 721-45.
[60] *Seventh Report of the Royal Commission on Historical Manuscripts, appendix* (London, 1879), 622.

and drasse of men ... to these muste the thirde be knit, withoute whiche all the rest runne to wracke and ruine. Chryst ought bee the Crest, the Fane and type of Nobylytie: Without whome, nothynge is Noble in this inferiour circle below the Moone.'[61] The true nobles must 'rule and governe ryghtlye thynges divynge', they must 'strengthen with theyr ayde empoveryshed religyon, to shield it forsaken with theyr patronage ... to root out superstition'. Humphrey advocates liberality towards the weak and needy but especially towards the learned, lamenting the passing of the golden age in which kings and all honourable men were the protectors and nurses of learning, the learned, and students. Now, he admits, there are many who seek by flattery, suit, or extortion, to lay their hands on the revenues set apart for students, and to divert them to private gain.[62] Theory and practice were often badly married in Humphrey, and the experience of his early years in Oxford seems to have turned him into a less than honourable example of the bounty and humility he had earlier advocated.

It was the new commoners who were largely responsible for the breakdown of collegiate enclosure and the discipline on which the godly set such great store. The deans and censors found it difficult to control them, when their statutory power did not extend beyond the scholars. As early as 1565, the Dean of Balliol had attempted to make commoners conform to the same pattern of religious services and academic exercises as the scholars and fellows.[63] When Bishop Cooper conducted his visitation of Magdalen in 1585, he found that the commoners were not subject to decanal discipline, and that Humphrey had reserved control of them to himself.[64] Commoners often had separate tables from scholars in hall, and breached the regulations about visiting the town with impunity. Nevertheless, Humphrey's Magdalen nourished a continual succession of gentleman commoners, electing some, in time, to demyships. Laurence Tomson, ally of the precise in the troubles of 1575, already a demy in the first year of Mary's reign, was elected a

---

[61] Humphrey, *The Nobles or of Nobilitye*, sigs. k v ᵛ - k vi ʳ.

[62] Ibid., sigs. l iiiᵛ, l viʳ, m viiʳ⁻ᵛ, p iii-iv.

[63] Balliol College Archives, Register (1514-1682), 108.

[64] Macray, *Register*, III, 20.

fellow in 1559 and remained a member of the college until 1568.[65] Francis Hastings, fifth son of the second Earl of Huntingdon, was Tomson's contemporary in early Elizabethan Magdalen, and became a firm supporter of Humphrey and later a prominent parliamentarian, anti-papist writer, and friend of godly ministers.[66] Francis Knollys, a member of the college in the reign of Edward VI, remained a staunch ally of the godly in Oxford throughout Elizabeth's reign, relying on the intellectual support of John Reynolds in his parliamentary campaign against *iure divino* episcopacy in the 1590s.[67] His son, Henry, a pupil at the grammar school, later became a commoner in the college. Erasmus Dryden, son of John Dryden of Ashby Canons in Northamptonshire, who appears to have been imprisoned for his support of puritan preachers in 1604-5, was a demy from 1571-5, and lived to be Sheriff of Northampton in 1598 and 1620.[68]

Outside Magdalen, Merton produced Thomas Bodley.[69] Across the road in Alban Hall, John Bruen with his brother, Thomas, matriculated just before Christmas 1577. John Brerewood, a gentlemen from Chester, seems to have drawn him away from papism, but his conversion to an advanced protestant position did not come until 1587. Bruen had returned from Oxford in 1579, the year of his father's death, but his life, published in 1641 by William Hinde, editor of Reynolds's sermons, attributed the beginnings of his change of heart to Oxford, 'that vineyard of the Lord', where his father, unlike most gentlemen, was minded to bring up two sons in love of truth, knowledge, and understanding. Bruen became the true model for all godly gentlemen. He renounced all pleasures and lived frugally; he set up religion in his family, provided and main-

---

[65] See above, 51-3.

[66] See above 49; and see Wood, *Athenae Oxonienses*, II, cols. 82-4; Claire Cross, *The Puritan Earl* (London, 1966), 35-48, 134; and *The Letters of Francis Hastings (1574-1609)*, ed. Claire Cross (Somerset Record Society, lxix, 1969).

[67] Wood, *Athenae Oxonienses*, I, cols. 653-4; Neale, *Elizabeth I and Her Parliaments*, II, 271-2; *Informations or a Protestation Offered to the Parliament...* (n.p., 1608), 73 f. and 88 f.

[68] Bloxam, *Register*, IV, 186-7.

[69] H. W. Garrod, 'Bodley of Merton', in Friends of the Bodleian Library, *13th Annual Report* (1937-8), 8-17; *Reliquiae Bodleianae* (London, 1703), includes Bodley's short autobiography and letters.

tained a preacher, and instead of tables, card, and dice, set up two Bibles, one in the parlour and another in the hall. Thus, rejoiced Hinde, the tables of the commandments of God took the place of the profane tables of men.[70]

[70] William Hinde, *A Faithfull Remonstrance of the Holy Life and Happy Death of John Bruen* (London, 1641), esp. 13-15, 42. Richardson, *Puritanism in North-West England*, 90-2, 122-4.

IX

'THE NECESSITY AND EXCELLENCIE OF DEVOUT AND HOLY PREACHING': THE GODLY AND THE PULPIT

Wee mislike also the length of a Leiturgie which cloyeth the Minister *prolixitate et multitudine precationem quotidie recitandarum* and which must not be omitted for studie to preach, or be shortened to have time for preaching ... even Baptisme it selfe must be omitted rather than that preaching should be hindered ... *Gregorie* commandeth to give over singing for the studie of preaching ... *Hierome* first cutt short the lessons ... that there might be time for preaching.

In the radical writing which provoked a royal warrant for his arrest and his flight into exile in Amsterdam, Robert Parker, fellow of Magdalen 1583-93, sets the word preached, 'the tree of life', against 'these ceremonies', particularly the sign of the cross, which are 'as bad as the serpent' and 'open the door to hirelings and idol shepherds'. While godly preachers are thrust out of their livings because they refuse the ceremonies and subscription, the ignorant are intruded, and even moderate men claim that 'preaching is not so much to be cared for as praying is', and that 'a praying ministerie wil doe well enough in a Church alreadie stablished if there be Preachers here and there to preach now and then'.[1] In starkest terms, Parker contrasted those who were content with the church by law established, its ministry and worship prescribed in the Book of Common Prayer, its episcopal government and discipline, all of which presented the face of a church 'halfly reformed', with the increasing number of more radical ministers, who in previous decades might have been drawn into the *classes,* but now diverted their attention to the pulpit, to Sabbath observance, and to practical, domestic godliness. In Oxford, this new emphasis also served to redirect concern to the corporate life of the colleges, the conduct of students, and the government of the societies and their elections.

[1] Parker, *A Scholasticall Discourse against Symbolizing with Antichrist in Ceremonies*, 175-9, 187-92.

This change in direction, in Oxford and in the country at large, was inevitable. Radical experiments had failed or been suppressed, although they were to enjoy a brief revival at the outset of the new reign in 1603-5. The puritan surveys of the ministry in the mid-1580s may mark the beginning of a change, with their dominant concern for a well-trained, resident, and adequately-maintained ministry, above all given to preaching.[2] Presbyterian course had ceased to be viable, and even the framers of the *Discipline* admitted its limited application.[3] As hope of attaining other objectives failed, preaching must have seemed once more the best available means of instruction, edification, and spiritual direction, though the ideals of the most fervent were rarely attained in practice.[4]

In the university, and wherever its graduates settled, this became the age of the preacher.[5] The formal arrangements for an increase in the courses of sermons and Leicester's attempts to control unruly preachers in the period 1582-4 have already been noted.[6] In 1584 the university set up a committee, which included Robinson, Humphrey, Cole, Culpepper, and the Vice-Chancellor and proctors, to review the privilege of granting licences *'ad annuntiandum verbum Dei per Universam Angliam'*. This right, dating back to *c.*1490, gave the university, alone among corporate bodies, the authority to grant licences under its Great Seal to preach throughout the country. The new decree on preaching licences, promulgated on 5 February 1584, required that graces for such licences should be asked in Congregation, and, if leave were granted, should be sealed at the next meeting of Convocation. Candidates were to be Masters of Arts *actualiter creatus,* who had disputed in theology at least once in the Schools or at the *Comitia,* and had preached before the university four times, either in Christ Church or St. Mary's, or in the Lenten course at St. Peter-in-the-East.[7] This was a further attempt to control

---

[2] The wider context of this transition is discussed in William Haller, *The Rise of Puritanism* (New York, 1938), ch. 1.

[3] Collinson, *E.P.M.*, 432-3.

[4] On the limited power of the sermon to convert Lancashire, see C. Haigh, 'Puritan Evangelism in the Reign of Elizabeth I', in *English Historical Review*, 1977, 30-58.

[5] For a general discussion of the role of the preacher in the Elizabethan church, see J. W. Blench, *Preaching in England in the Late Fifteenth and Sixteenth Centuries* (Oxford, 1964); Horton Davies, *The Worship of the English Puritans* (London, 1948).

[6] See above, ch. VI.

[7] Clark, *Register*, II, part i, 131-2. In April 1584, St. Martin's Carfax and All Saints were added to the churches where 'trial sermons' might be preached.

extremes in preaching, but its requirement for four sermons from each candidate may have provided additional opportunities both for preachers and congregations.

That such additional provision was needed, the godly preachers of Elizabethan Oxford did not doubt. Disputing for his DD in 1579, Reynolds described the nourishment of the true church by the word of God: where 'ministers doo preach the word of God, pure, sincere and uncorrupt ... those churches may we count to be sound, and whole'. Where it is corrupted, mixed with darnel, the people die of hunger.[8] In the Church of Rome, he maintained, where the word was not preached, or preached in a strange tongue, or where God's word was mixed with man's words, the body had become a carcass, destitute of the Spirit. He saw that preaching had a vital role in the construction of the church: catechizing laid the foundations, preaching built up the walls, and, finally, discipline covered the building with a roof. The sermons on Haggai are full of references to deficiencies in preaching. In April 1586, Reynolds portrayed the university as it had appeared to some 'strangers of godly zeale and good credit', who complained that there was not one sermon on a Sunday afternoon in the whole of Oxford, whereas at an earlier period there were fewer preachers, but more sermons.[9] Later that year, Reynolds encouraged his hearers to press forward with the implementation of the university's order 'for ordinarie sermons and preaching of the woord on our Sabbath-daies in the afternoone, not the forenoone onely', but the matter needed further regulation by a Convocation delegacy in February 1587 which provided for sermons to be preached on Sunday mornings in Lent and Sunday afternoons out of Lent throughout the year.[10]

For Reynolds, the preacher is a prophet, not because he is able to foretell things to come, but because he speaks the word of the Lord and applies it to his age. Though he was reputedly the most learned man of his generation, Reynolds opposes the stuffing of sermons with Hebrew and Greek by those who wish

[8] Reynolds, *Six Conclusions Touching the Holy Scripture and the Church,* at the end of *The Summe of the Conference betwene J. Rainoldes and J. Hart,* 720-6.

[9] Reynolds, *Haggai,* 18.

[10] Reynolds, *A Sermon upon Part of the Eighteenth Psalm,* preached 31 August 1586, sigs. C 2ᵛ-3ʳ. OUA/NEP *supra*/Register L, fo. 289ʳ.

to show themselves learned, rather than preaching in the vulgar tongue, for 'that preaching then is most warrantable, which is most profitable, and that most profitable which is most powerfull, and that most powerfull which best informeth the minde, enlightneth the judgement, affecteth the soule aright, and warmeth the heart with the comforts and contentments of it'.[11] The ministry of the word preached he also considered the ultimate weapon against Rome. In his series of anti-papist sermons, published as *The Discovery of the Man of Sinne,* Reynolds acknowledged that lack of preaching God's word 'is the reason why so many soules among us are not yet delivered from the power of Antichrist, why after so long calling so few are willing to come ... we have fought against spirituall adversaries more with the weapons of man, than of God'.[12]

Henry Airay, whose own course of sermons on Philippians is perhaps the best example of a preacher's persistence, continually reminded his hearers that, despite the adequate provision made for preaching, not all embraced the opportunities or otherwise 'how where the light of this knowledge [of Christ] shineth most clearly, men do yet love darknesse better than light? It may be spoken to the shame of this whole Towne or the shame of a great many of this congregation, that they love darknesse rather than light. ... Three or foure Sermons may commonly be heard weekely. ... How many scores come to heare them weekely, nay come to heare any of them weekely?'[13] Dullness, coldness, and slackness were Airay's continual complaint. In his view, this was especially grievous, since the gift of faith was given to man through the word preached. By this means, natural man, who does not have understanding, is renewed by the divine spirit.[14] Airay lamented that while men should gladly frequent places where they could hear sermons, they were careless, indeed 'not halfe of that congregation which should be here present have beene assembled in this house of the Lord at any one Sermon. Againe, a great slacknesse in coming of those that doe come.' Even those who do attend the preaching exercises must further

[11] Reynolds, *Haggai,* 87-8.
[12] Reynolds, *The Discovery of the Man of Sinne,* 17.
[13] Airay, *Philippians,* 652.
[14] Ibid., 71, 266-7.

persist in keeping the whole of the Lord's Day holy by reading, by hearing, and by meditating on the word of life. The preacher realizes that this advice will not be popular, and continues: 'Yea but this is too precise, and strait, and savours too much of Puritanisme. Well, be it as it will, thou must either be a Puritan in observation of the commandement, or else thou bringest upon thy selfe iudgement.'[15] Here is the hint of conflict which frequently recurs in Airay's writing, suggesting that the stricter reformed theologians, with their insistence on Sabbath observance and attendance at sermons, were under pressure in Oxford in the 1590s.

The experience of hearing a godly preacher was a *sine qua non* in the training of ministers and laymen. Dr Paul Seaver has argued that what was important in the training of puritan ministers was not what they learned formally, but the chances of hearing great preachers in the university towns. This was especially true in Cambridge, where men from the surrounding country, from London, and from Oxford flocked to hear William Perkins.[16] Oxford also had its corporation preachers. On 13 October 1579, the Council decided that a new pulpit should be set up at St. Martin's, Carfax, and maintained at the city's charge. A month later, all freemen and their wives and families were ordered to attend sermons on Sundays and Holy Days or forfeit twelve pence on each occasion they failed to do so. This order was reinforced in March 1582, and in February 1583 the Council agreed to set aside a stipend for a preacher to be chosen by the Mayor and aldermen. This was fixed at £10 in 1585, and Richard Potter of Trinity and John Prime of New College were appointed to deliver the sermons alternately. They were succeeded by Francis Mason, appointed in 1953 and later *vindex ecclesiae Anglicanae*, and Richard Field, then at Queen's, subsequently royal chaplain and Dean of Gloucester. Robert Brysenden, fellow of Merton and a disciple of Reynolds, held the lectureship from 1594 until 1603.[17] John

[15] Airay, *Philippians*, 445-53; see also 722.
[16] Porter, 264.
[17] P. S. Seaver, *The Puritan Lectureships* (Stanford, 1970), 112-13; C. J. H. Fletcher, *A History of the Church and Parish of St. Martin (Carfax) Oxford* (Oxford, 1896), 22-4; *Selections from the Records of the City of Oxford*, ed. W. H. Turner (Oxford, 1880), 405-6, 419-20, 431; *Oxford Council Acts, 1583-1626*, ed. H. E. Salter (Oxford Historical Society, lxxxvii, 1927), 17-18, 23.

Prime was certainly the most zealous preacher produced by New College in this period, an exception in that generally conservative society.[18] Some of his sermons appeared in 1583 under the title *A Fruitfull and Briefe Discourse in Two Bookes: the One of Nature, the Other of Grace.* Dedicated to his patron, Walsingham, they set out to confute the view of the Rhemists, in particular Stapleton, on grace, faith, and works.

Not all Oxford heads took the exercise of preaching as seriously as Airay and Reynolds. Martin Culpepper, Warden of New College 1573-99, and a member of the 1584 committee on preaching licences, was appointed Archdeacon of Berkshire in 1588. A puritan caricature of him survives in *A Dialogue, wherin is plainly laide open, the tyrannicall dealing of L. Bishopps against Gods children,* one of the tracts associated with the Marprelate controversy. Here is Culpepper at a sermon:

He is an Archdeacon, and going in his visitation, not far from *Oxford*: It is the ordinarye thing with them, to have a Sermon before they keep court, and alwaies the court is kept in the Church. The preacher somewhat troubling him, (in telling the spiritual fathers their duties) did sometimes nod at the preacher so as he did perceive him, to the end that he shoulde make an end of his Sermon: The preacher notwithstanding went forward with his text, which troubled Master Doctor sore. Then he fel a beckoning to the preacher, the precher would not see his signes, althogh the audience greatly marveled at him, then Master Doctor (being soare galled you must thinke,) spake to him and bad him come down: the precher thought it not long (though Master Doctor were weary to heare his dutie tolde him in so plaine a menner) and seeing he could use no means to get him out of the pulpit, caled the cryar to him, and bad him cry, *Ho yes,* and so he did. Then went he very reverently about his busines, and left the preacher in the pulpit: Nowe tel me I pray you, whether he had more minde to heare the worde preached, or to be with his kenell of hounds.[19]

Others, though not as careless as Culpepper, sought to impose a fairer balance between hortatory preaching and the other aspects of Christian devotion and discipline. Dr Richard Eedes, once Canon of Christ Church, a close friend of Dean Tobie Mathew, and Dean of Worcester from 1596, preaching in Oxford in 1604, announced that 'wee condemne that idle

[18] *New College Oxford, 1379-1979*, 51.
[19] *A Dialogue...*, sig. D 3ʳ.

and perfunctory hearing of sermons which too many make only the duty and fruit of ther religion as yf they ought nothing but their eares to the Lord'.[20] In a sermon preached on the anniversary of the Queen's accession in 1599, Thomas Holland attempted to restore the balance which zealous preachers threatened to disturb. Holland, concerned, as always, with the state of the ministry, was an establishment figure, promoted to the Rectorship of Exeter on the Queen's insistence, and supported by Buckhurst and Whitgift as grave, wise, and very learned.[21] His 1599 sermon, dedicated to Bancroft, is an apology and defence of church and commonwealth against their papist accusers. It not only justifies the observance of the Sabbath, which would have endeared Holland to the godly, but also those festivals which, like the Queen's accession, though not expressly ordained by God yet tended to his honour.[22] The preface, addressed 'To Al Faithful Christians and true harted subiects', explains that Holland has dealt with the arguments of his opposers, Nicholas Servarius, Nicholas Sander, William Reynolds, and 'the Anonymall' in a scholastic manner, where truth and falsehood appear more rapidly than in long discoursing. Holland was aware that two groups would dislike his method: first, those who would fear that he meant to reintroduce the 'olde Dunsery of the Schoolmen'; secondly, those who would suppose 'that this persuasion of mine, if it should take effect, would greatly hinder the unspeakable benefitte which godlie preaching worketh in the Church among Christian people'. God forbid, he exclaims, that he should 'hinder the gift of soule-saving preaching', which has three benefits, edification, exhortation, and consolation and is to be prized above the use of tongues and many other gifts in the church. However, he foresaw no danger that preaching would be prejudiced by the introduction of scholastic rather than discursive divinity, for 'in the Universities the greatest number of scholers desire to have their names in the register of the sonnes of the Prophets'.[23] If fifty of the 5,000 preachers, catechists, and

[20] BL, Sloane MS 848, fo. 8^r.

[21] Exeter College Muniments, A.I.5. Register, 1539-1619, 157. Letter of the Queen to the Sub-Rector and fellows, 28 March 1592.

[22] Thomas Holland, πανηγυρὶς D. Elizabethae, a sermon preached 17 November 1599 (Oxford, 1601), sigs. Q 4^r, R 1^r.

[23] Ibid., sigs. b 2^{r-v}, b 3^{r-v}, b 4^{r-v}, c 1^{r-v}, c 2^r.

exhorters in the realm could be employed in scholastic divinity, it would help preaching rather than diminish it, prophets and preachers would be multiplied, and the Roman adversary better answered. Holland's figure of 5,000 is an inflated estimate which, had it been realistic, would have provided half the parishes in the country with preaching ministers. His aim, to enhance the role of the preacher, was reaffirmed at the end of his dedication: 'I boldy may averre, as one that of the Lord has obtained mercy, that 50 armed in the studies of Divinity, furnished with the skil of tongues, laboriously exercised in the scriptures, studiously conversant in the fathers, wel acquainted with the history of times, practised in ready writing will be no more hinderance of the thousands of preachers of this land.'[24] Holland's view of the office and work of the preacher, if adopted, would have done much to improve educational standards and curb the fiery zeal of the radicals. Even in the 1590s, the problem of an unlearned ministry was still under discussion in the university. Alexander Cooke, of University College, in an academic exercise considered the question: 'Whether the ability to preach is necessarily required of a minister of the gospel?' In a careful synthesis, he quotes both those who claimed that lack of preaching nullified a ministry, and others who asserted that the calling of the church made a minister and that it would be possible to be a minister, though not a good one, without the ability to teach; integrity and honesty of life were equally necessary.[25] Cooke's is an academic, conciliatory view. There still existed in Oxford a fundamental opposition between those who were concerned with the stability of the church, bound to the Prayer Book with its calendar and ordered worship, and those who placed the pulpit at the centre.

The nomination of John Howson, student of Christ Church since 1577, as Vice-Chancellor in July 1602, formed part of a campaign by Chancellor Buckhurst to tighten the reins of his control. Howson had been an MA since 1581, but did not proceed BD and DD until 1601, the year before his appointment, which drew from the preachers the taunt that ' "he had to no other end and purpose got the Degrees of Bachelaur and Dr. of Divinity, without exercise done for them, but only that he

---

[24] Ibid., sig. c 2r-v.
[25] BL, Harleian MS 5247, fo. 44r.

might the sooner obtain the Vicechancellorship and conse-
quently shew his authority in unjust proceedings'''.[26] On 17
November 1602, the Vice-Chancellor preached in St. Mary's
on the anniversary of the Queen's accession. His doctrine of
grace and election, here outlined, seems not to have differed
from the general reformed synthesis which dominated Oxford
theology in this period. His view of creation and redemption
would have caused the assembled doctors no concern, for he
spoke of the 'general and admirable benefit which was done to
al mankind by the creation of man, and the whole world for
mans sake [which] is offered perpetually to the memory of al
mankind by the institution of the Sabboth'. Such sentiments
could only have created a favourable impression in the minds
of the godly hearers, who were much concerned with proper
Sabbath observance. Howson continued with a description of
'that general and admirable benefite of our redemption, which
was sufficient for the whole world, but efficient to al the elect of
God', and summoned his hearers to celebrate this gift, not only
in Sabbath observance, but also on the great festivals. This was
a slippery path, advocating the observance of the 'Conception,
Nativity, Circumcision, Passion, Resurrection, and Ascension
of Christ by the whole Church of God, dispersed farre and
neere over the face of the earth, to the honour of God with
praiers and thankesgiving for the special benefits particularly
called to minde and acknowledged uppon these solemne
daies'.[27] He encouraged the observance of the Prayer Book
calendar and of particular feasts which the more zealous might
have considered of little importance compared with the provision of sermons Sunday by Sunday. Theologically, however,
none would have challenged him. It was the Vice-Chancellor's
ecclesiology, not his soteriology, which fanned the flames of
controversy.

Shortly after he had defended the right of the magistrate to
institute religious observances and encouraged his hearers to

[26] Wood, *Annals*, II, 272. In fact, Howson did dispute for his DD. His chosen
subject, remarriage after divorce for adultery, brought him into conflict with
Reynolds, whose *A Defence of the Iudgment of the Reformed Churches. That a man may lawfully
not onelie put away his wife for her adulterie, but also marrie another* (1609) is a reply.

[27] John Howson, *A Sermon Preached at St. Maries in Oxford in Defence of the Festivities of the
Church of England* (Oxford, 1602), sigs. A 2ʳ⁻ᵛ, A 3ʳ.

celebrate the great festivals of their redemption, Howson turned
to a more general account of the place of worship in the service
of God. Hearing the word preached, he asserted, was not the
only end, or indeed the chief end, of the Lord's Day, which was
'*latriae cultu,* in praising, and magnifying, and lauding God in
the memory of his manifold blessings'. '*Latria*', he continued,
consisted of prayer and thanksgiving, which he defined as a
moral rather than an intellectual virtue. To despise and neglect
'*latria*', said the preacher, 'and to gad up and downe to heare
the word preached, as they cal it, is not onely against the lawes
of this land, the statutes of our colledges, but against the chiefe
Institution of the Lords day'.[28] Howson was clearly anxious for
the observance of the Prayer Book offices and communion, the
calendar and lessons, there prescribed. He was alarmed at the
way in which the balance had been distorted by 'the grand
enormities committed in preaching by many, if not the
generality, of Divines of the University'.[29] Against running up
and down to hear preachers, the principal activity of the
Sabbath in the eyes of many of the godly, he sets the liturgy;
the collects, epistles, gospels, homilies, and sermons suited to
themes of particular days. Howson did not fear to drive home
his message: '*oratoria*', houses of prayer, had been turned into
'*auditoria*', places of hearing. Churches had been turned into
schools, the people desiring first to be 'δαιμονες, knowers, then
Seraphim, hot and zealous'. Sabbaths were not spent '*in cultu
latriae,* the divine service of God, but in hearing of an exercise
as some call it; where sometimes the hour is consumed, *Nihil
dicendo* in speaking never a wise word, sometimes *aliud dicendo* in
speaking from the daie, from the season, from the text, and
sometimes *Male dicendo,* in speaking ill, and slaundring their
private governours or publike magistrates'.[30]

---

[28] Howson, op. cit., sig. A 3r-v.

[29] Wood, *Annals*, II, 272.

[30] Howson, op. cit., sig. A 3V. A similar contrast, but from the opposite viewpoint, is
drawn in a puritan reply to the Oxford *Answere* of 1603. Our preaching, its author
claims, is settled in one church and congregation, where we preach at least once, if not
twice or oftener. We expound one book of scripture until we have finished it. The
Oxford doctors, framers of the *Answere*, of whom Howson was one, he argues, preach
the epistle and gospel for the day and use examples, not only from the Scriptures, but
from ecclesiastical books, the fathers, and the schoolmen. Bodleian Library, MS
Bodley 124, 97, 100-1.

Howson's complaint was not only against the preaching exercise, but against lengthy hortatory sermons, unrelated to the church's calendar. Bancroft seems to have taken much the same line later at the Hampton Court Conference. Faced with demands that a preaching minister should be placed in every parish, he maintained that in a church which was newly founded, preaching was very necessary, but in a church as well established as that in England, it was by no means the only duty. While some maintained that the only duty of a minister was to speak openly, praying was neglected and condemned. James evidently approved, criticizing 'the hypocrisie of our time, which placeth all religion in the ear, through which there is an easy passage'.[31]

Evidence that the part of the sermon of November 1602 which caused Howson so much opposition was that related to the place of preaching is provided by a minor amendment which the Vice-Chancellor made to his printed text before a second edition in 1603. The new impression is identical with the first, apart from a small amendment opposite the reference to *'oratoria'* which have been turned into *'auditoria'*. Here Howson has added 'The authors opinion concerning the necessity and excellencie of devout and holy preaching is to bee read in a Sermon preached at Paules crosse, 1598 Maij 21. & printed at London. pag. 43.'[32] Even in 1598, Howson was touching a potentially explosive subject. The sermon, his second preached at the Cross, argues that the end and use of churches is the public worship of God. Prayer, he continues, excels all other religious actions, as the soul excels the body. Most people in the Church of England, however, neglect common prayer, 'holding it is the only exercise of the service of God to heare a Sermon'. Yet, there is an important caveat: 'I hope no man that heares me this day will be so iniurious to me, or preiudiciall to his owne knowledge and understanding, as to

---

[31] Barlow, *The Summe and Substance of the Conference*, printed in Cardwell, *A History of Conferences*, 191-2. See also Hooker on the excesses of hortatory preaching and the role of the liturgy, homilies, and read lessons in salvation, against the puritan derogation of 'bare reading', for '*sermons* are not *the only preaching* that doth save souls'. *Of the Laws of Ecclesiastical Polity*, V, xxi, 2-4; V, xxii, 9, 12.

[32] Howson, *A Sermon Preached at St. Maries in Oxford*, '*The second impression*' (Oxford, 1603), 6.

conceive that I speake against hearing or frequenting of sermons ... *the ordinarie meanes to live well, is to heare well.*' The
mature Christian requires a greater observance than the
catechumen or hearer, for 'I complaine not that our Churches
are auditories, but that they are not oratories: not that you
come to Sermons, but that you refuse or neglect common
prayer; not that you resort *ad porticum Solomonis,* to Paules
crosse, but that your parish churches are naked and emptie.'[33]
Preaching has its proper place in the service of God, but hearing must lead to knowledge and the intention to practise
religion. It is but a means to the *cultum Dei.* These sentiments,
when uttered by the Vice-Chancellor before the university in
1602, without the explanations and caveats of the Paul's Cross
sermon, were bound to occasion alarm and opposition.

Four days after Howson's sermon, a younger member of his
own house followed him into the pulpit of St. Mary's. John
Sprint had a long career of nonconformity ahead of him before
he eventually conformed, and his sermon of 21 November was
one of his first acts of defiance. Son of the Dean of Bristol, he
had come up to Oxford as a member of Christ Church in 1592.
His religious temper must be judged almost entirely from his
later writings, but it is evident that in 1602 he was already a
militant young man. His earliest published work, *Propositions,
Tending to Proove the Necessarie Use of the Christian Sabbaoth,* probably written while he was still at Oxford, shows him to be
thoroughly grounded in the continental reformed writers of the
second generation and the English Calvinist divines, especially
Fulke and Perkins. This work, refuting atheists and papists, is
conciliatory towards the establishment, and more indicative of
Sprint's fiery temper is a broadsheet entitled *The Anatomy of the
Controversed Ceremonies of the Church of England, Beeing Considered in
their Nature and Circumstances,* in which he draws the battle lines
between those who disclaim the ceremonies and those who retain them.[33a]

No detail of Sprint's St. Mary's sermon survives, though
Wood records that he made 'sundry points of Doctrine against
the Ceremonies and Discipline now established in the Church

---

[33] Howson, *A Second Sermon Preached at Paules Crosse...the 21 of May, 1598* (London,
1598), 40-4.

[33a] John Sprint, *Propositions* ... (London, 1607), esp. 8, 40-50.

of England ... also taxing by cavelling speeches the Vice-
chancellor, and other Governors of the University'.[34] Sprint
was immediately ordered by Howson to submit a copy of his
sermon and when he refused to do so was imprisoned. This
seems to have been the signal for the beginning of a sermon
campaign in the university. Wood ascribed to Airay the moving
force in this campaign, which was vigorously conducted. Robert
Troutbeck, a member of Airay's own college, a young man of
about the same age as Sprint and fellow of Queen's since
1599, found his way into St. Mary's pulpit on 21 December.
His sermon made two principal points: first, he deplored the
persecution of the godly in the university; secondly, he attacked
ministers who resided in the university whilst holding a benefice with cure of souls in which they were non-resident. A contemporary account depicts the general disorder caused by the
preachers:

Now since Mr. Sprint was imprisoned, the whole current of their Sermons is nothing but complaints of the afflication and persequution of the
godly, of hindering of the Word and stopping the course of the Gospel,
and that as bitterly in a manner as the Jesuits or Priests exclaime in their
books *de persecutionibus Anglicanis,* accounting the Magistrates no better
than tyrants and persequutors of Preachers. Lastly they are now come to
open and infamous libelling, affirming that sith preaching cannot have
its force, they may lawfully fly to that refuge. Which divilish humour, yf
by authority it be not repressed, will break out shortly into greater
outrage and inconvenience. They have consulted and consented to
preach non-residents out of their Benefices or Headships, or at least so to
rate and exagitate them in the pulpit, that they shall not dare for shame to
appeare at Sermon. And yf that will not serve the turne, they threaten
force, and all outreageous attempts. Yt is to be proved that one of them in
a Conventicle with applause of others, made his braggs that yf the
Vicechancellour had come in person to any of the three Congregatiohs,
his hood had been pulled over his eares and himself thrown down the
staires, as they say a Proctor was once served so in Cambridge.[35]

Despite the imprisonment of Sprint, the radical preachers still
had the use of the Oxford pulpits at the end of the year, and the
Vice-Chancellor was able to do little to control their libels.

[34] Wood, *Annals,* II, 272.
[35] BL, Harleian MS 4240, fo. 70; Magdalen College Oxford MS 280, item 53;
Wood, *Annals,* II, 277.

Through Buckhurst, he seems to have appealed to the Privy Council, and the undated 'Articles Against the Puritan Faction' clearly belong to this period. They appeal from the university for help to suppress the irregularities, depicting dangerous social upheaval. First, the preachers have been discovering the faults of magistrates, ministers, and non-residents, and any action taken against a member of the preachers' faction is immediately reported from the pulpit. Secondly, all non-residence, without exception, is bitterly condemned, and though no individual has been named, those so vilified from the pulpit can easily be identified. Thirdly, because the preachers have tired themselves with these factious courses, heresy and popery have grown in strength and are allowed to go unchallenged. Fourthly, 'the Pulpit and sacred function of preaching have become instruments of private revenge: our persons deeply disgraced: our authority greatly weakened; whilst the junior sort reprehending these odious imputations are easily drawn to an utter contempt of their lawful Governors, whom so openly and confidently they hear dayly depraved'.

Howson is attempting to present a case which has more than domestic implications. The university hierarchy was under attack and its ability to deal with the papist challenge gravely impaired. He now demanded that if the Council or the 'higher powers' were unable to deal with the matter, and since the university could not afford the costs of continual resort to the Privy Council, a commission should be issued to certain members of the university 'with sufficient authority from the sovereign power to hear, examine and censure such undiscreet and enormous persons'.[36]

Documentary evidence is incomplete for the course of events following Howson's appeal to the Privy Council. With Sprint in prison, Airay emerged as ringleader of the opposition. This was a curious development. Not only was he the non-resident incumbent of the Queen's College living of Charlton-on-Otmoor and therefore himself subject to the strictures of the radical preachers, but he was also a senior figure in the university, hardly to be associated with militant juniors. Some members of Queen's,

---

[36] BL, Harleian MS 4240, fo. 70; Magdalen College Oxford MS 280, item 53; Wood, *Annals*, II, 276-7.

Troutbeck among them, joined in the attack on non-residents and particularly on Howson as persecutor of the godly. Unfortunately none of Airay's ninety-five sermons on Philippians is dated, though he refers frequently to the problems of non-residence, lack of maintenance for poor ministers, and the likelihood of hardship for those who persist in godly courses.[37] Some of these sermons may easily relate to the campaign at the turn of the year 1602-3. Howson seems to have singled out Airay as the ringleader. Either on his own authority, or that of the commission which he had requested from the Privy Council, he began proceedings against him. This was a bold move, in some ways similar to that taken against John Reynolds in 1586, in view of the fact that Airay's college had assumed the mantle of principal seminary for godly preachers. Airay was now forbidden to preach or teach the word of God in the university. On 18 January 1603, he appealed to Congregation against the sentence, perhaps in the belief that among the younger masters, who dominated that body, he would have a strong lobby. The appeal is evidence of his hurt feelings and raised temper. Airay protested that Howson had deprived him without the customary warning, or any chance to appeal. He believed that the Vice-Chancellor, acting from personal hostility, had proceeded hastily and unconstitutionally against him. The petition is witnessed by some of his younger colleagues in Queen's, Thomas Todhunter, David Hechstetter, and Henry Woodward. Howson was wise not to attend the meeting of Congregation which considered the appeal, perhaps aware of the story circulating concerning the Cambridge proctor. Leonard Hutten, one of the pro-Vice-Chancellors and Canon of Christ Church, took the chair. He rejected Airay's appeal, but it was admitted *notwithstanding* by the proctors, Daniel Pury of Magdalen and Walter Bennett of New College, because it had the customary and statutory support of the house. The religious sentiment of the proctors is not known, but, in theory at least, they may be held to have represented the younger masters.[38]

Since disciplinary proceedings against Airay and others within the university itself were now either impossible or too dangerous,

[37] For example, Airay, *Philippians*, 122.
[38] OUA/NEP *supra*/Register M, fo. 149ᵛ.

Howson's only recourse was to external jurisdiction, even at the risk of infringing the university's jealously-guarded immunities. In a letter to Dudley Carleton, Ambassador in Paris, dated 11 February 1603, John Chamberlain provides the only evidence of the next stage of the proceedings. He writes, 'Doctor Howson Vicechancellor of Oxford made a sermon there on the Queenes day that is accused of false doctrine, and hath bred much brabling and raised such a dust there that I thincke will put out some of theyre eyes. Dr. Ayrie and divers others are sent up and imprisoned here and some there. I send you here the sermon.'[39] Airay, Sprint, and Troutbeck were probably at this point summoned to London to be examined by a commission of the Privy Council, Buckhurst himself, the ageing Whitgift, Sir John Stanhope, Vice-Chamberlain, Sir John Fortescue, Chancellor of the Exchequer, together with Bancroft and Sir Richard Swale, Chancellor of the diocese of Ely. No record of the enquiry survives, apart from the forms of submission to be pronounced publicly by the offending preachers, dated 26 February, probably the end of the proceedings in London. On 4 March, the examination ended, a letter was sent to Howson to be read to Convocation, stating that 'Wee send yow herein inclosed the several orders of submission for Dr. Airay, John Sprint and Robert Troutbecke, which wee uppon due consideration of the qualitie of their offences, have thought meet to enjoyne unto them; for the due performance whereof, wee have taken severall bonds with sufficient sureties for the use of her Majestie.'[40] These forms of submission were to be read in Oxford within the following two weeks. This did not take place, and it is difficult to resist the view that Howson found the summoning of a meeting of Convocation tiresome. However, on 17 March 1603, the assembly gathered, and the forms of submission for Sprint and Troutbeck are duly recorded in the register.[41]

Sprint made the following confession, supplied by the commissioners: 'Whereas I John Sprint have by my rash and indiscreet behaviour, as well in pulpitt, on the 21 day of November last past, as elsewhere, given publique scandall and offence, namelie by uttering sundry poynts of Doctrine against the Ceremonies and Discipline now established in the Church of England, as also

---

[39] *The Letters of John Chamberlain*, ed. N. E. McClure (Philadelphia, 1939), I, 185.
[40] Wood, *Annals*, II, 272.
[41] OUA/NEP *supra*/Register M, fos. 71ᵛ-72ʳ.

by my unreverent and undutifull taxing, by cavilling speaches, Mr Vicechancellor, and other Governors of this Universitie contraire to my dutie.' He confessed also his threat of revenge against the authorities after he had been punished. He promised that in future he would behave himself 'in a more modest, temperat and dutifull sort'.[42] His future career was to demonstrate that another fifteen years would pass before he reached that degree of conformity which the commissioners demanded in 1603. In the meanwhile, he continued to offer harsh criticism of the doctrine and ceremonies of the Church of England.

Troutbeck's form of submission, read at the same meeting of Convocation, acknowledged his unadvised action in supporting Sprint and his encouragement of turbulent spirits. He confessed that he had as much sought 'to deprave publique authority as to animate disorderly and factious persons'.[43] A similar promise of future good behaviour was made. The register of Convocation says nothing further about Airay, though the Vice-Chancellor, having initiated the external proceedings, can scarcely have ignored the form of submission sent down by the commissioners. Wood speculates that he 'through the favour he found, escaped a submission'.[44] The victory which Airay had won in January before Congregation may have made Howson very wary of further action. Airay, at least, had achieved a personal triumph.

Howson did not allow the indignity he had suffered to pass without ensuring that the university was furnished with a stricter rule for licensing preachers, which, at the same time, helped to check the renewed papist assertion to which he had referred in his letter to the Council. The statute of 19 October 1580 had required subscription to the Articles of Religion and the Book of Common Prayer from all those seeking a licence to preach in the university, as well as a year's experience preaching or catechizing in a hall or college. These regulations were primarily introduced to restrict the activity of crypto-papists. Now Howson provided 'Articles whereunto all such as

[42] OUA/NEP *supra*/Register M, fo. 71ᵛ; Wood, *Annals*, II, 273-4.
[43] OUA/NEP *supra*/Register M, fo. 72ʳ; Wood, *Annals*, II, 274-5.
[44] Wood, *Annals*, II, 275.

are admitted to preache, reade, catechize, minister the Sacraments, or to execute any other ecclesiastical function doe agree and consent'.[45] The first article asserted the absolute sovereignty of the monarch, both temporal and spiritual, and would appear to have been directed towards papists rather than radical protestant preachers. In the second article, the subscriber consented that the Prayer Book and Ordinal contained nothing contrary to the word of God, and that he would always use it in public services of the church. The third article was an agreement to the Articles of Religion.

The controversy was at an end, and Howson was able to re-establish some of the ground he had lost before he relinquished the Vice-Chancellorship in July 1603. By this time it had become the invariable custom for the Vice-Chancellor to hold office for one year only, so Buckhurst's failure to renominate him is of no significance. A letter from the Chancellor, dated 30 June 1603, was read at Convocation on 6 July. He noted that Howson had completed his term of office, and nominated George Abbot, Master of University College, to succeed him. He commended Abbot as a man of experience and dexterity of mind, and prayed that the university would aid and assist him in his office. He seized the occasion to lecture the scholars on their duties and indicated that the good of every one of them and of the commonwealth consisted of their dutiful and religious service of God, the administration of justice, and general peace and concord. Here Buckhurst added, 'the breach whereof lately made by some over-turbulent and troublesome spirites, whose names though I conceale are well enough knowne unto you, hath brought soe great an imputation to your whole universitie as that I feare it will not easely be abolished'.[46] Abbot was probably the best available candidate to reconcile the warring elements in the university. He had been Vice-Chancellor already in 1600 and was well known as a preacher. His course of sermons, delivered before the university in 1594-9, had been published under the title *An Exposition upon the Prophet Ionah*. The tone of these sermons differs from the more fervent and evangelical note which Airay sounds, but

---

[45] Ibid., 277.
[46] OUA/NEP *supra*/Register M, fo. 74ᵛ.

Abbot's concerns are often similar. He stresses the central role of preaching in the church, and the need for diligent ministers 'in these most perillous times, wherein Satan fretteth and rageth; wherein Papisme is little weakned, but Atheisme waxeth strong, and the sinnes of men doe crie; but on the other side pitie waxeth thin, and charitie groweth cold, This should be a lively motion to stirre up the Spirit of God in us, that with alacritie we may go forward, to the building up of Gods house and not to be wearied in well doing.'[47] Whilst Abbot can in no sense be considered a puritan, as Professor Trevor-Roper implies when he argues that Abbot preached puritan doctrines but rejected their implications, he was sometimes to be identified with the leaders of advanced protestant opinion in the university.[48] In 1600, when he was Vice-Chancellor, some of the citizens of London sought the opinion of the university on the re-erection of the Cross at Cheapside. Abbot's reply was eventually published in 1641, under the title *Cheapside Cross Censured and Condemned*. The chief plank in the argument seems to have been the danger of idolatry from the visual representation of the persons of the Trinity, and Abbot reported how in the previous summer, as Vice-Chancellor, he had burned in the market-place in Oxford 'a picture wherein was the image of God the Father over a Crucifix ready to receive the soul of Christ'.[49] He also records the destruction of a crucifix in a stained-glass window at Balliol, while he was an undergraduate, and concludes that the Cheapside Cross should not be re-erected, and the opportunity taken to strike a further blow against superstition.[50] He was supported, as co-signatories, in this opinion by Henry Airay and John Reynolds, and three other Oxford divines. Abbot was no friend of extreme courses, indeed his later ineffectiveness as Archbishop was in no small measure a result of his moderate opinions, but men like Airay and Reynolds knew that he stood on the side of the preachers and would never proceed against them as Howson had done. Airay's career seems to have been unaffected by this incident. He continued to serve on Convocation committees throughout

---

[47] Abbot, *An Exposition upon the Prophet Ionah*, 41.
[48] H. R. Trevor-Roper, *Archbishop Laud, 1573-1645* (2nd ed., London, 1962), 41.
[49] Abbot, *Cheapside Cross Censured and Condemned* (London, 1641), 4.
[50] Ibid., 6-7.

this winter of discontent. The militant preachers had been checked both by Howson's 'Articles' and by the reply to the Millenary Petition, the Oxford *Answere*, another product of Howson's Vice-Chancellorship, though published after his successor Abbot had taken office.[51] Nevertheless, while Howson had stood for the worship of the Church of England as conceived in the Book of Common Prayer, a balance of word and sacrament, where preaching was regulated by the restrictions of the calendar and the structure of the offices, at no point did he contest the preachers' view on basic questions of faith and salvation. The seriousness of that challenge was soon to be glimpsed in Oxford.

[51] For a further discussion, see below 228-9.

X

EPILOGUE: THE REFORMED TRADITION, ASSERTION AND CHALLENGE, c.1595-c.1606

In our Church what Cockatrice egges be now a hatching? what out-worne errors of Pelagianisme be now a broaching? Libertie of will, universalitie of grace, salvation of all men, and other like damnable errours must now be set on foot againe, though the whole Church bee set on fire therewith.[1]

With this warning, Henry Airay alerted his undergraduate congregation to the danger of dissent in church and common-wealth. He had little to fear. Throughout the 1590s, the Cal-vinist message rang loudly and clearly from the Oxford pulpits, with few to challenge it. In Cambridge, young William Barrett was suggesting to the learned doctors that the security of the elect, by which they set such store, might be a wicked presump-tion, and Peter Baro was extending the frontiers of the universe of grace to allow that God, by his primary or antecedent will at least, had created all men to eternal life. All, he claimed, possessed grace sufficient to salvation; each had freedom to accept or reject the grace offered, to embrace or turn aside from the benefits won by the death of Christ. The reprobate had only themselves to blame: they had rejected the offer. Their dam-nation was not the result of God's antecedent will, but of his consequent will.[2] Accounts of the Cambridge disturbances and the action launched there by the Calvinist doctors must have reached the ears of the Oxford divines.

Nevertheless, until 1606 there was little wavering in the message delivered from the Oxford pulpits. In two sermons, preached by George Abbot in 1595-6, the crucial years in Cam-bridge, the enemies are atheism and papism, not universalism or a doubting of salvation in the elect. In his subject, Jonah, Abbot detects the classic conflict between faith and fear. Jonah doubts that he is one of God's elect, or that he ever has been

---

[1] Airay, *Philippians*, 302.
[2] Porter, 382.

such. This cannot be true, since the divine decree is immutable; those whom God loves, he loves to the end, even though they have sometimes to wait until the ninth hour or even the eleventh hour before they apprehend the divine promises.[3] In a later lecture, Abbot insists again that in foreappointing some to eternal life, though there are sometimes 'shadowes and seemings to the contrary', God has worked unchangeably for a man's salvation.[4]

The Oxford undergraduate congregation suffered an unrelenting diet, without the occasional excitement of a Barrett or a Baro in the pulpit. Preaching in the same course of sermons as Abbot, Airay was constantly concerned to give hints for practical godliness, Sabbath observance, attendance at sermons, scripture reading, and sobriety of life, which might have been thought to verge on the semi-pelagian. He could preach like this because he was clear on essentials. He calls his hearers to beware of those who claim that men not begotten in the faith of Christ are able to do things which are good and pleasing to God. The good things which men do must be directed solely to the praise and glory of God, not so that they may merit heaven.[5] Aware that such preaching might mislead, Airay warned his congregation to 'beware of such as traduce us, and the doctrine which wee preach'. Good works are no part of salvation; we are exhorted 'to make an end of our owne salvation not for that we are able to doe so, but to teach us to flie unto him who worketh in us both the will and the deede'.[6] Good works, however, do have a secondary purpose: man's constant endeavour must be to demonstrate to himself and to others that he is a son of God. Much may also be based on feeling. An elect man will continually feel a strife within himself, because his sanctification in this life is imperfect.[7] Airay, like Perkins, places great stress on the knowledge of election which a man may gain from the workings of his own soul, 'an experimentall feeling and knowledge of Christ, whereby we feele and know in our own soules that he is such a one as the scriptures describe him to be'.[8] He

---

[3] Abbot, *An Exposition upon the Prophet Ionah*, 232.
[4] Ibid., 271. Compare Perkins and Robert Some; Porter, 301-3, 319.
[5] Airay, *Philippians*, 151-4.
[6] Ibid., 394, 400.
[7] Ibid., 432-6.
[8] Ibid., 683.

calls his hearers to try their hearts to see how many of them possess this knowledge of Christ. Yet there is a catholicity of outlook in Airay, often found in early seventeenth-century Calvinist theology, for example in John Preston and the earlier thought of John Cotton. Man will also find assurance of his election within the church and especially in the bread and wine of the supper. These are seals of the mystical union with Christ; they give assurance and strengthen faith, but only when a man has duly prepared himself to receive them.[9]

If theological controversy had come to Oxford in 1595-6, Airay would have been ill-equipped to deal with it. His sermons give little evidence of a powerful or original mind; he accepts the reformed synthesis without ever needing to state it clearly, and there is practically no point at which he needs to defend it. One young fellow of Corpus would, however, have risen to the challenge. Sebastian Benefield was just 26 when he mounted the pulpit of St. Mary's on 14 December 1595 to preach before the university. His sermon survived because he later became Lady Margaret Professor, and it found its way into print in 1614, long after delivery. The date of the first of the *Eight Sermons Publikely Preached in the University of Oxford* is worth noting. In December 1595, Cambridge had already been involved for eight months in the controversies following Barrett's sermon. The Lambeth Articles, Whitgift's attempt to bring peace to the university, had been issued on 20 November. The seventh article was especially relevant to Benefield's theme: 'Saving grace is not granted, is not made common, is not ceded to all men, by which they might be saved if they wish.'[10] The first eight pages of Benefield's sermon are devoted to refuting the idea of universal election. It is the first of very few signs, if sign it is, that the Lambeth Articles and the controversy which produced them had any immediate impact upon Oxford. Benefield first weighs the scriptural evidence. He sets up, in apparent opposition, 1 Timothy 2:4, 'God desires all men to be saved', and Romans 9:18, 'God will have mercy on whom he will have mercy, and whom he wills he hardeneth', and asks whether these two texts indicate a divine mutability.

---

[9] Ibid., 688-9; see also BL, Harleian MS 4048, fos. 6ᵛ-12ʳ.
[10] Porter, 371.

God forbid, declares the preacher, and proceeds to a series of justificatory arguments. Rapidly, he falls back on the acknowledged English authority and his constant mentor, William Perkins. Perkins had proposed, for refutation, the erroneous thesis that 'there is an universall election by which Almighty God, without any restraint or exception of persons, hath purposed by Christ to redeeme or reconcile unto himselfe all mankind'.[11] For Benefield, as for Perkins, this is a fundamental error. God teaches all men to come to Christ and be saved, not because all men therefore come, but because no man who comes is saved, unless he is called by God. And this calling is selective; God chooses some and not all. How then are the ways of God to be justified to men? Benefield avoids this difficulty by recourse to the teaching of Calvin himself: 'Such busie and too curious demanders may learne of S. *Paul,* that Gods will and pleasure is the onely chiefe cause, why hee *electeth* some, and *reproveth* the rest; that this point of doctrine is to be beleeved by faith, not to be examined by reason.'[12] Benefield returns to this theme in sermons which he preached in 1596-7: that Christ died for all the elect while they were still sinners; that it is an error, as some claim, that the elect and regenerate do not sin; that the elect may fall, but not finally; and that the golden chain of the causes of salvation can never be broken.[13]

The increasing emphasis given to good works as the fruits of salvation in Oxford writers reached its climax in a 1604 treatise by one of the chaplains of Merton, Jeremy Corderoy. *A Short Dialogue, wherein it is proved, that no man can be saved without good works* is conceived as a debate between an Oxford scholar, 'of the old stamp ... which ... all the Elect of God have bin ... zealous of good works and studious to approve their calling therby; yet ... far from the blasphemous conceit of the Papists', and a gallant, who has heard that strong faith, a 'bare faith' without works, is sufficient. On their journey to Oxford they are joined by a church-papist who maintains that by his works a man can gain divine reward.[14] Corderoy's aim is to refute

[11] *The Workes of that Famous and Worthie Minister of Christ in the Universitie of Cambridge, Mr W. Perkins* (Cambridge, 1608), I, 109-10. (*A Golden Chaine*, ch. 54, error 1.)
[12] Benefield, *Eight Sermons*, 4-8.
[13] Ibid., 80, 90-1; Benefield, *The Sinne against the Holy Ghost Discovered*, 11-12.
[14] Jeremy Corderoy, *A Short Dialogue* (Oxford, 1604), 2-4, 16, 27.

presumption and false security. The scholar, probably intended as a self-portrait, explains that for justification strong faith without works is sufficient, but that for sanctification more is required. First comes predestination, then an effectual vocation, by the preaching of the word externally, and the internal operation of the Holy Ghost. Strong faith on its own turns to strong presumption. Predestination is an excellent doctrine, yet it is a stumbling-block to many and an incentive to live carelessly. Frequenting sermons and having conference with the godly, for example, must be the ordinary means of salvation in the elect. The gallant, with his strong faith, not suprisingly becomes tired of the scholar and they join company with a church-papist, also riding in the direction of Oxford. The papist maintains that it is clear from the Scriptures that bad works are the cause of a man's damnation, but that by his good works he merits heaven. The scholar will have none of this, protesting that no works are perfectly good, and that even those good works which the elect do perform are not their own, but the special gift of God. Held in this balance, the reformed synthesis was maintained in Oxford throughout this period, even when, from the pulpit at least, pelagian tendencies sometimes appeared to throw doubt on the strict doctrine of election.[15]

In the Schools, however, where pastoral care did not dictate a moderate approach and where no appeal to the tender consciences of the hearers was necessary, a student might have expected to find the doctrine of election reigning supreme in all its grandeur and purity. Such is not the case. By far the most prominent category of thesis defended there concerned the doctrine of justification by faith in general, and, particularly in the early 1590s, the relative place of faith and works. The authority of the Scriptures and the nature of the presence in the eucharist were also prominent, and anti-papal themes, for example, attacks on papal headship, invocation of the saints and private masses, and defences of the legitimate ministry of the Church of England, were more popular in the period 1595-1605 than the doctrine of election. Some interest in this doctrine had however been evident well before the Cambridge debates of 1595-6, or the first edition of Perkins's *A Golden Chaine* in 1591.

---

[15] Ibid., 44, 47, 73, 76-8.

In 1581, Nicholas Bond, the future President of Magdalen, had defended for his DD the thesis 'Is God's will immutable?', and in the following year, William Souch, student of Christ Church, had discussed 'None of the elect can perish'.[16] There is some evidence, though it is slight, that the Lambeth Articles determined the course of debate in Oxford in the period immediately following their formulation, and that the doctrine of election, in less precise terms, became a growing preoccupation in these years. 'Are the elect justified through faith without works?' had been defended in 1590, and in 1591, a similar thesis 'Are good works the cause of our predestination?' was prescribed.[17] However, from 1595, the discussions take on a more technical appearance. The first of the Lambeth Articles, 'God from eternity hath predestined some men to life, and reprobated some to death' was defended in almost precisely these terms by Robert Abbot in 1597. In 1596, Henry Parry discussed 'A just man cannot finally fall away from faith', though he was required to debate using the term *'justus'* not *'electus'*. He may have denied the second thesis, 'A just man cannot for a time fall away from faith' and affirmed the third, 'A just man can be certain (*certus*) of the continuance of his faith'. In the same year, the subjects prescribed for debate at the *Comitia* revealed a continuing emphasis on this controversial subject: 'Is election free without foregoing works?', 'Is justification by faith alone?', 'Do works merit eternal life?'.[18] After 1595-7, a more general treatment of the doctrine of election seems to have attracted some attention, though there is little evidence that any disputant adopted a line other than that of the orthodox Calvinists except to set up a case for demolition. At the *Comitia* of 1602 disputants were still considering 'Whether God gave every man sufficient grace for salvation?', 'Whether the regenerate may wholly fall from grace?', 'Whether the sacraments bring grace by the work wrought?'.[19]

The first signs that the reformed synthesis was seriously in question are slight, though hints of the coming troubles may be discerned in the Howson-Airay controversy of 1602-3. Another

---

[16] Clark, *Register*, II, part i, 194-207.
[17] Ibid., 196-7.
[18] Ibid., 198-9.
[19] BL, Sloane MS 848, fo. 26ʳ.

index of the theological temperature of the university is afforded by the debates at the Hampton Court Conference in January 1604. For the more radical members of the national movement, it was a disaster that John Reynolds emerged as 'the Principall mouthe and speaker', and Professor Patrick Collinson has argued that moderates like Reynolds were far from dominating the proceedings at the puritan conference held in London to prepare for the meeting.[20] Reynolds's contribution to the conference indicated both his essential moderation and his fundamental preoccupation with doctrinal issues. He was not, for instance, committed to the radical demands for the abolition of the surplice, though he did protest that, together with the cross, it was a teaching ceremony and not merely a thing indifferent. His own view had been formulated in a letter to the Lancashire ministers of 1590.[21] He nevertheless advocated most of the points in the puritan programme, and had he achieved them, there would have been little cause for complaint. His most radical suggestion, which he had previously canvassed in the 1586 sermons, for clergy meetings, prophesyings, and episcopal synods, where the bishop and ministers could decide contentious issues, was, according to the *Summe and Substance,* misunderstood by the King, who seems to have believed that the abolition of episcopacy was intended, and that Reynolds aimed at Scottish presbytery, which 'as well agreeth with a monarchy as God with the Devil'. In fact, what Reynolds intended was presbytery-in-episcopacy.[22] His refusal to subscribe the Three Articles, brought forward by Bancroft at the conference and reinforced through the Canons of 1604, was based on the doctrinal ground that subscription to the Prayer Book involved consent to the use of the Apocrypha in church.

---

[20] Usher, *The Reconstruction of the English Church*, I, 310-33; Collinson, *E.P.M.*, 455-9; 'An anonymous account in favour of the Bishops', Cambridge University Library, MS Mm I.45, fos. 155-7, printed by Usher, op. cit., II, 337.

[21] Queen's College Oxford MS 280, fo. 174ʳ, Reynolds to Edward Fleetwood, 30 November 1590. Reynolds advised the Lancashire ministers to conform and wear the surplice, rather than be deprived of their ministry.

[22] Barlow, *The Summe and Substance of the Conference*, in Cardwell, *A History of Conferences*, 201-2; M. H. Curtis, 'The Hampton Court Conference and its Aftermath', in *History*, xlvi (1961), 1-16.

For this refusal, he was willing to risk expulsion from the university, and it may have been the intercession of the Earl of Salisbury alone which prevented this.[23]

In the discussions on the second day of the conference, Reynolds gave the highest priority to the reassertion of the reformed doctrine in all its fullness. His four points were, that the doctrine of the church might be preserved in purity according to God's word, that good pastors might be planted in all the churches to preach it, that church government might be sincerely ministered according to God's word, and that the Book of Common Prayer 'might be fitted to more increase of piety'. This order of priorities was far from the balance of the Millenary Petition.

The Oxford *Answere* to the petitioners had appeared on 7 October 1603, published in the names of the Vice-Chancellor, the doctors, both the proctors, and other heads of houses. Its stated intention, in the face of the slanders of the 'Humble Petition', was 'to shewe ourselves as truly zealous and carefully religious in the defence of the Church'.[24] By the time that it came from the press, George Abbot had begun his second term as Vice-Chancellor, though the original initiative for publication may have come from his predecessor, John Howson, who held office until the middle of July. Christopher Dale of Merton and William Laud of St. John's were the proctors. Of the heads of houses and doctors, it is inconceivable that Reynolds subscribed and highly improbable that Airay would have done so. The *Answere* gives no indication that there had been doctrinal disputes in Oxford, though it refers to the Petitioners' desire for doctrinal uniformity against the continued defence and teaching of popish opinions. No intimation of the university's general theological climate emerges. One of the 'puritan replies', however, indicates that disquiet had been caused by the public affirmation in the pulpit and in the Schools of the following doctrines: that justifying faith could be lost, that such faith is not proper to the elect, that a man cannot be sure of his own salvation, that a

[23] Historical Manuscripts Commission, *Calendar of the Manuscripts of the Marquess of Salisbury at Hatfield House*, XVII, 422-3, 431; Lambeth Palace Library, MS 929, fo. 121; Cardwell, op. cit., 194-5. Reynolds was willing to conform in the matter of the surplice and square cap.
[24] *Answere*, sig. ¶ 3ᵛ.

man has free will to believe or not, and that Christ did not die only for the elect.[25] These points of doctrine would seem to relate more closely to events in Cambridge than Oxford, but a second reply, a manuscript copy of which was in the possession of William Burton of Queen's College in 1626, has a definite bearing on Oxford, although its provenance is unknown. It substantiates the holiness and justness of the puritan request that conformity of doctrine be prescribed and that popish opinions be no more taught or defended, and traces the initial corruption of doctrine to two strangers in the universities, one, a Spaniard, at Oxford, the other, a Frenchman, at Cambridge. The reply gives Corro much less emphasis than Baro. The writer refers to the Spanish preacher's commentary on Romans, and his other writings which were 'knowen to have byn full of manye erronious and fantasticall opynions'. A final point also makes quite clear reference to the sermon campaign of 1602-3 against Vice-Chancellor Howson. The same persons who have maintained doctrines ·contrary to predestination have also preferred prayer before preachihg and have complained 'that Oratoryes were turned into Auditoryes' and have extolled Holy Days above the Sabbath.[26] Both these points have suffered distortion, but clearly spring from Howsons's sermon, based on a general suspicion that he inclined towards a less strict view of predestination than the dominant Oxford opinion.

Reynolds's failure at Hampton Court to provide the additional doctrinal safeguards which he desired must not be attributed to disaffection on the part of most of the other participants. Several of the bishops involved, Babington of Worcester, Robinson of Carlisle, Rudd of St. David's, and Tobie Mathew of York, all supported the Calvinist cause, as did George Abbot, Dean of Winchester and James Montagu, Dean of the Chapels Royal. Bancroft may assume a more than justified dominance of the proceedings in Barlow's *Summe and Substance,* together with Dean Overall of St. Paul's, Lancelot Andrewes, Dean of Westminster, and Barlow himself; and he probably determined to rebut all puritan requests and to oppose a closer definition of Calvinist theology.

---

[25] BL, Additional MS 8978, fo. 47ʳ.
[26] Bodleian Library, MS Bodley 124, 59-63.

On the second day of the conference, opening his speech, Reynolds first asked that certain obscurities in the Articles of Religion might be removed. For example, he desired that in Article XVI, following the words 'after we have received the Holy Ghost, we may depart from grace and fall into sin', should be added 'yet neither totally nor finally', in order to ensure that no doubt be cast on the final perseverance of the elect. He also attempted to elevate the Lambeth Articles, intended by Whitgift for the settlement of a private dispute in the university of Cambridge, to the status of a confessional document appended to the Articles of Religion. It was not until Reynolds had proceeded with some other small amendments to the Articles that Bancroft interrupted, much to the King's irritation, attacking Reynolds's desire to have the doctrine of predestination more closely defined. 'How very many in these daies', he said, 'neglecting holiness of life, presumed too much of persisting of grace, laying all their religion upon predestination, If I shall be saved, I shall be saved; which he termed a desperate doctrine, shewing it contrary to good divinity, and the true doctrine of predestination, wherein we should reason rather *ascendendo* that *descendendo*, thus "I live in obedience to God, in love with my neighbour, I follow my vocation, etc., therefore I trust that God hath elected me, and predestined me to salvation: not thus, which is the usual course of argument, God hath predestined and chosen me to life, therefore though I sin never so grievously, yet I shall not be damned: for whom he once loveth, he loveth to the end." '[27] Dean Overall also desired to speak on this subject, believing that Reynolds had attacked him personally in his reassertion of the doctrine of predestination.[28]

Reynolds was checked at Hampton Court, and his desire to bolster the Calvinist doctrinal statements rejected. Outside the university, where his theoretical radicalism had flourished for thirty years, he failed to satisfy the demands of those who had sent him to the conference. James seems to have realized that away from the Schools, he and his companions were out of their depth. The King reported to a Scottish friend, 'they fled

[27] Barlow, *The Summe and Substance of the Conference*, in Cardwell, op. cit., 178-81.
[28] Ibid., 186.

me from argument to argument', and added that if any of their scholars had behaved in this manner, they would not have escaped unpunished. He told Reynolds himself that 'he was a better college man than a states man'.[29] Yet Reynolds and his supporters were almost destined to fail. Bancroft and the bishops had not wanted the conference, and they were ultimately responsible for the implementation of its decisions; the Archbishop himself drafted the amendments to the Book of Common Prayer. However, he was an isolated figure among the episcopate, and the failure of Reynolds at Hampton Court in no way affected the Calvinist dominance of the university and of the country in general. Bancroft was succeeded by the Calvinist George Abbot, and Calvinists continued to weigh down the episcopal bench throughout the reign of James.[30] For the next two decades, the reformed synthesis still dominated Oxford theology, but no longer did it go unchallenged. Oxford theologians at last found it necessary to assert their doctrines and the nomination of Henry Airay as Vice-Chancellor in 1606 may be seen as part of a stiffening resistance.

Buckhurst wrote to Airay on 12 June 1606, noting that his chief aim had always been to provide for the university's government 'men of learning and integrity and such as have been comfortable to the ecclesiastical discipline established in this land'. Of Airay's conformity, he claimed that he had no doubt. 'I acknowledge you to be one of that number what-soever hath been surmised or suggested to the contrarye; for the better confirmation and encouragement in that course, I take you to my protection.' Buckhurst is making a clear point: that there has been some concern about Airay's conformity, perhaps justified. In nominating him as Vice-Chancellor, he must have realized that he was taking a calculated risk; yet Airay, for all the troubles of 1602-3, was a comparatively safe man, which John Reynolds never was.[31] His Vice-Chancellor-ship might have passed into quiet obscurity had he not found himself in conflict with a young fellow of St. John's, William Laud.

---

[29] Ibid., 161, 189.
[30] N. R. N. Tyacke, 'Puritanism, Arminianism and Counter-Revolution', in *The Origins of the English Civil War*, ed. C. Russell (London, 1973), 120-7.
[31] Bodleian Library, MS Rawlinson A 289, fo. 76.

For the Calvinist divines, Laud was a marked man. He had
come up to Oxford from Reading School in 1589, was chosen
scholar of St. John's in the following year, and elected fellow in
1593. A decade later, he was one of the proctors. In St. John's,
Laud absorbed a quite different tradition from that of Airay's
Queen's, Reynolds's Corpus, or even Thomas Holland's
Exeter. The religious tradition of the college had been conservative from its foundation and in the 1570s and 1580s, it was a
home for several crypto-papists, including Edmund Campion,
already on his way to Rome. John Buckeridge, once Whitgift's
chaplain, was Laud's tutor and became President of the college
in 1605. He was an admirer of Lancelot Andrewes, and would
have ensured that Laud was thoroughly grounded not only in
the Scriptures, but also in the patristic writers.[32] Peter Heylin,
Laud's first biographer and Chaplain to Charles I, maintained
that it was during Laud's year as proctor, 1603-4, that he first
ran into conflict with the Calvinist divines. In a divinity lecture, he seems to have maintained the perpetual visibility of the
church of Christ, descending from the apostles to the Church of
Rome, and continued in that church until the Reformation.[33]

Independently of Laud's lecture, George Abbot had produced in 1604 a work entitled *The Reasons wh. Doctour Hill hath
Brought*. This was primarily designed as a reply to the papists'
question, 'Where was your church before Luther?' Abbot put
forward an argument not only diametrically opposed to that of
Hill, but also at variance with that of Laud. He found the true
church not in the papal succession, but in England, Italy,
France, Spain, and even Rome itself, God's secret and *invisible*
company.[34] In the remainder of the work, he maintained that
the Church of England was not divided into sects, and went so
far as to claim that the university had no divisions and that its
preachers did not differ. All the preachers and graduates, he
explained, subscribed the confession and the Articles, and
those called puritans by the papists did not differ from the rest
in any point of substance, but only in circumstances and

---

[32] Peter Heylin, *Cyprianus Anglicus, or the History of the Life and Death of William, Lord
Archbishop of Canterbury* (London, 1668), 48.

[33] Ibid., 53.

[34] Abbot, *A Treatise of the Perpetuall Visibilitie and Succession of the True Church in All Ages*
(London, 1624), 20-1, 30 ff., 94-6.

ceremonies, the cap, the surplice, and ecclesiastical government.[35] Abbot must have been aware that this united front was
a dream. He may well have known of Laud's views, and the
young fellow of St. John's was shortly to demonstrate that the
divisions in the 'religion of protestants' could not be ignored.
In July 1604, Laud proceeded BD. The theses he chose were
controversial. William Prynne later reported: 'His supposition
when hee answered in the Divinity Schooles for his degree,
concerning the efficacie of Baptism, was taken *verbatim* out of
Bellarmine, and hee then maintained, there could bee no true
Church without Diocesan Bishops: for which Doctor *Holland*
(then Doctor of the Chair) openly reprehended him in the
Schooles for a seditious person who would un-Church the
reformed Protestant Church beyond Seas, and now sow division between us, and them, who were brethren, by this novell
popish position.'[36] Laud subsequently denied that this was his
intention.[37] Holland was no puritan, but would have reacted
violently against any hint of popish leanings at the expense of
English links with the continental reformed tradition. Heylin
admitted that Holland was theologically better principled than
his predecessor in the chair, Humphrey, but allowed himself to
be borne along by the violent current of the times.[38] In the
Schools, Laud was not alone in the case he attempted to present for *iure divino* episcopacy. In 1602, William Swaddon of
New College also affirmed that episcopacy in the church was of
divine institution.[39]

Laud invested the 1606 clash with Airay with some significance; it was one of the very few events in his Oxford career
which he noted in his diary: 'Quarrel Dr. Ayry picked with
me about my Sermon at St. Mary's, Octob. 21, 1606.'[40] The
subject of Laud's sermon is unknown, though Heylin sug-

[35] Abbot, *The Reasons wh. Doctour Hill hath Brought for Upholding Papistry Unmasked*
(Oxford, 1604), 101-2.
[36] William Prynne, *A Breviate of the Life of William Laud* (London, 1644), 2. Prynne's
account, forty years after the event, may, however, be considered an unreliable
witness.
[37] Trevor-Roper, op. cit., 39.
[38] Heylin, op. cit., 51.
[39] Clark, *Register*, II, part i, 203.
[40] *The History of the Troubles and Tryall of the Most Reverend Father in God, the Blessed
Martyr, William Laud* (London, 1695), 2.

gests, unoriginally, that there were 'sundry scandalous and popish pasages in it', remarking that Airay found popish everything that was not to be located in Calvin's *Institutes*. Sir William Paddye, once a member of Laud's college, physician to James I, and MP for Thetford 1604-11, kept a keen eye on his career. Paddye was present at the October sermon, and immediately informed Buckhurst that Airay intended to proceed against Laud, adding his own opinion that there was nothing in the sermon to have caused offence. Paddye suggested that the Chancellor could rescue Laud without causing Airay to lose face by reserving the case to himself. The Chancellor justified this to his commissary on the grounds of avoiding disturbance in the university. His letter to the Vice-Chancellor, probably of November, cannot have pleased the recipient, who nevertheless wrote a courteous reply, justifying his own course of action. On Christmas Eve, Buckhurst wrote again, pleased at the mild manner in which Airay was dealing with Laud. 'I am fully content', he said, 'to remit the cause to your great judgment, learning, justice, equity, moderation and discretion.'[41] Flattery evidently worked, for nothing more was heard of the proceedings against Laud. Such a warning was not, however, sufficient to check a man so determined and self-assured. When he took his DD in 1608, Laud chose the defence as another occasion to strike a blow for his doctrine of the visible church based on the apostolic succession and enshrined in the historic episcopate.[42] The final triumph of Laud's Oxford career lies outside the scope of this study. In 1611, by a majority of one and in the most controversial circumstances, he was elected President of St. John's. This college, so exceptional in its religious complexion, could still sustain a man like Laud, who would not have survived in one of the public posts of the university.[43]

The Calvinist doctors were now however alert and seeking to close their ranks. A man who lacked Laud's powerful patrons found himself effectively silenced by the assertive hierarchy. In view of his later admission to the Society of Jesus, Humphrey Leech's dispute with the Oxford divines, initiated by a sermon

---

[41] Bodleian Library, MS Rawlinson A 289, fos. 78, 80.
[42] Clark, *Register*, II, part i, 206.
[43] SP 14/64/35-6; SP 14/65/68; SP 14/66/25.

which he preached in Christ Church in 1607, may seem
nothing more than a crypto-papist defending himself against
the protestant establishment. The reality is more subtle. In
Leech's consideration of the evangelical counsels of perfection,
he distinguished four categories in the human race: some who
are to be judged and damned, some who are judged and damned
already, some who are to be judged and saved, and some who are
already saved without judgement. This last class, he maintained,
was composed of those who had transcended the moral
precepts of the law by due performance of the counsels of
perfection. They endeavoured not only to obey the Decalogue,
but added to it spiritual poverty, angelical chastity, and humble obedience.[44] Leech thus laid bare the heart of the Calvinist
synthesis, the doctrine of election. From 1607 to 1609, he provoked a detailed discussion of the finer points of election,
unknown in almost all the anti-papist writing of the last quarter
of the sixteenth century, and revealed the diversity of opinion
among the Oxford divines, from Benefield and Airay, rigid in
their adherence to Calvinist orthodoxy, moderates like John
King, Dean of Christ Church, and the Sub-Dean, Leonard
Hutten, to Leech himself, who claimed that he held to the common faith of the ancient church which was also the faith of the
Church of England. He protested his love for the university
which he could not bear to see perverted, yet 'the perfit hatred,
that from my innermost soul I ever conceived against
Puritanisme (the very bane of ancient Christianity) ... could not
suffer me ... to sit still and be silent'.[45] He also argued that
those who opposed him in the university were a faction of strict
Calvinists, a 'purer strayne', led by Sebastian Benefield, and
that without their prompting, proceedings would not have been
taken against him.

In the Easter Term 1608, Benefield took the opportunity of
his solemn lectures for the DD to reinforce the narrow,
Calvinist view. He denied that either the fathers or the Scriptures upheld Leech's case that the evangelical counsels were of
a higher standing than the divine precepts.[46] Leech himself
continued to claim that King had heard his original sermon and

[44] Humphrey Leech, *A Triumph of Truth* (?Douai, 1609), 2-4.
[45] Leech, op. cit., 27.
[46] Benefield, *Doctrinae Christianae Sex Capita*, 35-40, 145-208.

had made no complaint against it, and that many in Oxford not only sympathized with his position, but indeed covertly held the same view. No supporters, however, came out into the open or have been subsequently identified. Leech was not immediately denied access to the Oxford pulpits and on 27 June 1608 he launched into a spirited expansion of his earlier theme. In this, like William Barrett in 1595, he drew a distinction between *certitudo*, which, with reservations, a Christian might possess, and *securitas*, which he regarded as presumption.[47] He also thrust a deeper wedge between the precepts of the Christian life which all men need in order to remove what is contrary to the will of God, and evangelical counsels performed by a small minority of men whose salvation is already certain.[48] None of the Oxford doctors, strict Calvinists or moderates, would have been happy with this distinction. Having thus cast doubt on the Christian's security, Leech compounded the error by referring to Calvin as 'a blasphemous interpreter'. It may well have been at this point that the strict Calvinists and moderates joined forces against him. Leech was summoned before a committee which consisted of Airay and Benefield, John Harding, President of Magdalen, John Algionby, and Leonard Hutten. The establishment was determined to silence him. Excluded from preaching in the university, he appealed to Bancroft, but even the Archbishop now appeared to him to favour Calvin's opinions.[49] Eventually, Leech withdrew himself from the university; he had crossed the frontier and nothing now separated him from Rome.[50]

Leech, though he is scarcely representative of the opponents of rigid Calvinism within the Church of England, produced in the opening decade of the seventeenth century the first serious challenge in Oxford to the Calvinist doctors. His theology of evangelical counsels may, as he claimed, have had its roots in the doctrine professed by the ancient church; at least it had grown out of the same general understanding of election as that of the orthodox divines. Hence, perhaps, men like Benefield

---

[47] Leech, op. cit., 31-5.
[48] Ibid., 39, 149, 169.
[49] Ibid., 116.
[50] For a detailed discussion of the Leech case, see C. M. Dent, 'Protestants in Elizabethan Oxford', unpub. Oxford D.Phil. thesis, 1980, fos. 407-22.

and Airay were not content to dismiss Leech as a simple
crypto-papist, but deemed it necessary to present a formal
defence of their own position. For another two decades, however, the majority of the clergy, high and low alike, were to
maintain the Calvinist synthesis, with Benefield as Lady
Margaret Professor, Airay in control at Queen's, and the two
Abbots, Robert as Regius Professor and George at Canterbury.
The shaking of this foundation, by those who placed greater
emphasis on the sacraments and the Christian life to the detriment of preaching and the strict doctrine of election, foreshadowed, perhaps, in Howson in 1602-3, in Laud in 1604-8,
and in Leech in 1607-9 would have to wait for Laud to become
chancellor of Oxford on Pembroke's death in 1630 and eventually to succeed George Abbot at Canterbury three years later.

CONCLUSION

During the reign of Elizabeth, the university of Oxford and a number of individual colleges established a significant place within a broad continental reformed tradition, influenced by a wide range of reformed writing and the example of a variety of more perfect schools of Christ in the European cities. The roots of this broad, hybrid outlook may be found in the reign of Edward VI. Despite Oxford's failure to rebuild the alliance on Elizabeth's succession, when Peter Martyr was unable to return to his chair in the university, the link with the continental churches was effectively re-established and Oxford found its place within what has often, and too narrowly, been called 'Calvinism'. Its theology was by no means exclusively based on the Genevan development of Calvin's thought by Beza and its English popularization by William Perkins. That the Oxford reformed tradition was not solely Genevan in inspiration is attested by the broad spectrum of texts prescribed in the 1579 Catechetical Statute, a turning-point which marks the end of the generation of the exiles and the beginning of a new, more active phase of theological exploration. Although Calvin held an important place in the formation of generations of students, more detailed work on the contents of college libraries, such as has already been done on Grindal's collection in Queen's, Jewel's in Magdalen, and the library of Corpus, might reveal more accurately patterns of influence and development. The present study has attempted to demonstrate that the writings of the reformers of Zurich and later of Heidelberg held a very high place both in collegiate and in private collections in the second half of the reign.

Since there was no necessity in Oxford, until the early years of the seventeenth century, to defend this synthesis of reformed theology against alternative interpretations of the doctrine of salvation, Oxford theology remained less rigid, less insistent, less precise than that hammered out in Cambridge in the attempts to discredit Peter Baro and William Barrett. Corro was not a significant threat to the dominant theology of the 1570s. Leicester's attempt to introduce him into the university had the important result of prompting the young John Reynolds to assume the leadership of the coming generation of divines, who now took the place of men like Humphrey and Cole who had settled into a conforming mediocrity, but Corro did not threaten the doctrine of election as understood in Oxford. He was not an Arminian before his time. Like Pucci before him, he was an arrogant, naïve, and insensitive free-thinking intellectual. He wished to be allowed to speculate freely, to reject narrow theological categories in favour of a universalist approach. He derided the confessional outlook not only of the London French, but also of the universities. His position contrasted not only with that of Oxford, but with the much stricter emphasis on discipline and polity which would have been found in Zurich, Geneva, Heidelberg, and Cambridge.

When the university of Oxford was disrupted in 1602-3, controversy was occasioned by questioning not of the doctrine of election, but of the prevailing understanding of the church, its ministry, and worship. By the end of the sixteenth century, more radical activity had ceased and Oxford divines focused their attention on the provision of a learned, resident ministry, above all given to preaching the word. In his sermon of 17 November 1602, Vice-Chancellor Howson had no intention of attacking the role of preaching in general. Like the heads of advanced protestant colleges, Airay and Reynolds, as well as the more moderate Holland, he no doubt saw the university as an important seminary. Yet he objected to *oratoria* being transformed into *auditoria* by lengthy and sometimes disruptive hortatory preaching. His concept of the church demanded a balanced liturgy, centred on the Prayer Book calendar and lectionary, and including the observation of Holy Days. The significance of Airay's leadership of the opposition to the Vice-Chancellor lies in the fact that it was his college, Queen's, which had established the most dominant tradition of providing preaching ministers, particularly for the dark corners of Cumberland and Westmorland.

Since Oxford largely avoided soteriological controversy, the ministers trained in this school were not normally rigid or extreme in outlook, but rather were concerned with high standards of education, pastoral care, and evangelism. Oxford did produce its nonconformists, but it is a mistake to see Field and Oxenbridge in one generation, Barebon, Gellibrand, Wight, and Stone in another, and Sprint and Troutbeck at the end of the century, as typical. Oxford provided far more ministers of the calibre of William Hinde and Robert Mandevil, who were primarily concerned, not with promoting reform of the church from above, but with peaceably advancing the godliness of their own lives and those of their flocks. Here it is simply a confusion to comprehend all these men under the title 'puritan', however convenient. The activity of Oxford men in parochial ministry might be more clearly discerned by further local studies, such as have already been made in the dioceses of Chester, Chichester, and Peterborough. Yet such studies could also disappoint. George Wilton's letter-book, besides recording a crucial moment in the history of Magdalen College, also gives tantalizing glimpses of the relationship between Barebon and his pupils after he withdrew to Northamptonshire; of Wilton's involvement with a godly gentleman, Urian Verney; and of his continuing correspondence with his Oxford tutor after he moved to Crediton in the 1590s. But Wilton became a schoolmaster, not a minister, and it has been impossible to trace the network of his career and relationships further. Frequently nothing more can be known of an Oxford man after he left the university unless he came into conflict with episcopal or civil authority, or unless he became a preaching minister who, perhaps through the generosity of a patron, was enabled to publish his sermons.

These hindrances direct the study back to the closed, or relatively enclosed, world of the university and its individual colleges. The history which has been described here is narrow in its confines and, in large measure, that must always be its nature. The university looked inwards, jealously protecting its privileges and deeply resenting outside interference, whether from the Queen, the Council, the ecclesiastical commissioners, or even the Chancellor. Inwardness was a particular characteristic of the more advanced protestants and here at least the generation of new and more radical men in the later 1570s resembled the monks of old to whom John Foxe had likened them.[1] They regarded their colleges as protective enclosures,

---

[1] See above, 61.

not only safeguarding their liberties, but providing a controlled, strictly-governed microcosm of the world, limited by statutes interpreted by a Visitor and internal regulations which ensured purity of life.

Such enclosure encouraged faction, as is massively exemplified in the turbulent history of Magdalen College. It also allowed a latitude of opinion and freedom of practice impossible for parochial ministers under the eye of bishops and archdeacons. When Humphrey told Leicester that his college was 'out of the universitie ... separate and exempte', it was only a slight exaggeration.[2] The President survived the troubles of 1564-6 because Magdalen was a place apart, while Sampson lost his deanery. In the succeeding twenty years the members of the college, despite the intervention of the Visitor and, in 1575, the influence of Walsingham and his secretaries, were able to develop their radical courses largely unchecked. It was because of the constitutional and geographical isolation of the college that, at least in part, Magdalen had such a tumultuous and exceptional history which cannot be paralleled elsewhere in this discussion.

One man intervened in the affairs of the university throughout the period, its Chancellor for twenty-four years, Robert Dudley, Earl of Leicester. Apart from his letters recorded in the Convocation registers, his activity in the university emerges tantalizingly seldom. When it does, it is sometimes enigmatic, often unexpected. Leicester is frequently considered to have been the friend of more convinced protestants, a man concerned to advance the careers of godly ministers. To Thomas Wood, anxious at the rumour that Leicester had been instrumental in suppressing the prophesying at Southam in 1576, Leicester defended his activity, citing his influence in the advancement of religion and in the preferment of bishops and deans. He advised Wood, if still perplexed, to 'looke into the University of Oxford lykewise, whereof I am Chancelor, and see what heads of houses be there now in comparison of those I found. And do but indifferently examine howe the ministry is advanced there, even where were not long agoe not only many ill heads, but as many th'worst schollers for religion.'[3]

---

[2] See above, 38.
[3] *The Letters of Thomas Wood, Puritan, 1566-77*, xviii-xxi, 10-13.

Leicester himself claimed that he had consistently promoted the interests of reformed religion and its ministers, but in his dealings with Oxford there are some curious anomalies which might seem to indicate that the charges in *Leycesters Commonwealth* and from Anthony Wood, that he acted out of self-interest, were not entirely without foundation.[4] Leicester certainly exercised strong control over the university, taking the appointment of the Vice-Chancellor into his own hands after 1570, and he cannot be exonerated from the charges that he damaged college estates by securing long leases of them for his friends. At the beginning of 1561, even before he became Chancellor, he was willing to heed the plea of the canons and Students of Christ Church and aided the advancement of Thomas Sampson to the deanery, but shortly before he had helped his Chaplain, Francis Babington, a crypto-papist, to the Rectorship of Lincoln College and, when he was deprived of all preferments in 1563, Leicester appointed in his place another of his domestic chaplains, John Bridgewater, also a man deeply conservative in religion. Professor Collinson claims that 'it was only after the readjustments in the pattern of domestic and external politics between 1569 and 1572 that Leicester's public image became thoroughly infused with progressive protestantism'.[5] He then helped John Harmar, who had sat at the feet of Beza in Geneva, to a fellowship at New College, he probably advanced John Reynolds, and he placed his confidence in Lawrence Humphrey as his Commissary from 1571 to 1576. Nevertheless, it was as late as 1576 that Leicester attempted to promote Corro when Villiers might have seemed a much more obvious protégé for an advanced protestant. Perhaps the Chancellor did not realize how much unease Corro's opinions would cause in Oxford, since his principal dealings there were with the senior doctors, men like Humphrey and his generation, who do not seem to have been alarmed, initially at least, by Corro. It needed a man of the coming generation, John Reynolds, to sound the warning. Yet it looks suspiciously as if Leicester intended to obtain here what suited him best, perhaps to rid himself of the embarrassment of a persistent Corro.

---

[4] *The copie of a leter*, 77-80; Wood, *Annals*, II, 231.
[5] *The Letters of Thomas Wood, Puritan, 1566-77*, xxv.

If Oxford and some of its colleges were places exempt, places apart, there is one other place in England with which they may be compared. Studies in the protestant history of the university of Cambridge are more advanced than those for Oxford. For twenty-five years, students have had access to the most interesting areas of the general field in Dr H. C. Porter's *Reformation and Reaction in Tudor Cambridge*. Recently, the detailed study by Dr P. G. Lake, *Moderate Puritans and the Elizabethan Church* has discovered a more continuous tendency of theological development in the university.[6] Dr Lake sees a pattern, a tradition closely defined by two characteristics: first, the rigorous assertion of anti-papist polemic, using the scholarly resources of the university, which emphasized the reformed purity of the English church; secondly, on the domestic front, action and argument to achieve the completion of the reform in England according to the rule of scripture.

Oxford, from time to time, had among its divines men who would have insisted that their lives and ministries were directed to these goals. Yet the present study makes no claim for a consistent pattern or tradition. John Reynolds may have been the Chaderton of Oxford, as Professor Collinson claims, but his career was a series of responses to particular crises and incidents.[7] Above all, Reynolds was a university man; his radicalism of the 1580s was bred of an academic cast of mind. Ministers who had been his pupils turned to him for advice when pressed with the need to conform, but Reynolds himself was strangely out of his depth when removed from the Schools. The theoretical radicalism which emerges most clearly in the sermons on Haggai and Obadiah was not robust enough to survive the debates at Hampton Court and when Reynolds faced the outside world, he feared that, with the demand for subscription, he might lose his place in Oxford altogether. This study reflects, rather, in a microcosm, the discovery made by H. A. L. Fisher, who, having surveyed a far larger canvas, admitted that 'one intellectual excitement has ... been denied me. Men wiser and more learned than I have discerned in

---

[6] I regret that Dr Lake's book appeared too late to be considered here. I have been grateful for the opportunity to refer to his unpublished Cambridge Ph.D. thesis.

[7] Collinson, *E.P.M.*, 129.

history a plot, a rhythm, a predetermined pattern. I can only see one emergency following upon another, as wave follows upon wave ... only one safe rule for the historian: that he should recognise in the development of human destinies the play of the contingent and the unforseen.'[8]

---

[8] H. A. L. Fisher, *The History of Europe*, 3 vols. (London, 1935), I, vii.

SELECT BIBLIOGRAPHY

Note: An extensive bibliography of the manuscript and printed sources will be found in my 'Protestants in Elizabethan Oxford', unpublished Oxford D.Phil. thesis, 1980.

PRIMARY SOURCES

(1) *Manuscripts*

British Library
  Cottonian MSS
  Harleian MSS
  Lansdowne MSS
  Egerton MSS
  Sloane MSS
  Additional MSS
Dr Williams's Library, Morrice MSS
Inner Temple Library, Petyt MSS
Lambeth Palace Library MSS
Public Record Office
  State Papers Domestic Edward VI (SP 10)
  State Papers Domestic Mary (SP 11)
  State Papers Domestic Elizabeth (SP 12)
  State Papers Domestic James I (SP 14)
  State Papers Domestic Elizabeth, Addenda (SP 15)
  State Papers Domestic, Supplementary (SP 46)
Oxford, Bodleian Library
  Bodley MSS
  Gough MSS
  Rawlinson MSS, A, C, and D
  Tanner MSS
  Top. Oxon. MSS
Oxford, Corpus Christi College MSS
  Magdalen College MSS
  Queen's College MSS

Oxford, University Archives (OUA)
  College Archives
    All Souls
    Balliol
    Christ Church
    Corpus Christi
    Exeter
    Magdalen
    Merton

New College
Queen's
University
Cambridge University Library MSS
Cambridge, Corpus Christi College MSS
Huntington Library, San Marino California, Hastings MSS

(2) *Printed Works* (published before 1650)

Note: The place of printing is London, unless otherwise stated.

Abbot, George,	*An Exposition upon the Prophet Ionah* (1600)
——	*The Reasons wh.Doctour Hill hath Brought for Upholding Papistry Unmasked* (Oxford, 1604)
Airay, Henry,	*Lectures upon the Whole Epistle of Saint Paul to the Philippians* (1618)
Bagshawe, Edward,	*The Last Conflicts and Death of Mr. Thomas Peacock* (1646)
Bancroft, Richard,	*Daungerous Positions and Proceedings* (1593)
——	*A Survay of the Pretended Holy Discipline* (1593)
Benefield, Sebastian,	*Doctrinae Christianae Sex Capita* (Oxford, 1610)
——	*Eight Sermons Publikely Preached in the University of Oxford* (Oxford, 1614)
——	*The Sinne against the Holy Ghost Discovered* (Oxford, 1615)
Bisse, James,	*Two Sermons, the One at Paules Crosse the Other at Christes Church* (1581)
Bolton, Robert,	*A Discourse about the State of True Happinesse* (1611)
——	*Mr. Boltons last and learned worke. Of the last four things. With his life* [by E. Bagshawe] (1632)
Bullinger, Heinrich,	*Catechesis pro adultoribus scripta* (Zurich, 2nd ed., 1599)

The copie of a leter wryten by a master of arte of Cambridge to his friend in London (1584) (= *Leycesters Commonwealth*)

Corderoy, Jeremy,	*A Short Dialogue* (Oxford, 1604)
——	*A Warning for Worldlings* (1608)
Corro, Antonio del,	*Dialogus theologicus, quo epistola Divi Pauli ad Romanos explanatur* (1574)
——	*An epistle or godlie admonition* (1569)
——	*Epistola Beati Pauli ad Romanos e Graeco in Latinam μεταφρασιχως* (1581)
——	*Tableau de l'oeuvre de Dieu* (Norwich, 1569)
Crakanthorpe, Richard,	*A Sermon of Predestination* (1620)
——	*A Sermon of Sanctification* (1608)

A Dialogue, wherin is plainly laide open, the tyrannicall dealing of L. Bishopps against Gods children (?La Rochelle, 1589)

Gosson, Stephen,	*The Shoole of Abuse* (1579)
[Heidelberg Catechism]	*A catechisme, or short kind of instruction*, ET T. Sparke and J. Seddon (Oxford, 1588)

Hinde, William,   *A Path to Pietie* (Oxford, 1613)
Holland, Thomas,   πανηγυρὶs D. *Elizabethae, a sermon preached
                            17 November 1599* (Oxford, 1601)
Howson, John,   *A Sermon Preached at Paules Crosse ... the 4 of
                            December* (1597)
——   *A Second Sermon Preached at Paules Crosse ... the 21 of
                            May* (1598)
——   *A Sermon Preached at St. Maries in Oxford in Defence
                            of the Festivities of the Church of England* (Oxford,
                            1602)
——   Second impression (Oxford, 1603)
Hubert, Conrad,   *Historia vera: de vita, obitu, sepultura ... Buceri et
                            Fagii* (Strasburg, 1562)
Humphrey, Lawrence,   *Jesuitismi Pars Prima: sive de praxi Romanae curiae*
                            (1582)
——   *Jesuitismi Pars Secunda* (1584)
——   *J. Juelli Episcopi Sarisburiensis Vita* (1573)
——   *The Nobles or of Nobilitye* (1563)
——   *Optimates, sive de nobilitate* (Basle, 1560)
——   *De religionis conservatione et reformatione vera* (Basle,
                            1559)
——   *A View of the Romish Hydra and Monster* (Oxford,
                            1588)
Hutten, Leonard,   *An Answere to a Certaine Treatise of the Crosse in
                            Baptisme* (Oxford, 1605)
Jefferay, Richard,   *The Sonne of Gods Entertainment by the Sonnes of
                            Men: a Sermon* (1605)
King, John,   *Lectures upon Jonas, delivered at Yorke in the yeare of
                            our Lorde, 1594* (Oxford, 1597)
Kingsmill, Andrew,   *A Most Excellent and Comfortable Treatise*, ed.
                            F. Mylles (1577)
——   *A view of mans estate*, ed. F. Mylles (1574)
Leech, Humphrey,   *A Triumph of Truth* (?Douai, 1609)
Mandevill, Robert,   *Timothies Taske: or a Christian Sea-Card* (Oxford,
                            1619)
Massie, William,   *A Sermon Preached at Trafford* (Oxford, 1586)
[Oxford, University]   *The answere of the Vice-Chancellor, the doctors bothe
                            the proctors, and other the heads of houses in the univer-
                            sity of Oxford* (Oxford, 1603)
[Parker, Robert,]   *A Scholasticall Discourse against Symbolizing with
                            Antichrist in Ceremonies* (?Amsterdam, 1607)
*A parte of a register, contayninge sundrie memorable matters, for the reformation of our
    church* (——, ? 1593)
Prideaux, John,   *Certaine Sermons Preached by John Prideaux* (Oxford,
                            1637)
Prime, John,   *A fruitfull and briefe discourse in two books, the one of
                            nature, the other of grace* (1583)
——   *A short treatise of the sacraments generally* (1582)

Reynolds, John, *The Discovery of the Man of Sinne* (Oxford, 1614)
—— *A Letter of Dr. Reinolds to his Friend, Concerning his Advice for the Studie of Divinitie* (1613)
—— *Th'overthrow of Stage-Playes* (Middleburg, 1599)
—— *The Prophecie of Obadiah Opened and Applyed in Sundry Sermons* (Oxford, 1613)
—— *The Prophesie of Haggai, Interpreted and Applied in Sundry Sermons* (1649)
—— *A Sermon upon Part of the Eighteenth Psalm* (Oxford, 1586)
—— *Sex Theses de Sacra Scriptura et Ecclesia* (Oxford, 1580)
—— *The Summe of the Conference betwene J. Rainoldes and J. Hart* (1584)
—— *The Judgement of Doctor Reignolds concerning Episcopacy* (1641)
Sprint, John, *The Anatomy of the Controversed Ceremonies of the Church of England* (1618)
—— *Propositions, Tending to Proove the Necessarie Use of the Christian Sabbaoth* (1607)
Stubbes, Philip, *The Anatomie of Abuses* (1583)
Ursinus, Zacharias, *A Collection of Certaine Learned Discourses* (Oxford, 1600)
—— *The Summe of Christian Religion*, ET H. Parry (Oxford, 1587)
Zanchius, Hieronymus, *H. Zanchius: His Confession of Christian Religion* (Cambridge, 1599)

SECONDARY SOURCES

(1) *Printed books*

Babbage, Stuart S., *Puritanism and Richard Bancroft* (1962)
[Blaurer, A. and
  Blaurer, T.,] *Briefwechsel der Brüder Ambrosius und Thomas Blaurer, 1509-67*, ed. T. Schiess, Band III, 1549-67 (Freiburg-i-Br., 1912)
Bloxam, J. R., *Register of the Presidents, Fellows, Demies ... of St. Mary Magdalen College, Oxford*, Vol. II (Oxford, 1867). Vol. III (1873); Vol. IV (1873)
Boas, F. S., *University Drama in the Tudor Age* (Oxford, 1914)
Boehmer, Edward (ed.), *Bibliotheca Wiffeniana*, Vol. III, *Spanish Reformers of two Centuries from 1520* (London and Strasburg, 1904)
Brodrick, G. C., *Memorials of Merton College* (Oxford Historical Society, iv, 1885)
Bush, M. L., *The Government Policy of Protector Somerset* (1975)
Buxton, E. J. M. and
  Williams, P. H., *New College Oxford, 1379-1979* (Oxford, 1979)

Calendar of State Papers, Domestic Series, 1547-1625, eds. R. Lemon and M. A. E. Green, 9 vols. (1856-72)

Calfhill, James,   *An Answere to John Martiall's Treatise of the Crosse,* ed. R. Gibbings (Cambridge, Parker Society, 1846)

Cardwell, Edward,   *Documentary Annals of the Reformed Church of England, 1546-1716,* 2 vols. (Oxford, 1844)

——   *A History of Conferences and Other Proceedings Connected with the Book of Common Prayer from the year 1558 to the year 1690* (Oxford, 1849)

Clark, Andrew (ed.),   *Register of the University of Oxford, 1571-1622,* Vol. II, part i, Introductions (Oxford Historical Society, x, 1887), part ii, Matriculations and Subscriptions (Oxford Historical Society, xi, 1888)

Clasen, C.-P.,   *The Palatinate in European History, 1555-1618* (Oxford, 2nd ed., 1966)

Collinson, Patrick,   *Archbishop Grindal* (1980)

——   *The Elizabethan Puritan Movement* (1967)

—— (ed.),   *The Letters of Thomas Wood, Puritan, 1566-1577* (*Bulletin of the Institute of Historical Research,* Special Supplement, 5, 1960)

Cooper, C. H. and T.,   *Athenae Cantabrigienses, 1500-1609,* 2 vols. (Cambridge, 1858-61)

Costin, W. C.,   *The History of St. John's College, Oxford, 1598-1860* (Oxford Historical Society, new series, xii, 1958)

Cremeans, C. D.,   *The Reception of Calvinist Thought in England* (Urbana, Illinois, 1949)

Cross, Claire,   *Church and People, 1450-1660* (1976)

——   *The Puritan Earl* (1966)

—— (ed.),   *The Letters of Francis Hastings (1574-1609)* (Somerset Record Society, lxix, 1969)

Curtis, Mark H.,   *Oxford and Cambridge in Transition, 1558-1642* (Oxford, 1959)

Dickens, A. G.,   *The English Reformation* (1964)

Dictionary of National Biography, ed. Leslie Stephen and Sidney Lee, 21 vols. (1908-9)

Firpo, Luigi,   *Gli Scritti di Francesco Pucci* (Turin, 1957)

Fletcher, J. M. (ed.),   *Registrum Annalium Collegii Mertonensis, 1521-67* (Oxford Historical Society, new series, xxiii, 1974)

——   *Registrum Annalium Collegii Mertonensis, 1567-1603* (Oxford Historical Society, new series, xxiv, 1976)

Foster, Joseph,   *Alumni Oxonienses, 1500-1714,* 4 vols. (Oxford, 1891-2)

Fowler, Thomas,   *The History of Corpus Christi College Oxford* (Oxford Historical Society, xxv, 1893)

Gee, Henry,   *The Elizabethan Clergy and the Settlement of Religion, 1558-64* (Oxford, 1898)

Gibson, Strickland,   *Statuta Antiqua Universitatis Oxoniensis* (Oxford, 1931)

Gorham, G. C.,   *Gleanings of a Few Scattered Ears* (1857)

Green, V. H. H.,   *The Commonwealth of Lincoln College, 1427-1977* (Oxford, 1979)

Grindal, Edmund,   *Remains*, ed. W. Nicholson (Cambridge, Parker Society, 1843)

Hauben, P. J.,   *Three Spanish Heretics and the Reformation* (Geneva, 1967)

Haugaard, W. P.,   *Elizabeth and the English Reformation* (Cambridge, 1968)

Hessels, J. H. (ed.),   *Ecclesiae Londino-Batavae Archivum: Epistulae et Tractatus* (Cambridge, 1889-97)

Hill, J. E. C.,   *Economic Problems of the Church from Archbishop Whitgift to the Long Parliament* (Oxford, 1956)

Historical Manuscripts Commission,   *Calendar of the Manuscripts of the Marquis of Salisbury*, 18 vols. (1883-1940)

——   *Report on the Pepys Manuscripts, Preserved at Magdalene College, Cambridge* (1911)

Hotman, Francis and Jean,   *Francisci et Johannis Hotomanorum Patris ac Filii et Clarorum Virorum ad eos Epistolae* (Amsterdam, 1700)

Kearney, H. F.,   *Scholars and Gentlemen: Universities and Society in Pre-Industrial Britain, 1500-1700* (1970)

Kendall, R. M.,   *Calvin and English Calvinism to 1649* (Oxford, 1979)

[Ker, N. R.,]   *Oxford Libraries in 1556* (Catalogue of an exhibition held in the Bodleian Library Oxford, 1956)

Knappen, M. M.,   *Tudor Puritanism* (Chicago, 1939)

Lake, P. G.,   *Moderate Puritans and the Elizabethan Church* (Cambridge, 1982)

Léonard, E. G.,   *A History of Protestantism*, ET H. H. Rowley (1967)

Loades, D. M.,   *The Reign of Mary Tudor* (1979)

McConica, J. K.,   *English Humanists and Reformation Politics, under Henry VIII and Edward VI* (Oxford, 1965)

Maclure, M.,   *The Paul's Cross Sermons, 1534-1642* (Toronto, 1958)

Macray, W. D. (ed.),   *A Register of the Members of St. Mary Magdalen College, Oxford, new series*, Vol. II (1897); Vol. III (1901)

Madan, F.,	*The Early Oxford Press: a Bibliography of Printing and Publishing at Oxford, 1468-1640* (Oxford Historical Society, xxix, 1895)
Magrath, J. R.,	*The Queen's College*, Vol. II (Oxford, 1921)
Mallett, C. E.,	*A History of the University of Oxford*, Vol. II (1924)
Mitchell, W. T. (ed.),	*Epistolae Academicae 1508-1596* (Oxford Historical Society, 1980)
Morgan, Paul,	*Oxford Libraries Outside the Bodleian* (Oxford Bibliographical Society, 1974)
Mozley, J. F.,	*John Foxe and his Book* (1940)
Neale, J. E.,	*Elizabeth I and Her Parliaments*, Vol. I: 1559-1581 (1953); Vol. II: 1584-1601 (1957)
Nowell, Alexander,	*A Catechisme, or First Instruction and Learning of Christian Religion*, ed. G. E. Corry (Cambridge, Parker Society, 1853)
O'Day, Rosemary,	*The English Clergy: the Emergence and Consolidation of a Profession, 1558-1642* (Leicester, 1979)

Original Letters Relative to the English Reformation, ed. Hastings Robinson, 2 vols. (Cambridge, Parker Society, 1846-7)

Parker, Matthew,	*Correspondence of Archbishop Parker*, ed. J. Bruce and T. T. Perowne (Cambridge, Parker Society, 1853)
Peel, A. (ed.),	*The Seconde Parte of a Register*, 2 vols. (Cambridge, 1915)
Perkins, William,	*The Work of William Perkins*, ed. Ian Breward, (Appleford, Oxon., 1970)
Porter, H. C.,	*Reformation and Reaction in Tudor Cambridge* (Cambridge, 1958)
Primus, J. H.,	*The Vestments Controversy* (Kampen, 1960)
Pucci, Francesco,	*Lettere, Documenti e Testimonianze*, ed. Luigi Firpo and Renato Piattoli, 2 vols. (Florence, 1955-9)
Richardson, R. C.,	*Puritanism in North-West England* (Manchester, 1972)
Roper, William,	*Vita D. Thomae Morie* (1716) (pages 69-179 = *Epistolae et Orationes Aliquammultae Academiae Oxoniensis*)
Rosenberg, E.,	*Leicester, Patron of Letters* (New York, 1955)
Salter, H. E. and Lobel, M. D. (eds.),	*The Victoria County History of the County of Oxford*, Vol. III, *The University of Oxford* (1954)
Sepp. C.,	*Polemische en Irenische Theologie* (Leiden, 1881)
Shiels, W. J.,	*The Puritans in the Diocese of Peterborough, 1558-1610* (Northamptonshire Record Society, xxx, 1979)
Simon, Joan,	*Education and Society in Tudor England* (Cambridge, 1966)

The Statutes of the Colleges of Oxford (1853)
Stevenson, W. H. and
   Salter, H. E.,   *The Early History of St. John's College, Oxford* (Oxford Historical Society, new series, i, 1939)
Stone, L. (ed.),   *The University in Society*, Vol. I, *Oxford and Cambridge from the 14th to the early 19th century* (Princeton, 1975)
Strype, John,   *Annals of the Reformation ... during Queen Elizabeth's Happy Reign*, 2 vols., each in 2 parts (Oxford, 1824)
——   *Ecclesiastical Memorials, relating chiefly to religion and its reformation, under the reigns of King Henry VIII, King Edward VI and Queen Mary*, 7 vols. (Oxford, 1817)
——   *The History of the Life and Acts of the Most Reverend Father in God, Edmund Grindal* (Oxford, 1821)
——   *The Life and Acts of Matthew Parker, Archbishop of Canterbury*, 3 vols. (Oxford, 1821)
——   *The Life and Acts of John Whitgift*, 3 vols. (Oxford, 1822)
——   *Memorials of the Most Reverend Father in God, Thomas Cranmer* (Oxford, 1853)
Usher, R. G.,   *The Reconstruction of the English Church*, 2 vols. (New York, 1910)
Venn, J. (ed.),   *Grace Book △, Containing the Records of the University of Cambridge, 1542-89* (Cambridge, 1910)
Venn, J. and
   Venn, J. A.,   *Alumni Cantabrigienses, Part I, from the earliest times to 1751*, 4 vols. (Cambridge 1922-7)
White, F. O.,   *The Lives of the Elizabethan Bishops* (1898)
Williams, P. H.,   *The Tudor Regime* (Oxford, 1979)
Wood, Anthony à,   *Athenae Oxonienses*, ed. Philip Bliss, Vol. I (Oxford, 1813); Vol. II (Oxford, 1815)
——   *The History and Antiquities of the University of Oxford ... The Annals*, ed. John Gutch, Vol II (Oxford, 1796); *Appendix ... Fasti Oxonienses*, ed. John Gutch (Oxford, 1790)
The Zurich Letters, 1558-1579, ed. Hastings Robinson (Cambridge, Parker Society, 1842)
The Zurich Letters, Second Series, 1558-1602, ed. Hastings Robinson (Cambridge, Parker Society, 1845)

(2) *Articles*

Backus, Irena,   'Laurence Tomson (1539-1608) and Elizabethan Puritanism', *Journal of Ecclesiastical History*, 28, no. 1, January 1977, 17-27.

Collinson, Patrick,	'John Field and Elizabethan Puritanism', in *Elizabethan Government and Society*, ed. S. T. Bindoff, J. Hurstfield, and C. H. Williams (1961), 127-62.
Costin, W. C.,	'The Inventory of John English, BCL, Fellow of St. John's College', *Oxoniensia*, xi and xii, 1946-7, 102-31.
Cross, Claire,	'Continental Students and the Protestant Reformation in England in the Sixteenth Century', *Studies in Church History, Subsidia*, 2, ed. D. Baker (1979), 35-57.
Curtis, Mark H.,	'The Hampton Court Conference and its Aftermath', *History*, xlvi, 1961, 1-16.
Firpo, Luigi,	'Francesco Pucci in Inghilterra', *Révue Internationale de Philosophie*, 5, 1951, 158-73.
Hall, Basil,	'Calvin against the Calvinists', *Proceedings of the Huguenot Society of London*, xx, 1962, 284-301.
——	'Puritanism: the Problem of Definition', *Studies in Church History*, II, ed. G. J. Cuming (1965), 283-96.
Haugaard, W. P.,	'The Episcopal Pretensions of Thomas Sampson', *Historical Magazine of the Protestant Episcopal Church*, xxxvi, 1967, 383-6.
Ker, N. R.,	'The Library of John Jewel', *Bodleian Library Record*, ix, no. 5, 1977, 256-65.
——	'Oxford College Libraries in the Sixteenth Century', *Bodleian Library Record*, vi, 1959, 459-515.
McConica, J. K.,	'Humanism and Aristotle in Tudor Oxford', *English Historical Review*, xciv, 1979, 291-317.
——	'The Social Relations of Tudor Oxford', *Transactions of the Royal Historical Society*, 5th series, 1977, 115-34.
Myres, J. N. L.,	'The Painted Frieze in the Picture Gallery', *Bodleian Library Record*, 3, 1950, 82-91.
——	'Thomas James and the Painted Frieze', *Bodleian Library Record*, 4, 1952, 30-51.
Parker, T. M.,	'Arminianism and Laudianism in Seventeenth Century England', *Studies in Church History*, I, ed. C. W. Dugmore and C. Duggan (1964), 20-34.
Tyacke, N. R. N.,	'Puritanism, Arminianism and Counter-Revolution', in *The Origins of the English Civil War*, ed. C. Russell (1973), 119-43.

(3) *Unpublished theses*

Collinson, Patrick,	'The Puritan Classical Movement in the Reign of Elizabeth I', London, Ph.D., 1957

Lake, P. G.,   'Lawrence Chaderton and the Cambridge
                        Moderate Puritan Tradition, 1570-1604', Cam-
                        bridge, Ph.D., 1979
Liddell, J. R.,   'The Library of Corpus Christi College, 1517-
                        1617', Oxford, B.Litt., 1936
McFadden, W.,   'The Life and Works of Antonio del Corro,
                        1527-91', Queen's University, Belfast, Ph.D.,
                        1953
Tyacke, N. R. N.,   'Arminianism in England in Religion and
                        Politics, 1604 to 1640', Oxford, D.Phil., 1968.

INDEX